CHINTAMANI CRYSTAL MATRIX

"This is a work of extraordinary depth, scholarship, and esoteric knowledge, revealing the interface of consciousness-intention and the world of matter. The authors are multidimensional explorers returning from the inner and outer frontiers to report on the wonders they have seen. *The Chintamani Crystal Matrix* is historically fascinating, profoundly spiritual, and absolutely practical—an illuminating study of stones of power through the lens of history, myth, science, and quantum energy, with additional revelations from the authors' own research. This is a unique can't-put-it-down guidebook that by its very nature shines with an astonishing light. A joy to savor and be grateful for."

CATHERINE DEES, SENIOR EDITOR AT ST. LYNN'S PRESS,
COPRODUCER OF *CONTINUUM: THE IMMORTALITY PRINCIPLE* EXHIBIT,
AND COAUTHOR OF *OMM SETY'S EGYPT*

"A fascinating book that blends mythology, history, and philosophy into the quest for the sacred wish-fulfilling jewel. The authors weave the lore of the chintamani with modern-day crystal wisdom to create a book that truly stands out. Whether you love history, esotericism, or crystal healing, this book is sure to delight."

NICHOLAS PEARSON, AUTHOR OF *CRYSTAL BASICS*
AND *CRYSTALS FOR KARMIC HEALING*

"Unlike most books on crystals that seek to persuade readers to buy crystals to attain their heart's desires, here is actual instruction on how to invoke the consciousness of the crystal known as the wish-fulfilling jewel—and become that jewel! This is an ancient secret of not only alchemy but also Tibetan Buddhist tantra. Having journeyed to Tibet myself in search of this jewel, I found, as the authors did, that it is within you."

PETER MT. SHASTA, AUTHOR OF
MY SEARCH IN TIBET FOR THE SECRET WISH-FULFILLING JEWEL

"Incredibly well researched and highly documented, demonstrating the dedicated interest of the authors on the mysteries, legends, and authenticity of the stone. The content of this book is the best I have read on the chintamani stone. *The Chintamani Crystal Matrix* is a beautiful book and well worth taking the time to read."

JOLEEN D. DUBOIS, PRESIDENT OF
WHITE MOUNTAIN EDUCATION ASSOCIATION, INC.

"One of the most comprehensive, amazing books I've ever read. It expands upon the connections between crystals and feng shui to help you personalize your spiritual journey. The authors' insights explain how to build your own unique practice in a way that is not only easy to understand but easy to achieve."

LESLEY JOAN LUPO, AUTHOR OF *REMEMBER,*
EVERY BREATH IS PRECIOUS

"If the power of crystals, the energy of sound and resonance, and the history of alchemy, astrology, and ancient wisdom fascinate you, you will want to read *The Chintamani Crystal Matrix*. Johndennis Govert and Hapi Hara have written an exciting, well-researched, and unforgettable book that explores spiritual forces through mythical and historical material. A book you can't live without."

TRYSHE DHEVNEY, SOUND ENERGY EXPERT,
BESTSELLING CRYSTAL SINGING BOWL RECORDING ARTIST,
AND AUTHOR OF *SOUNDSHIFTING*

"The scope of the book is astonishing—part history, part science, part legend—held together with the practical application: *intention.* Spirit and science truly come together."

CLEAR ENGLEBERT, AUTHOR OF *FENG SHUI FOR REAL ESTATE*
AND *FENG SHUI FOR LOVE AND MONEY*

THE
CHINTAMANI
CRYSTAL MATRIX

QUANTUM INTENTION AND
THE WISH-FULFILLING GEM

Johndennis Govert and Hapi Hara

DESTINY

BOOKS

Destiny Books
Rochester, Vermont

Destiny Books
One Park Street
Rochester, Vermont 05767
www.DestinyBooks.com

Destiny Books is a division of Inner Traditions International

Copyright © 2022 by Johndennis Govert and Hapi Hara

All rights reserved. No part of this book may be reproduced or utilized in any form or
by any means, electronic or mechanical, including photocopying, recording, or by any
information storage and retrieval system, without permission in writing from the publisher.

Cataloging-in-Publication Data for this title is available from the Library of Congress

ISBN 978-1-64411-314-1 (print)
ISBN 978-1-64411-315-8 (ebook)

Printed and bound in the United States by Versa Press, Inc.

10 9 8 7 6 5 4 3 2 1

Text design and layout by Virginia Scott Bowman
This book was typeset in Garamond Premier Pro with Albertus used as the display
typeface
Illustrations on pages 72 and 221 copyrighted work available under Creative Commons
Attribution-only license CC BY 4.0, page 147 by Fjgdh5, page 199 by Thincat, page 203
(bottom) by WikiPedant, page 212 (bottom) by Cmdndms, page 256 from Joyofmuseums:
CC BY 4.0, http://creativecommons.org/licenses/by/4.0. Photos and illustrations on
page 125 from Franzy89, page 130 by 350z33, page 146 by Ammerycan Muslim, page 158
by Carles Millan, page 188 by Rob Lavinsky, iRocks.com, page 224 by Parnassus: CC
BY-SA 3.0, https://creativecommons.org/licenses/by-sa/3.0. Page 144 by kevinzim/Kevin
Walsh and page 203 (top) by Stephen Branley, geograph.org.uk/p/1236575: CC BY 2.0,
https://creativecommons.org/licenses/by/2.0

To send correspondence to the author of this book, mail a first-class letter to the author c/o
Inner Traditions • Bear & Company, One Park Street, Rochester, VT 05767, and we will
forward the communication, or contact the authors directly at **chintamanimatrix.com**.

Contents

Foreword

LET ME BEGIN BY CONGRATULATING Hapi Hara and Johndennis Govert for writing *The Chintamani Crystal Matrix: Quantum Intention and the Wish-Fulfilling Gem.* This is because the book brings together, in an inspirational and comprehensive manner, the many faceted aspects associated with the study and significance of crystals, physical and metaphorical, in human existence—including crystal skulls, birth stones, planetary stones, and even stone circles. The authors have cleverly combined their different knowledges and experiences of crystals, science, astrology, and meditation in a very readable and instructive manner.

At the outset of the book, the authors ask the reader a question: "What would you wish for if you were certain your most heartfelt wish would unfold in front of you now?" From there, the reader is taken on a journey that recounts an actual mysterious pilgrimage of the Roerichs to find the mystical location of Shambhala, a kingdom somewhere between the Himalayan Mountains and the Gobi Desert, and their search for the chintamani stone—a wish-fulfilling jewel within both Hindu and Buddhist traditions, that may also be equivalent to the Philosopher's Stone in Western alchemy. Then the journey continues through an examination of the spiritual power of crystals. Ultimately, we are taken through an exploration of the science of crystallography, the branch of science that deals with the structure and properties of crystals, including the electrical properties, as well as the broader subject of mineralogy, and, via reference to the publications of Professor Robert Temple, the ancient significance of meteorites and connections to Sirius are also explored.

The title of the book may seem a little strange, but in chapter 8 the concept of a matrix in the context of crystal structure is explored. Whilst a matrix can be many things, in the context of this book, the authors are thinking of it as a multidimensional material object of great power from which something takes its form, origin, or is enclosed. It is posited that perhaps a chintamani crystal has the yet undiscovered power even to generate tachyons—particles faster than light—hence the discussion of the potential of tachyolithic crystal technology!

But most importantly, the authors' search for the chintamani stone goes well beyond the physical nature of a three, four, or even more dimensional material physical object, and explores the possibility of a personal internal chintamani—one which perhaps aids our search for the power of true nonmaterialistic spiritual happiness.

In the seventeenth century, at the beginning of what is known as the Age of Enlightenment, scientific investigation began taking humanity down the path of intellectual rationalisation and the fragmentation of our material existence. Science achieved this by breaking down the study of the whole being or, for that matter, the whole universe, into the study of ever smaller aspects of our physical existence. Now in the twenty-first century it is as if we are nothing but biological machines—we have placed great emphasis on our mechanism rather than emphasising the fact that we are a living organism contained in a living universe. As a result of such an approach, today we live in a world all too often devoid of spirituality. We exist, for the most part, in a mechanistic and materialistically focused existence where it is generally accepted that all there is to be experienced is simply only that which we can see or interact with through our other senses. This mechanistic approach has led to some terrible human travesties—the two world wars, for example.

The authors challenge the materialist and analytic paradigm of the Enlightenment by transporting the reader to a kind of pre-Enlightenment holistic thinking, that once again combines the spiritual aspects of our being with the science of nature. The truth is that we all desire inner peace and tranquility—that peace and tranquility that brings with it the sleep of the just. So I hope that reading this book will help bring you, the reader, closer to the discovery of, as the authors say, "chintamani awareness" to discover your personal chintamanistic reality. To paraphrase the authors, through the tachyolithic energy state of the chintamani, you become lighter in every sense over the course of your life and transform any remaining karma into golden light.

PROFESSOR MARTIN W. B. JARVIS, OAM, PH.D., FRSA, FIMT
PROFESSORIAL FELLOW, COLLEGE OF INDIGENOUS
FUTURES, ARTS AND SOCIETY
VISITING PROFESSOR, ANHUI NORMAL AND
HAINAN UNIVERSITIES, CHINA
EMERITUS ARTISTIC DIRECTOR, DARWIN SYMPHONY ORCHESTRA

MARTIN JARVIS is a professorial fellow at Charles Darwin University in Australia and visiting professor at Anhui Normal University in Wuhu, China. He has traveled frequently to China since 2010 and was the director of the Confucius Institute at Charles Darwin University for eight years. He has a keen interest in Confucianism and its history, as well as Taoism and Traditional Chinese Medicine. He has a long career in music and was the conductor for the Darwin Symphony Orchestra. His research field is the application of forensic handwriting examination to handwritten music manuscripts, particularly those of the eighteenth century, and he is carrying out new research in Rosicrucianism, music, and Mozart's connection to alchemy.

Acknowledgments

THIS BOOK WOULD NOT HAVE BEEN POSSIBLE without the help and expertise of several people who assisted us. In research, we gained valuable insight from Gvido Trepsa, director at the Nicholas Roerich Museum in New York. We appreciate Joleen DuBois for her time, information, and insight during a personal interview. We extend our gratitude to Darlene Randolph and Martin Jarvis, who provided extensive assistance with editing and feedback about the text. We appreciate images provided by the Very Reverend Gregory Dunstan, Donald Lightner, Jan Eisen from VitaJuwel, and photography by Sloane Ehnat. We are greatly indebted to the assistance provided by Kaleigh Brown, who spent several hours on photography, illustrations, digital compilations, photo editing, and text editing. As the years of writing unfolded, we appreciate all the support of family and friends who listened patiently to our stories and experiences and encouraged us to continue. Finally, we thank the staff at Inner Traditions for their work on this book, and we extend appreciation to Jon Graham who reviewed our initial text with encouraging feedback. We want to express our appreciation to Jamaica Burns Griffin, Mallory Hennigar, and Ashley Kolesnik at Inner Traditions for their work in editing this book. Last, we wish to thank Martin Jarvis for agreeing to write the foreword.

Introducing
the Chintamani

Masses of lamps lit by suns, moons, and radiant gems,
Shine ecstatic light rays to illumine the billion worlds.

ROBERT THURMAN, *THE JEWEL TREE OF TIBET*

CHINTAMANI. WHAT WOULD YOU WISH FOR if you were certain your most heartfelt wish would unfold in front of you now? What would you wish for if you had in your hands the certain means to manifest your wish on Earth? The chintamani is the wish-fulfilling gem known in a variety of legends from around the world. Its power can transform the Earth negatively or positively depending on the character of whoever directs it by intention. Possessing the chintamani has inspired soldiers-of-fortune, despots, and kings to search the ends of the Earth for it through the annals of history. Wielding the power of the chintamani has driven gods, titans, and men to risk everything for the promise of securing their own supremacy. Diminishing injustice and suffering to benefit all beings has inspired heroes, saints, and sages to engage in the battle of good versus evil, even at their own extreme peril. What discourages most people from seeking the chintamani is doubt that its mythical origins describe something useful, let alone tangible, or doubt that it might function on a global scale. Perhaps most incapacitating is doubt that any of us personally should enter the fierce competition to shape the future of the Earth.

At first, folklore seems to suggest that there has been just one single chintamani. As we untangle mythology, history, and philosophy through time, we discover that there have been multiple chintamanis from prehistory

1

into the present. The image of one great earth gem expands to include a number of other dizzying possibilities:

1. The chintamani is from outer space and either randomly or purposefully landed on Earth as a meteorite or tektite.
2. There are an indefinite number of chintamani-like gems that appear and disappear through the course of time.
3. The chintamani is the Philosopher's Stone.
4. The chintamani is a system or grid of gems with particular qualities and focused energy.
5. The chintamani is a technology embedded in crystals, not an item.
6. The chintamani transcends time and is multidimensional.
7. The chintamani activates by the power of intention.
8. The chintamani is a primal archetype.
9. The chintamani is a tool for spiritually realized beings to guide humans and Earth herself along a more positive evolutionary trajectory.
10. The chintamani is inherently a subtle essence embedded in the root of consciousness itself.
11. The chintamani is a means to transform limited awareness into the realization of supreme enlightenment.
12. The chintamani is a quantum expression of great compassion, wisdom, and skill.

Since it is likely there is more than one mysterious chintamani, you may want to consider how important a personal quest for a physical or spiritual chintamani may be for you. As the chintamani has the ability to stimulate Earth's evolution to bring uncountable blessings for all, you may want to examine carefully the practical and transcendental value the chintamani may be for all of us. In William Butler Yeats' poem "The Second Coming," he squarely sets forth the challenge of his era as well as ours:

> *The best lack all conviction, while the worst*
> *Are full of passionate intensity.*
> *Surely some revelation is at hand.*[1]

In this book, we will explore myth and history to understand who has quested for the chintamani across space and time and what they intended and accomplished with the wish-fulfilling gem. We will consider the physical and metaphysical basis and use of gems along with a deeper exploration of crystals and gems used as the chintamani. We will present chintamani spiritual practices based not just on our research but on our direct experiences as well. We invite you to follow the skein of investigative threads over space and time and sort the evidence with us. There is a very practical value to the chintamani path. We aim to inspire and encourage you to experiment with chintamani practice to accelerate, manifest, and evolve your heart's desire.

The Roerich Chintamani

The chintamani is as much a quest as it is a destination. It is as much a key to resolve life's mysteries as it is a precious prize to guard. In chapter 1, we introduce you to Helena and Nicholas Roerich and their two sons George (Yuri) and Svetoslav. Together, from the 1890s into the 1950s, this family embarked on a number of spiritual quests through India, the Gobi Desert, the Altai and Kunlun Mountains, Mongolia, and Tibet, crisscrossing the Himalayan mountains many times before they settled in Kullu, India, in the shadows of the great mountain range. They were an immensely talented family involved in the fine arts, particularly oil painting, archaeology, cultural anthropology, and the comparative study of languages and religions. They were world adventurers who had left their native Russia just months before the Russian Revolution in 1917. They were involved in international politics, especially in efforts to preserve cultural sites worldwide, as well as to promote peace on the planet in the era of both world wars and their chaotic aftermath.

We present the story of the Roerichs in the first chapter because of their quest using the chintamani to discover the kingdom of Shambhala. Although many consider Shambhala a myth, it is noteworthy that the United States government was a contributing sponsor of one of the Roerichs' Asian treks. In fact, Franklin D. Roosevelt called his presidential retreat "Shambhala" during that era. Later, Dwight D. Eisenhower renamed it "Camp David." The Roerich quests were tracked by Russian and Nazi spies and complicated by tense interactions with local warlords whom they encountered in the thousands of miles of hard travel across environmentally and politically harsh terrains. We present the Roerich story not because we want to chronicle their fascinating adventures, but rather because the chintamani was central to their quest. In treks across decades and continents, the Roerichs experienced the chintamani in the full range of possibilities, from worldly power stone to true mystical key.

The First Chintamani

The chintamani appears both personally and collectively more as mysticism than as fact. Lore of its origin points to the depths of the Milky Way and not immediately to Earth. Since we cannot offer a generally accepted historical timeline, let us start in the mists of myth before the appearance of humankind with a chintamani origin story from three converging Hindu sources: the *Bhagavata Purana,* the *Vishnu Purana,*[2] and the epic Mahabharata. The story is known either as the *samudra manthana* or *kshirasagara manthana,* or in English, "churning of the milk ocean."

In Hindu mythology, Lakshmi, devi of prosperity and beauty, vanished into the cosmic ocean due to a curse devised by the wronged sage Durvasa to punish Indra, chief of the devas, or gods. Along with Lakshmi vanished the vitality, grandeur, grace, wealth, and power of the entire deva realm. The devas consulted among themselves and with the supreme trinity of God. Vishnu, the sustaining manifestation of God, advised the devas how to recover Lakshmi and, consequently, the former greatness of their realm. The cosmic ocean of existence needed churning in order to release Lakshmi from its great depths. In order to accomplish this vast task, all the devas had to cooperate with all the *asuras.* The asuras, sometimes referred to as titans or demons, were involved in perpetual competition and battle with the devas. Under the leadership of Bali, the asuras had gained control of the universe, supplanting the devas. To entice the asuras, Vishnu disclosed that churning the ocean would not only return Lakshmi but would also produce *amrita,* the elixir of immortality. The great desire to gain amrita of immortality was enough to motivate the asuras to cooperate with their detested enemies. Vishnu secretly assured the devas, however, that he would prevent the asuras from ever becoming immortal.

The grand plan required the celestial mountain Mandara be used as a churning rod. The king of serpents, multiheaded Vasuki, would be used as a rope to spin Mount Mandara. The ancient sea turtle Kurma would become the base to float the mountain in the ocean waters. Vishnu himself would center the axis so the mountain could spin stably in place. Vasuki was the most venomous serpent in existence. Vishnu advised the devas to hold the serpent's tail, leaving the asuras to wield the serpent's head as both sides pulled Vasuki back and forth to provide the power needed to spin the mountain and froth the ocean. The asuras resisted the poison released during the spinning, but great clouds of *halahala,* the ultimate poison, soon threatened the devas as the poison began to fall as rain. Shiva, the third manifestation of the supreme trinity of God, drank all the *halahala* poison. This act of compassionate valor earned him the epithet of Nilakantha, "the blue necked one," because his neck turned blue from drinking but not swallowing the poison.

The immediate result of churning the cosmic ocean was the emergence of fourteen *ratnas.* Both *ratna* and *mani* in Sanskrit refer to gems, jewels, and more broadly anything precious or of great value. The fourteen precious ratnas that emerged were:

1. Amrita, elixir of immortality;
2. Dhanavantri, the physician of the devas bearing a jar of amrita;
3. Mahalakshmi, *mahadevi* of prosperity, beauty, and wealth;
4. Ratnas, chintamani gems including the *kaustubham;*
5. Rambha, the Apsara queen and celestial beauty renowned for her dance skill;
6. Chandra, the moon;
7. Gada, Vishnu's mace weapon known as *kaumodaki;*
8. Parijata, a great, fragrant tree planted in Indra's paradise realm;
9. Airavata, a multi-tusked elephant for Indra;
10. Kamadhenu, the wish-fulfilling cow;
11. Kalpavriksha, the wish-fulfilling tree;
12. Sankha, the victory conch of Indra;
13. Uchchaihsravas, the white horse of Indra;
14. Mada, or Sura, another devi, creator of wine and fermentation.

After all the fourteen ratnas appeared, the asuras demanded their share of amrita to obtain immortality as reward, but Vishnu frustrated their desires. With Lakshmi's return to the gods' realm, Indra's *devaloka* returned to its former glory and power, reenergizing the devas who then repulsed the asuras and reasserted control. Having nowhere left to go in *svarga,* "the high heavens," nor on Earth, the asuras were forced to inhabit *patala,* "the underworld." Assuring their immortality, the devas took all the amrita and kept what they didn't consume. Four celestial beings came from the milky ocean: Lakshmi (transformed into Mahalakshmi), the Apsara queen, Dhanavantri, and the goddess Sura. Indra, king of the devas*,* received gifts for his realm of Indraloka, which included two of the five trees of paradise. Personally, Indra also received a victory conch, white horse, mighty elephant, and a wishfulfilling cow. All beings benefitted from the cooling effects of the moon's emergence from the oceanic depths. Shiva transformed the deadly *halahala* poison and protected the environment. Last, Vishnu received the mighty mace weapon, Gada, and the *kaustubham* gem. This fourth ratna was one of many chintamani gems that also emerged from the cosmic ocean with the kaustubham. This myth points to a time when not one but many chintamani gems were invoked by Vishnu and arose from the vastness of the cosmos.

Details about all the chintamani gems produced in churning the milk ocean are sparse. More is revealed about the most archetypal chintamani, the kaustubham gem that Vishnu wore around his neck as a garland from that time forward. In Sanskrit, *kaustubham* means "pervading the universe." It is a solid essence of pure consciousness that radiates brilliantly in every direction like the sun. It is a blue jewel resembling a great and flawless sapphire. The kaustubham also radiated a number of qualities such as creating powerful protection, vast wealth and splendor, and infinite and unimaginable benefit toward all beings. Vishnu was the only one who could possess and wear the kaustubham uncorrupted and remain able to use its complete power and brilliance to maintain the entirety of creation. As we explore more of chintamani history, we will discover that corruption and misuse of power is a central moral dilemma throughout time concerning all those who attempt to wield a chintamani. The kaustubham was believed to possess high consciousness itself, so much so that a later Tamil emperor of the Chera dynasty was considered a reincarnation of the kaustubham.

Wish-Fulfilling Power

Chintamani in English is most often called the wish-fulfilling gem. This translation, however, misses the heart of the meaning. A more apt and succinct translation is "thought gem." The second part of the word is easy, as *mani* means jewel, gem, or precious treasure. It is the first half of the word phrase that requires clarification. *Chinta,* or its root, *chint-*, has a range of usages:[3]

> *Chint,* verbal root: to think, to have a thought or idea, to reflect, to consider, to direct thoughts toward, to care for, to take into consideration
>
> *Chinta,* noun: thought, consideration, care, anxiety, anxious thought

These meanings suggest not a whimsical wish, but rather a thoughtful, more thorough exploration of intention.

To properly use a chintamani then, the holder's intention should be well-considered and invoked not merely to indulge a momentary urge or advantage for the ego. If we power our intentions with a chintamani, our intentions need to make sense and offer benefit in many directions simultaneously, like waves rippling in the total ocean of being. This implies the chintamani holder should be a very knowledgeable and wise person who has attained higher spiritual realization. This is also a moral from the churning of the milk ocean myth. The asuras have the least regard for any but their own collective and personal self-interests. The devas have a greater view and produce a wider beneficial effect in the universe, but they too have limiting, collective self-interests for control. Only Vishnu, the sustaining God, who has the interests of the entirety of creation in mind, can and ought to bear the kaustubham, which is the primal chintamani.

Chintamani Matrix Topics

In chapters 2 and 3 we will explore more of the myths, legends, and history of the chintamani in the Vedic and Buddhist traditions, which interconnect to form a more extensive and deeper understanding of the wish-fulfilling gem. We will learn about those who have worked the most harmoniously with a chintamani versus those who have been the actual chintamani bearers through history. There is a stark contrast between these groups, which we will also explore in this book. In chapter 4, we reexamine the theme of the chintamani in relation to the quest for Shambhala. This sets the Roerichs' unique and modern adventures into a longer historical perspective and describes the axis of the physical and spiritual dimensions that cross in Shambhala. In chapters 5 and 6, we look at how power crystals have been used in the global-scale battle for world dominance and review some of the most notorious gems in the world. In chapter 7, we look at crystal science: where it began and how it has developed at an accelerated pace in the last century. We explore the scientific qualities inherent in crystals and gems as well as crystal spiritual technology. We consider, among other topics, how DNA itself is an aperiodic crystal and what that means for conscious human evolution. In chapter 8, we consider astrological qualities of birthstones. We look at the related phenomena of grids of jewels assembled in crowns, breast-plates, and arrays to increase the aggregate power of gems. We extend this discussion to include the enigmatic field arrays of ancient stone circles.

The Chintamani Crystal Matrix is this book's title and theme. We are suggesting that there is not a single gem, but that in fact there is a matrix of gems that are chintamani in nature. These gems, as they are dispersed around the Earth, and perhaps the whole galaxy, interact with one another, as well as with conscious beings. All the intentions, gems, and conscious beings interact together in a great cloud of mind and energy to co-create the *Chintamani Crystal Matrix.* As each one of us is a node in the *Chintamani Crystal Matrix,* we will describe ways to access chintamani gems and how to practice with them to produce great benefit for self and others simultaneously.

We have subtitled this book *Quantum Intention and the Wish-Fulfilling Gem* because the chintamani highlights the journey that proves to be an endless knot that leads to your heart energy and out into the world again, folding ever in and ever out. The chintamani is the core of an extremely ancient and yet very advanced future technology simultaneously. It operates faster than the speed of light at the speed of thought. We are just beginning to explore the scientific evidence to explain the nature of quantum entangle-ment. Are there faster-than-light subatomic particles, the hypothetical tachy-ons? If so, the chintamani is tachyolithic, the stone that can move energy faster than light. Or does quantum entanglement create instantaneous connections in time and space through intention? If this is the case, the chinta-mani coupled with intention can open access to an infinite set of potential alternate realities.

It is not enough to know about the incredible promise that chintamani crystals and gems encode if we do not use their energy to unlock our own potential. The last four chapters deliver our more urgent message, which is why and how you can work more successfully for your own and others' benefit with tangible and intangible crystals. In chapter 9, we consider alchemical systems, Western and Eastern, in which gems, minerals, and elements form an integral part of many methods for self-transformation. Chapter 10 arose as a surprise during our research. We discovered a category of created chintamanis from alchemical science, glass, and medicines to elaborate combinations of rituals and ingredients as treasure vases. These two chapters provide a greater, philosophical context for crystal and chintamani practice. Chapter 11 is much more tangible; we offer methods of using crystals for personal practice. It discusses the basics of working with crystals in selecting, purifying, and programming intention. It also describes crystal meditations for personal transformation, as well as how to assemble crystals in grids. Last, chapter 12 provides details about more advanced chintamani yoga practices with which you can experiment to bring about both your spiritual development and personal altruistic intentions. It is our intention to help shine the reflected and refracted light rays from the chintamani realm on the hero's quest, which is the central quest of each and every one of us.

1

The Chintamani Quest

The Chintamani and the Roerichs' Search for Shambhala

We do not know. But they know. The stones know.

NICHOLAS ROERICH, *FLAME IN CHALICE*

THE SEARCH FOR THE CHINTAMANI STONE, or the wish-fulfilling gem, is also the search for Shambhala, the place of peace and happiness. In modern times, the discovery of the mythical chintamani stone and the search for the legendary Shambhala has not been better exemplified than by the epic adventures of Nicholas Roerich and his family in their quest through Asia in the late 1920s. Nicholas, born in St. Petersburg, Russia, in 1874, was an intriguing real-life Indiana Jones. His efforts led to the signing of the historic Roerich Pact, or the Treaty on the Protection of Artistic and Scientific Institutions and Historic Monuments, whose purpose was to protect cultural heritage and objects during war. The Roerich Pact eventually led to the creation of UNESCO. While there are conflicting and controversial theories about the Roerich family, they left an undeniable impact on the twentieth century, leaving behind a spiritual-cultural-social movement called Roerichism. A Renaissance man, Nicholas was an artist, archaeologist, philosopher, poet, and, because of his political affiliations, perhaps a spy working for more than one government. Curiously, one of Nicholas' expeditions was purportedly a secret commission by the U.S. government to locate the kingdom of Shambhala in Asia.* Shambhala is the inspiration for stories about Shangri-La,† a fabulous land in a hidden valley where people live in a paradise on Earth in perfect peace and harmony.

Nicholas wrote extensive travel journals that describe the Roerich family's perilous and arduous journey through the Himalayas, Mongolia, Tibet, and India during the early twentieth century. Nicholas trekked with his wife Helena, a writer and mystic, and his son George (Yuri), a linguist and prominent Tibetologist. While travel journals and other published works provide tantalizing glimpses regarding the chintamani and Shambhala, Nicholas does not divulge specific information about either, and after reading his travel log we are left with the sense that Shambhala was either not found or that if an important clue regarding its existence was discovered, it was not divulged openly. Nicholas' travel log is matter-of-fact and dry in many respects, simply discussing the many obstacles with respect to grueling weather conditions, deadly altitude sickness, violent bands of thieves, packs of man-eating dogs, long periods of imprisonment, and endless delays involving corrupt officials and travel documents. The travel journals record Nicholas dutifully searching for and cataloguing items of cultural heritage while brazenly opening Western consciousness to remote regions of the East.

By contrast, a review of Nicholas' paintings graphically portrays an altogether different perspective. Many of Nicholas' artworks were painted while on a caravan through difficult travel conditions, a testament to his tenacity and determination. While recognizing the practical importance of the written record, we think Nicholas' paintings more vividly represent the truth of his physical and spiritual journey. Andrew Tomas, a contemporary of

---

*This agricultural commission was initiated by the U.S. Secretary of Agriculture, Henry Wallace, with the approval of Franklin D. Roosevelt. There is much controversy about this U.S. commission and rumors that it involved a secret political agenda to locate Shambhala before another rival nation found it. (Walker, "The New Deal and the Guru.")

†In 1933, James Hilton wrote *Lost Horizon,* a novel, describing Shangri-La as a utopian paradise in Asia's Kunlun Mountains, which was made into a famous film of the same name directed by Frank Capra in 1937.

the Roerichs, reported that Nicholas may have hidden cryptograms among the mountains and rocks in his paintings.[1] Though a written account of Nicholas' journey is found in other books, including his own writings, we found it incomplete compared to what he pictorially presented in his paintings.[2] Here, we present the story through the lens of an artist and a poet. This lens may reflect an inner journey for Nicholas, but often our inner journey is reflective of our outer journey, a reflection not unlike those made by the facets of a gem. We hope the reader will forgive us as we take creative license to present a narrative style exploring more fully the impact of the chintamani stone on the consciousness of Nicholas as expressed in his works of art.

The Chintamani Stone

The Roerich family's journey with the chintamani began on October 9, 1923, a brisk autumn day in Paris. George Roerich solemnly made his way to the Banker's Trust in Paris to retrieve a package held securely by the bank. When George saw the label on the package, he was filled with excitement. The sender of the brown paper-wrapped package wrote only the initials "M. M." in formal, cursive letters. The mysterious "M. M." was an agent who had been communicating with his parents, Nicholas and Helena, that they would receive a package with an auspicious gift that was to assist them in a very unusual commission. For the past several weeks, the Roerichs had waited for the arrival of the package while residing in their suite at the Lord Byron Hotel in Paris.

George eagerly made his way back to the Lord Byron, located in an exclusive area of Paris near the Arc de Triomphe. He felt a sense of excitement as he delivered the treasure to his famous parents, who had made a name for themselves in the art world. His father, Nicholas, had become an accomplished artist internationally. Nicholas' paintings achieved worldwide recognition for their modern approach to mystical themes. Nicholas was funded by government groups to carry out expeditions that, on the surface, seemed purely cultural in nature, but ultimately would have far-reaching ramifications in global politics and power in the tense era of the Russian Revolution and two destructive world wars. Under a shroud of political maneuvering and secrecy, the Roerichs had been commissioned to find the mythical realm of Shambhala that was legendarily believed to exist in the Himalayas. Nicholas was selected to lead the expedition because of his knowledge of Tibetan Buddhist monasteries and their connection with the Buddhist mysteries of the Kalachakra and Shambhala.* He was an ideal candidate for this special mission due to his depth of knowledge, indefatigable energy, and personal passion for the quest.

Promoting his unique approach to the mystic arts was not the only reason for Nicholas' time in Paris. The Roerichs were waiting to receive instructions about an object that was to aid them on their journey. Nicholas was a middle-aged man, bald, with a long, pointed beard. His intense, piercing eyes carried an age and gravity that was older than his years. His wife, Helena, famous in her own right, was far more than the wife of an internationally acclaimed artist. In many ways, while her husband was the artist and the philosopher, she was the mystic and clairvoyant. She was regarded in their circles as having the uncanny ability to communicate with spirits and possessed remarkable spiritual vision. Indeed, such were her intuitive gifts that she was chosen by their guru as the bearer of a singular, precious treasure. It was hoped that her uncanny intuition would attune her clairvoyance to the treasure and guide their small band through the treacherous mountains during their ambitious and dangerous Himalayan trek.

An attractive woman with dark hair, she was both refined and educated. Coming from a noble family that included generals,† poets, and musicians, she was related to Russian composer Modest Mussorgsky. With artistic and poetic genius in her blood, she was a suitable and well-matched companion to Nicholas, with the ability to support and appreciate her husband's work

---

*Kalachakra is a complex Tibetan Buddhist practice and mandala considered the highest teaching leading to enlightenment. The practice helps in accessing Shambhala (see chapter 4).

†Helena Roerich was related to field marshal Mikhail Kutuzov, who defeated both the Turks in the Russian Ottoman Wars and Napoleon in the War of 1812. According to Wikipedia, which cites a Russian source, Kutuzov was a member of several masonic orders, including a German lodge called "Three Keys" and a Moscow lodge called "Three Banners."

in the art world. They shared a deep philosophical interest in Asian religions and eventually became the spiritual leaders of a mystical philosophy that was to become Agni Yoga (Fire Yoga). Helena was beautiful and dignified, with a cool composure that helped to offset Nicholas' intensity. Her serene eyes also shone with a quiet knowing. Her eyes conveyed an older wisdom that seemed ageless. She had a furtive, coy glint in her expression that showed that she could be amused by life too. Indeed, this unassuming quality helped her remain resilient during their daunting travels over the next several years.

So it was to these famous parents that George Roerich was now delivering the important package. He knew that his parents' aspirations were tied to the contents of the package. George himself remained close to his parents and joined their expeditions in Asia. Among other works, George Roerich wrote an eleven-volume *Tibetan-Russian-English Dictionary with Sanskrit Parallels,* which is considered a significant contribution to Tibetan dialectology. As a Tibetologist, his contributions during the Asian expeditions were invaluable. His brother, Svetoslav, also accompanied the family on expeditions and became an artist like his father, painting important portraits of Nicholas and Helena standing or sitting next to an antique box referred to as "the casket" (figures 1.1 and 1.2).

George found his father in his room at the hotel and, barely suppressing his excitement, showed Nicholas the package with its simple inscription from a mysterious "M. M." Father and son mutually decided to wait for Helena to return from her walk, as the precious contents were really intended for her. The two men put the enigmatic package aside and waited patiently.

Helena was on her morning walk strolling the well-to-do areas of Paris close to the Lord Byron Hotel. She had not been feeling well, but the walks gave her the opportunity to clear her thoughts and open her visionary channel without interference. Of a naturally nervous and sensitive disposition, she found walking soothed her. For months, they had been waiting for some word from their guru, Master Morya, about the enigmatic treasure he was sending them. As she walked the neighborhoods of 1920s Paris, she reflected on the communications she had received from Master Morya over the past few months.

Master Morya was an accomplished mystic who had profoundly influenced the Roerichs. He had guided them in their quest toward Shambhala

Figure 1.1. Svetoslav Roerich, *Nicholas Roerich Holding the Casket*, 1928, Nicholas Roerich Museum, NY.

Figure 1.2. Svetoslav Roerich, *Mme. Helena Roerich*, 1924,
Nicholas Roerich Museum, NY.

and had appeared to both during meditations. Morya, also known as El
Morya and M. M., figured strongly in the Theosophical movement, considered an ascended master of the first ray and chief of the Darjeeling Council
of the Great White Brotherhood. In a stroke of synchronicity, they recognized him in a chance meeting on Bond Street in London in 1920. Since
that time, Morya and Helena connected in thought transmissions that were
quite extensive and continued throughout her lifetime. She had received
both thought transmissions and tangible telegraphs about the precious treasure. Indeed, the arrival of the stone was a sign to initiate their journey to

India. Helena had been told that she was to be the receiver and bearer of the stone as a symbolic "Mother of the World," and to use the stone for guidance and the transmission of spiritual messages.

Nicholas painted *Mother of the World* in the 1930s, portraying the painting subject as the divine feminine peace goddess garbed in mystical blue with rings of white illuminating her. She sits atop a mountain surrounded by the feminine earth power. Later, in 1932, Nicholas was to paint *Madonna Oriflamma,* also a medieval Madonna, but holding the peace banner of the Roerichs, with its iconic interlocking three circles encircled by a fourth larger one (figure 1.3 on the following page). The divine feminine was embraced by the Roerichs, and Helena actualized the divine feminine in their travels and in their work. Undoubtedly, her spiritual devotion to the quest in addition to her innate psychic gifts made her apt to act as an agent of Sophia, the paragon of timeless feminine wisdom. Streaks of white were visible in Helena's hair, adding to her appearance as a mystic sage, and she wore a blue sapphire wedding ring, a stone of wisdom that activates the third eye and visionary gifts.

Now she contemplated the next stage in her spiritual evolution in the fascinating life path with her artist-philosopher husband, Nicholas. As she approached the Arc de Triomphe de Etoile (The Triumphal Arch of the Star), she was reminded of the symbolism of their stay in Paris, as the Arc and its radiating wheel of twelve avenues were not dissimilar to the diagram and layout of the mythical central city of Shambhala. Master Morya had told them there would be many symbols and reminders of their quest to illumine and guide them on their journey. It was one of the reasons Helena was walking now—to encounter symbols of their quest and to reignite enthusiasm so their patience would endure and faith renew. She chose to walk down the Champs-Elysees undoubtedly inspired by the obelisk at the end of the avenue, Place de la Concorde, aligned with the Arc and the rays of the sun. The obelisk, twenty-two and a half meters high, was a granite phallus protruding into the sky. One of a pair of the two largest obelisks in the world, its companion still stands in front of the Luxor Temple in Egypt. The inscriptions on the obelisk are a prayer to the sun as the gnomon symbolically guides the sun across the heavens. The obelisk foreshadowed the impending journey that would take them to India via Egypt, where they would visit the

Figure 1.3. Nicholas Roerich, *Madonna Oriflamma*, 1932,
Nicholas Roerich Museum, NY.

Great Pyramid and the Sphinx, symbolic of their own initiation. Luxor
was associated with kingship, and the pharaohs were crowned there, as was
Alexander the Great. Luxor was famous for its Opet Festival that united
Luxor with nearby Karnak in a fertility ritual during the king's coronation.
The sensitive Helena would have noticed the theme as she approached the
obelisk praising the sun overhead.

Turning to her left from the obelisk, she would have faced l'Eglise de la Madeleine down the avenue Place de la Madeleine. The symbolism was obvious. The sun god was aligned with the Lunar Temple before her. A temple built in the Roman neoclassical style, it resembled the Ancient Temple of Artemis. This particular Roman Catholic church in Paris is dedicated to Mary Magdalene, who had been marginalized historically and labeled a prostitute without Biblical authority. Controversially, she was also the possible wife of Jesus.

In the 1920s, Paris led a renaissance for the liberation of women. This was the ideal place for Helena to receive a spiritual honor as the symbolic "mother of the world." Their initiation into secret societies may have led the Roerichs into information concerning the Gnostic belief that the Magdalene was Jesus' wife or consort with whom he had a child. The resulting bloodline was considered by some Gnostics and secret societies to be the real grail. These themes must have struck a chord with Helena, who was herself challenging traditional notions of Christianity and spirituality. As she walked, the alignment between the obelisk and white temple devoted to the Magdalene was obvious, and the auspicious symbols allowed her to reflect on alchemical unification, the pending grail quest, and enlightenment.

Making her way back to the Lord Byron Hotel, Helena found Nicholas and George expectantly waiting for her with the package from Master Morya. Her excitement and anticipation rose, and she quickly commanded George to open the mysterious package. This was the sign that a special treasure was being entrusted to them that would initiate and guide their quest. The package was a simple pine box with ornate script lettering typical of the period. It was addressed to Mme. and Ms. N. Roerich. The "Madame" was written first and longer than "Monsieur," clearly showing that the package was intended for Helena foremost. Curiously, in the lower left corner of the address was written "on behalf of MM." For the Roerichs, this could only be Master Morya.

George ceremoniously opened the box in front of his parents, full of anticipation. Inside was another box, dark with ornate brocade. It was a dark brown leather with pictures and symbols on the side and an antique metal latch on the front. The casket felt ancient. It was the sort of casket that could be the repository for the secrets known only to adepts and shared with the chosen few. George had carefully laid out the contents of the pine box and the inner casket on the dark wooden desk near a window. The light was shining auspiciously through the window onto the casket. Without a word, Nicholas ceremoniously approached the desk and antique casket. Slowly unlatching the metal clasp, he pulled out a creamy white brocade silk scarf to reveal a mysterious stone sitting on a silk pillow in the casket. It was a dark pitted stone a few inches in diameter. He looked over at Helena and made a gesture to her with his hand out toward the stone as though he were offering it to her.

She pensively approached the casket and gingerly reached for the stone. She thought it surprisingly light to the touch. Intuitively, she held it up to the sunlight streaming through the window. The sunlight ignited the stone from a dark black color to a brilliant, fiery green ray—the purest green ray that Helena had ever beheld. It was as though the light had activated the stone. Helena gasped in surprise, and as she continued to wonder at the intense green color of the stone, she felt the green fire ray move through her eyes and down into her heart. She felt flushed by the green fire. The stone had the light of the green eyes from a fire dragon, and her heart became "awake." She bid Nicholas and George look with her at the green flash of the stone. They too were surprised by its dramatic change of appearance. They each, in turn, held the stone, but when it was not lit from behind by the sunlight, it returned to its somber dark color. The stone needed illumination for the green ray to appear. The stone seemed magical to the Roerichs, and they were entranced by its mystical green fire. Helena felt transformed the moment she beheld the green fire of the stone. The arrival of the chintamani stone was the sign that started their quest for Shambhala.

The Path to Shambhala

The caravan meandered its way slowly, languidly along the path hugging a ridge. On the right was a spectacular gorge. The pathway was narrow, and the caravan of riders and horses squeezed to the left to avoid the cliff edge. The caravan gradually made its ascent as Nicholas reflected on their journey. Their caravan had traversed some of the highest mountain passes in the world in the Himalayas. The middle-aged adventurer was tired. Travel had been exhausting amid illnesses and deaths in their caravan party caused by the extremely high altitude. The Roerichs, though, were energized by a motivation and an inner, indefatigable fire. There was an intense drive that kept the Roerich family moving forward through treacherous mountain passes, ravines, and canyons that seemed unending. Yet the artist and poet in Nicholas saw more than unforgiving, insurmountable heights. His very soul engaged with the breathless beauty and magnificence of the Himalayas. In many cultures, there is a belief that climbing mountain peaks allows one to move closer to a higher, spiritual source. Thus, climbing peaks is a pilgrimage, and the more daunting the obstacles, the more the soul ascends. In those trials, Nicholas must have developed a strong spiritual connection during his Himalayan ascension.

Master Morya had informed them that they would see signs along their journey. Nicholas' visionary eye not only saw the signs but also interpreted them, while his mystic's soul drew faith from them. He did not doubt the signs. For him, they were living testimony. Roerich was a treasure seeker. He was seeking Shambhala, but he also saw much other treasure on his excursions through the East. He was an archaeologist uncovering great antiquities and ancient cultures throughout his travels, which he dutifully recorded. He appreciated their value to such an extent that he was moved to create the Roerich Pact, which was signed on April 15, 1935, by Franklin Delano Roosevelt to protect the great antiquities and archaeology of the world.[3] He deeply appreciated treasure on many levels. He understood and "saw," with the keen observation of an artist, the color and shape of the mountain peaks that so inspired him. Nicholas painted the mountain peaks, canyons, and crevices with such attention to detail and nuance of color that, later, members of Sir Edmund Hillary's 1953 Everest expedition recognized certain glaciers from his paintings. He knew there were splendid treasures in the mountains and that this was the reason why many hermits, lamas, and the true teachers were living there. His many paintings of the mountains showed respect for these tall peaks and, in some paintings, he even painted the cliffs with shamanic faces, suggesting that the rocks were living watchers during the Roerichs' epic journey. There were deep treasures in the foreboding mountains, and Nicholas decoded the language of the stones and nature. He found treasures in the Himalayan mountains, not only Shambhala. In the Altai foothills, he found sentient forests: "Their roots know what riches, what innumerable treasures, are guarded in the stony depths of the mountains, for the future prosperity of mankind."[4]

The Roerichs carried with them the chintamani stone in its casket on a horse, which inspired Nicholas to paint *Treasure of the World* (1924) (figure 1.4). He painted a living symbol because this is how his mystic's eye saw the energy of the stone. In the painting, it is burning with a blue auric flame far beyond its casket, energizing him, Helena, George, and their caravan on their quest to find Shambhala. During their long stay in Leh, Ladakh, they investigated stories about a guidebook to Shambhala titled *The Red Path to Shambhala,* which was said to be secreted in Hemis Monastery. They neither found this hidden volume nor confirmed its existence. The deep connection between the physical and spiritual was confirmed to Nicholas in his interview with a secret Lama about the location of Shambhala.[5] The interview tested Nicholas because the Lama did not give up his secrets about Shambhala easily. Nicholas' frustration and insistence are evident in his own writings: "Lama, tell me of Shambhala!"[6] The Lama was circumspect and dodged direct questions, brushing him off with notions that he was merely a curious, disrespectful Westerner who did not understand Shambhala. Nicholas was insistent during his interview and countered the Lama's arguments and dismissive accusations with his intense desire for the truth and his passion to find the treasure.

Nicholas mused on the Lama's comments while continuing the journey through the mountain pass. They ventured through the canyon and found a campsite. That night, in the bitter cold, Nicholas went outside and meditated under the luminous stars. They had reached a higher altitude in the Himalayas and were as close to the starry heavens as mortal man could reach. The luminous jewels of the sky undoubtedly inspired Nicholas in the creation of his many paintings with star themes (figure 1.5, page 24). The clarity of the skies allowed him to see the colors of the sky: deep blue sapphire, fiery red ruby, warm yellow topaz, sparkling white diamond. They were so close, thrumming with twinkling starlight, that he could almost

Figure 1.4. Nicholas Roerich, *Treasure of the World*, 1924,
Nicholas Roerich Museum, NY.

pluck the jewels from the sky with his shivering hand. There was an unyield-
ing purity in the cold white snow of the Himalayas and in his breath that
matched the purity of the heavens above him. He felt like Abraham and Job
of old peering into the heavens and talking directly to God. The brilliant
constellation Orion was luminous above the gleaming white mountains. Its
stunning purity awakened him ever more deeply to his mission. He was mes-
merized by the combination of the gleaming snow and glimmering stars in
the dark liquid sky. He was awakened from the contemplative moment by
the startling movement of a shooting star from Orion, streaking over the
white mountain before him. Master Morya said he would see signs, and he
felt this was pointing his way both metaphorically and geographically. As
the star faded into the dark sky, it pointed ahead where they were going
beyond the mountain toward a valley. Nicholas felt like he became one with

Figure 1.5. Nicholas Roerich, *Star of the Hero*, 1936,
Nicholas Roerich Museum, NY.

the stars, and the next moment he remembered his horse again traversing the mountainous, cold trail. The rising sun had turned the mountains into blazing, colored brilliance. The light was especially radiant in the direction of the previous night's shooting star. They headed in this direction, pushing further north. He beheld the stunning sunrise, observing the subtleties of the color with his artist's eye and remembering them for a future painting. He opened himself to the heat of the fire colors that warmed his soul while they traversed freezing mountain glaciers.

The caravan made its way through more mountain passes. Roerich saw large rocks with stern, austere faces peering down at them as their caravan passed underneath. The rocks seemed like ancient sages that had been there for eons. Roerich felt humbled by the rock faces and listened to them, but not in an ordinary way. He silenced himself out of respect to be

Figure 1.6. Nicholas Roerich, *Great Spirit of the Himalayas*, 1934,
Nicholas Roerich Museum, NY.

quiet enough to "hear" the rock voices. They spoke the language of silence
and were slow watchers who revealed little, but only because most passing
through had not the time or patience to listen (figure 1.6).

The rocks talked to Nicholas and to others who would listen. He cop-
ied the ancient tradition of painting a sacred mantra on the rocks. Called
"mani stones," Tibetans paint the mantra of Avalokiteshvara on rocks:
Aum Mani Padme Hung! The mantra translates as "the jewel in the lotus."
Nicholas created several paintings depicting mani stones. One of his most
famous mani stone paintings depicts a chintamani fire stone ablaze on the
back of a horse showing the Roerich Pact symbol of three circles (figure 1.7
on the following page). These three circles also symbolize the Tibetan
three jewels of Buddha, dharma, and sangha. A sign of enlightenment, the
sacred wind horse carries those ready to enter Shambhala.

Figure 1.7. Nicholas Roerich, *White Stone*, 1933,
Nicholas Roerich Museum, NY.

The Pearl of Great Price

The Roerichs and their caravan passed through the valley of rock beings into a
shrouded valley. They camped, and Nicholas separated himself from the group
to listen and rest. He sat on some rocks on the ground and looked into the
mist hovering on the white crested mountains. He must have fallen asleep,
because he suddenly awoke and, looking into the distance, saw a figure appearing from the distant, snow-covered mountains. The figure was a slim, white
clad woman wearing a robe suggestive of a priestess. She walked with such
grace she almost glided above the ground, but she seemed to appear out of
the mist from nowhere (figure 1.8). There was a pathway that he perceived
between the high peaks of the soaring, snow-encrusted mountain tops, and
the rocky clefts below where he was sitting. She moved slowly down to the

Figure 1.8. Nicholas Roerich, *From Beyond*, 1936,
Nicholas Roerich Museum, NY.

rocky area toward Nicholas as though in a dream and became more real as she neared. Nicholas blinked to clear his eyes because she seemed like a mirage. When he blinked again, she was much closer, and he was stunned when she was suddenly in front of him. She handed him a vessel and said "open" with a melodious voice. When he opened the vessel, there was a pearl inside. She said, "The treasure you seek is real and is in the stronghold of the mountain. Take the chintamani stone and go to the stronghold in the abode of Kanchenjunga." She signaled toward Kanchenjunga. "There you will find what you are seeking. You will need to be strong, for the path is fraught with danger. Stay on the path. This will make you stronger for your journey." Roerich removed a single pearl from the vessel, the pearl of great price. It seemed to glow with an inner radiance, and he clutched it toward his heart with great affection. It glowed a golden light from his hand and into his heart.

Nicholas jolted awake. He looked up at the path toward the mountains. It was gone, along with the graceful woman in white. His fist was tightly clenched over his heart with the golden pearl. He opened his fist, and the precious pearl had vanished. He took a sharp breath, feeling stunned because the experience had seemed more real than his present state where he was alone. He looked around and found no evidence remaining of the woman, the path, or the treasure. He slowly stood to return to the camp but looking back at the mountains he noticed that Kanchenjunga was glowing with the same golden light as the pearl. He knew this was a sign from beyond to reinforce him on his journey (figure 1.9). He wondered if the apparition of the woman in white was White Tara, the Bodhisattva who sometimes appears to guide the sincere to Shambhala.*

As the caravan continued, he told Helena about his vision, and they both agreed it was a sign that their journey was taking them to their spiritual destination. Helena had been in contact with Master Morya while holding the chintamani stone. Master Morya had told her that there would be an incoming sign as to their direction in the mountains. Nicholas' visitation by the guide confirmed Helena's psychic channeling with Master Morya. Nicholas looked at the green stone in Helena's hand. While they were traveling in high altitudes in the Himalayan mountains, the stone exuded an energetic glow that was perceived by Nicholas' subtle vision. He could feel its energetic resonance, and the chintamani glowed more intensely from within while in the mountains. Sometimes, in his mind's eye, Nicholas perceived the chintamani in its casket glowing with an intense flame on the back of the horse, just as he had painted.

Through its vibrational resonance, Nicholas sensed the stone's energy increasing, as though it continued to increase the closer he moved toward his destined path. He felt strangely energized and connected to the stone even amid the grueling conditions of the steep mountains. He sensed that there was an energy surrounding the stone that protected and energized their caravan like the pillar of fire in the wilderness guiding the Children

---

*During their trek, a Lama approached the Roerich party with a statue of White Tara. The Lama told them that White Tara appeared in a dream and instructed him to take the statue from his altar and give it to the Roerichs. (Roerich, *Altai-Himalaya*, 24.)

Figure 1.9. Nicholas Roerich, *Path to Shambhala*, 1933,
Nicholas Roerich Museum, NY.

of Israel. Indeed, their patience was tested like the patience of the wanderers in the wilderness. They followed signs, wonders, clues, and legendary myths about Shambhala for three years. Supernatural moments occurred. The stone caused a spontaneous combustion in the tent. They saw strange lights in the heavens glowing in the mountains and moving like the star that guided the three wisemen. A mysterious horseman appeared while they were in the Gobi Desert, after which they saw an unidentified flying object. Although there are many stories and clues pointing to the Gobi Desert as the location of Shambhala, upon Nicholas' return from his journey, he concluded his travel log with mysterious commentary about Kanchenjunga. It was at the Tashiding Monastery in the foothills of Kanchenjunga that he could have had a conversation with a Lama about the location of Shambhala.

Treasure of the Mountain

After an arduous journey through Mongolia and Tibet, Nicholas returned to Sikkim in 1928. He had consulted a Lama who had given him clues as to the whereabouts of a secret cave entrance into Shambhala where he was to return the sacred chintamani. Adepts, led by Nicholas, proceeded solemnly into the mountains. The mountains were a foreboding fortress of the most pristine white, the cragged peaks peering down at them like ancient, timeless sages of old. Dressed in white and bearing the casket, the adepts entered the sacred cave (figure 1.10). They were trained in the ancient, secret teachings of Kalachakra.

They descended into the cave, meditatively walking into its icy interior. It was difficult to distinguish the crystals in the cave from the icicles. The adepts entered a crystal enclave within the cavern. The candlelight refracted off the crystal faces so that the cave glowed with a soft brilliance. The adepts prayed and chanted, resonating with the crystals in the cave, invoking the ancient mantra of Kalachakra. The chintamani was in the center of the

Figure 1.10. Nicholas Roerich, *Burning of Darkness*, 1924,
Nicholas Roerich Museum, NY.

Figure 1.11. Nicholas Roerich, *Most Sacred*
(Treasure of the Mountains), 1933,
Nicholas Roerich Museum, NY.

Kalachakra ritual, the stone glowing green during the ceremony. There were ancient beings of wisdom living in the crystals; activated by the sound and the light, they awakened from their cavernous sleep and joined the chanting. In the deep caverns of the earth, the crystals know the location of Shambhala. One merely needs to listen and tune into the crystals, becoming one with them, to find Shambhala (figure 1.11).

During the meditation in the secret crystal cave, Nicholas connected with the chintamani and noticed the brilliant green stone enter his heart. The crystal seemed to float with the resonating chanting in the crystal chamber. He blinked slowly as the chanting and energy of the crystal room had created a trance state. When he opened his eyes, the chintamani was in front of his heart and then dissolved inside of him. Nicholas felt his heart become a brilliant green emerald, a green truer and purer than any color he had ever seen. He blinked again and saw a golden door appear through one of the large crystals in the cave. The door was large and intricately carved and glowed a brilliant gold. He saw the door open and walked through as though he were in a trance.

Nicholas entered the temple of Kalachakra and on the other side of the golden door met with the priest-king of Shambhala, the Kalki King. He was dressed in white and had a tall, cylindrical golden crown on his head set with many jewels. The Kalki King asked Nicholas who he was. Nicholas did not respond. The King handed him a white stone with mysterious characters written on it. The King told him that the stone had an inscription of his new name, his true name, and he spoke the name with a mellifluous and lyrical tone, sounding like a harp in water. When Nicholas heard his new name, he recognized the sound and it blended with the green energy of the chintamani in his heart. The Kalki King took Nicholas into another chamber in the Kalachakra palace where there was a hall of scrolls. The priest-king took a scroll down and slowly unrolled it in front of him. It had mysterious and unrecognizable characters glowing in a golden script. As the priest showed him the scroll, Nicholas became the golden characters floating off the scroll to make a spiral in front of him. Then Nicholas opened his mouth and swallowed the spiral flow of the mysterious letters.

They entered another passageway into a room of blue light with golden walls where the priest told him to dress in a white robe. The robe was glowing. They entered another room glowing with a golden light and the priest picked up a vessel filled with golden oil and poured it on Nicholas. The fluid was like a golden essence of light, and he felt his entire body glowing with the essence. They left the temple and the priest-king showed him Shambhala. Nicholas noticed that they had left the interior temple in the cave and they were now outside in a valley surrounded by mountains and mountain passes he had traversed with his caravan. These mountains had made a deep impression upon him while he painted, and as he looked at the peaks and valleys now, he wondered if he had missed this secret valley because it had been covered by mist (figure 1.12).

His present experience was so real and vital that his earlier travels through the mountains seemed like a dream. As the Kalki King showed him the land of Shambhala, it seemed that he could see all of it in his mind's eye. It was arranged in a lotus of eight petals surrounded by the

Figure 1.12. Nicholas Roerich, *Kanchenjunga*, 1936,
Nicholas Roerich Museum, NY.

peaks of the mountains. He was filled with a deep serenity and joy that was difficult to describe, and he felt like this place was his true home. The trees and flowers were graceful and pleasant and were so alive that he could see them move mellifluously in harmony. He noticed that when he turned to them, they toned a melodious tune. Water from the Jambu River, filled with gold, flowed gracefully and emanated a golden, glistening light. The structures in Kalapa, the central city of Shambhala, were not ordinary. Their shapes and forms seemed to organically blend into the landscape, and they were built with all types of gemstones and precious materials such as gold, silver, emerald, pearl, turquoise, and other gems.[*] He noticed people in Shambhala moving with a slow grace in a harmonic, synchronous state of perfect joy. There was a melodic tune in the air, and this blended with a fragrance that was floral and rapturous. He saw a luminous blue flower open in front of him, and as he entered the universe of the flower,

---

[*]Place names and specific jewel names are from the teachings of Geshe Lhundub Sopa, an experienced Kalachakra practitioner.

it showed its essence to him, and it entered his heart in a perfect harmony. Through the interior of the flower, he connected to a distant galaxy and saw billions of stars spiraling.*[8]

Absorbed by the flower, Nicholas was not sure where he was when he refocused his attention. The Kalki King looked at him as though he could see into the core of his soul and called him by his true name. The priest-king opened the vestment on his chest and Nicholas saw the stone of fire that he was wearing. The jewel was like a blue flaming star, more brilliant than the sun. Nicholas perceived that the Kalki King was wearing the sacred kaustubham, the primordial chintamani, the gem that pervades the universe. The light from the brilliant blue gem pierced Nicholas' eyes, and he was suddenly transported to another place, standing in front of a large brilliantly shining clear crystal, the diamond crystal heart center of Shambhala. This was the source of light for the mystical valley shrouded by the mists of the mountains, transmitting beams of light out into the world from a high tower. The stone invited him to blend with the essence of all. Nicholas realized he was not only in the center of Shambhala but was also in the sacred center of the Earth, the galaxy, and the universe, all connected and moving fluidly in a sacred dance. In a flash, he saw and knew everything and saw how infinitesimally insignificant and important he was at the same time. For the first time in his life, he felt complete, centered, and connected to the core source, as though he had always known.

After his initiation with the source chintamani, the Kalki King led Nicholas to a beautiful garden in the sacred land. The King discussed with him his role and mission in bringing Shambhala to the world through his understanding of the Kalachakra. They discussed ethical government, rightful rulership, and divine power, and he was instructed to keep the energy of the chintamani activated in his heart so that he could complete his sacred mission. He was told to use the sacred stone embedded in his heart to con-

---

*Roerich recorded a mysterious flower in his travel diary: "on the road to Kinchenjunga grows a precious plant, the black aconite. Its flower lights up at night, and by its glow one locates this rare plant. Here again is the trace of the legend of the Russian fire flower, that enchanted blossom which fulfills all wishes—and which leads us not to superstition but to that same source wherein so much still lies concealed." (Roerich, *Altai-Himalaya*, 59–60.)

tinue their journey and to spread the wisdom of peace on Earth to others for inspiration and hope.

Nicholas felt himself drift off to sleep while the Shambhala Kalki King was talking. He tried to stay awake because what the Kalki was saying was like music to his ears. The words he heard aligned with his own sense of his soul's inner truth and urgings. When he opened his eyes, he was chanting in the crystal cave with the others and the green stone was laying on its silk brocade pillow. He stopped and wondered how much time had elapsed while he was in a meditative state. He realized that the Kalachakra ritual opened the Wheel of Time. Now he more clearly understood the operations of the Wheel of Time and that he had temporarily broken off the wheel and had entered another dimension where Shambhala was very real, just as real as the ordinary Earth plane, but he had found it in a timeless state.

Nicholas, Helena, and the adepts left the cave holding the casket with the chintamani. It was night when they left, and they walked out solemnly, entranced by their mystical experience with Shambhala. Orion, the spectacular winter constellation, was overhead, its twinkling light brilliant over the white snow of the Himalayas. Nicholas felt like he had visited another star system when he went into crystal heart of Shambhala. Now he did not feel so far from Orion, but felt a deep and abiding connection with the star system. The stars were as precious jewels to him, and their light was shining deep in his heart.

Legacy of the Chintamani

The Roerichs' journeys through the Himalayas had helped them realize on a more vitally important level that their mission was less about politics than they first understood. They had seen a deep spiritual reality that could not be converted to the politics and play for power in their time. Indeed, Nicholas had tried to establish the League of Nations following World War I, but it had failed due to the world leaders' lust for power that resulted in a second world war in the twentieth century. The world was not yet ready for the peace of Shambhala. But the truth of Shambhala burned in the Roerichs' hearts. Helena channeled the teachings of Agni Yoga and she remained in psychic contact with Master Morya throughout her life, maintaining a piece of the chintamani stone to guide her and connect with her master. The Roerichs moved to Kullu, in the foothills of the Indian Himalayas, near the mountains they so loved. Nicholas died there in 1947 at the age of seventy-three. Helena continued to write and establish more firmly the truth of the reality of Shambhala in spirit so that the legacy of their journey would not be forgotten.

With respect to the chintamani stone, the story of Shambhala is important, as the two are closely interrelated. The legacy of the Roerichs is intimately tied to their physical search for the mythical Shambhala in remote regions of the East. In their quest, the Roerichs were guided by a mysterious chintamani stone as a light on their path to the sacred land. The higher path of the chintamani is associated with activating enlightenment that paves the way for humans to return to their spiritual home found in their truest self.

2

Chintamani and Intention

Ancient Wish-Fulfilling Gems and the Universal Jewel Net

I beheld the shining tree of jewels, decked with living jewel beings.
I recognized the jewel tree as the world tree, Yggdrasil, the great
ash tree extending over the entire earth, growing from the well of
wisdom, where Odin, the highest god, had cast one eye as sacrifice
in order to receive the eye of wisdom from the goddess of the tree.

ROBERT THURMAN, *THE JEWEL TREE OF TIBET*

Vedic Jewel Net of Indra

In his introduction to *The Jewel Tree of Tibet* Robert Thurman compares the Norse and Tibetan world trees, with their leaves and branches covering all of creation. In the Tibetan emphasis, the leaves are jewels, and the jewels are all the enlightened teachers that have ever transformed the illusory human condition into its highest expressions. The jewel tree is an image of all the individual connections to greater consciousness available to everyone. This reveals the chintamani not only as a great earth gem but as a mind gem as well.

Throughout the ocean of time, we on Earth's shore can make out misty shapes from here to the horizon. Each of the shapes has a range of names, an underlying truth, and multiple unfolding storylines intertwining with one another. There appear to be a number of timeless gems tangled in an endless knot in and out of time. This image evokes another view of the chintamani, arising from a fusion of the Hindu and Buddhist traditions, the jewel net of Indra, or *indrajala*. The *Atharva Veda* depicts the palace of Indra, maharaja of the devas, atop Meru, the sacred mountain. Suspended above the palace is a vast net that extends in every direction, covering all creation below. At every intersecting node on the net there is a jewel. Each jewel reflects every other jewel on the net, displaying limitless refracting brilliance and endless reflecting illusion. The chintamani in this scheme is not one great gem but every gem that exists interconnected in every dimension.

The Hindu moral of the *indrajala* differs from the moral drawn in Buddhist teaching. The Hindu view expressed in the *Atharva Veda,* composed between 1200 and 1000 BCE, presents the jewel net in two aspects. It is an emblem of Indra's splendor as king of the gods, which reveals the vast extent of his power and wealth. The jewel net is also Indra's weapon, with which he can threaten, snare, and control his subjects and enemies alike. Emanating from his celestial palace, the net covers his dominion completely. It envelops his realm in a force field that embeds his will into the fabric of natural order.* These lines from the *Atharva Veda* describe the weaponized aspect of Indra's jewel net:

> Great is the net of thee, great Indra, hero that art equal to a thousand, and hast hundredfold might. With that (net) Sakra† slew a hundred thousand, ten thousand, a hundred million foes, having surrounded them with (his) army. This great world was the net of great Sakra: with this net of Indra I infold all those (enemies) yonder in darkness. With great dejection, failure and irrefragable misfortune; with fatigue, lassitude, and confusion, do I surround all those (enemies) beyond. To death do I hand them over, with the fetters of death they have been bound.[1]

---

*For discussion of a modern equivalent of the jewel net of Indra, explore the dominion and weaponization of space in Elena Freeland's *Under an Ionized Sky: From Chemtrails to Space Fence Lockdown.*
†*Sakra* is an epithet that refers most often to Indra, meaning "mighty one."

Even though Indra is powerful within this realm, other realms exist below and above on the vast sacred mountain of existence. Even within his realm, Indra cannot exercise capricious power, because the order of creation itself limits his rule. Just as much as the jewel net projects Indra's intents, it also protects every being at every node on the net from disruption that may be contrary to natural order, which is called dharma. The *indrajala* also represents sham, illusion, delusion, magic, sorcery, the art of magic, juggler, and sorcerer.[2] The entire universe appears as an illusion resting upon the base of ever-aware consciousness. The *indrajala* gem net is the connectedness of the universe, its protection, as well as its unreal projection. This is the deeply metaphysical symbol of how the chintamani is bound in the paradox of quests for worldly power and dominance or spiritual realization and benefit.

Examining Intention

With any chintamani, it always comes down to the wisdom of the wish. As children, we made many wishes intended to bring immediate delight and entertainment. For instance, when we overindulged the urge for chocolate ice cream, it was intended as a positive experience, but may have had the unintended result of causing us to feel badly afterward. This stage is about acting on likes and dislikes, which is barely an intention. There are five levels of true intention and motivation above this that were presented by Chan/Zen Master Guifeng Zongmi. He referred to them as deep motivations to practice the Zen path, but they refer not to specifics but to the root of any intention. As you will see, the intender must already have a particular perspective in order to intend actively on any of the five levels.

First, there is ordinary intention. This can be equated with concern to solve the challenges posed by everyday living. The sum of collective problems at some moments, like wave piling on wave, can overwhelm any of us. Having the decisiveness and power to master these challenges is intention of the first level. The next intention level arises from comparative competitiveness as we strive to excel at some skill, attribute, or accomplishment that raises us well above the rest of humanity, like a sports heroine or superhero. The super-skill can be cultivated and used to benefit self or others, but the motivation is not generosity, instead arising from a will to dominate. The third level of intention is to eradicate our most difficult challenges at their roots, which means that in order to succeed at the intention, we have to understand the root problem. Is the root problem one we share with our family, community, nation, or the entire human race? This level means intending to resolve archetypal impasses. The next level of intention springs from the awareness that all beings are intimately interconnected in the ecology of life. To resolve our individual discontents, ultimately we have to resolve the collective difficulties of the matrix of all living beings. Finally, there is the intention of no intention, which can only arise once all dualistic thinking collapses into integrated awareness. The mind of no intention arises from recognizing the perfection of everything as it is and everything as the same as self. A parallel thought from the seventh poem of the *Dao De Jing* states:

> *thus the sage pulls himself back*
> *but ends up in front*
> *he lets himself go*
> *but ends up safe*
> *selflessness must be the reason*
> *whatever he seeks he finds.*[3]

Understanding the Breadth of Dharma

Why is wisdom that accords with the natural order important in working with the wish-fulfilling gem? The answer pervades Hindu spiritual philosophy. It is central in the religious and yogic practice traditions that rely both on the ancient Vedic teachings and also on traditions that don't hold the Vedas as ultimate spiritual authority. A shared core theme for all traditions is dharma, a term layered with many meanings and interpretations. It is a word that is now used freely in common English. Though it is common, it is important because it concerns truth, natural order, destiny, duty, and the return path to wholeness. The following lists set out the many meanings for the Sanskrit word *dharma*.[4]

English Meanings of *Dharma*

Duty	Religious merit	Justice
Virtue	Good works	That which is established
Morality	Steadfast decree	Natural law
Religion	Statute or ordinance	Yama, god of death & final judgment
Law	Customary observance	Attendants of the sun
Right	Prescribed conduct	Houses 1, 5 & 9 in Vedic astrology
Practice	Essential quality	

On a personal level, there is dharma that combines destiny and duties into your right path. Whenever you deviate from that course, whether by accident or choice, you are moving out of harmonic resonance with the universe near and far. When you are resonant with your dharma, it creates positive life momentum in which the world of all possibilities can unfold favorably for you. When out of resonance with your dharma, obstacles arise, impeding your progress to accomplish the false goal you are mistakenly pursuing. Another way of describing your dharma is by answering the question: Are you actively walking your right path? That path may be a good path in general, such as the path of a physician, but if it is not your path, then it is not right no matter how valuable that profession may be. Underlying your life path is the overall choice of direction you have determined—that is the most important intention you have set in motion. So were you to hold the chintamani and make a wish, it must accord with your dharma and all the layers of intentions you are directing to accomplish your chosen destiny. Otherwise, you will be broadcasting confusion into a confused world.

Consider discerning what constitutes good or bad events in our lives. There is often a dramatic disconnect between what we experience as good or bad initially, and later what we reflect upon as actually having produced good or bad in our lives. People in our lives are a great example because we like some and dislike others. We can like people that are good for us, but also we can and do like people who cause us short- or long-term problems. We can dislike people that injure or impede us or are difficult, even though they actually cause us to improve ourselves in response to their challenges. As we consider whether our careers, for example, are aligned with our dharma, we simply can't prove it by counting the immediate, apparently good and bad events we attract.

If my dharma broadly is to be a teacher, but instead I decide to work in mortgage banking because it pays much better, I have headed in an incompatible direction. A grave difficulty for me is that my culture does not value teachers and compensates them like unskilled laborers. To follow my dharma in this case will create all manner of economic hardships for me and those who depend upon me. By contrast, as I pursue mortgage banking, there will be those I was meant to teach who did not receive any benefit from me. Perhaps, because I failed to teach, I missed the opportunity to help a great many people who may have caused harm to themselves or others because I was not there to influence them toward the good. I probably will never know all those I have harmed inadvertently by not performing my rightful dharma. The Vedic teachings assert that even if we are unaware of what we have caused, we nonetheless are responsible for the good and bad results that may occur because we have not followed our dharma.

One of the great Indian epics, the Mahabharata, offers many specific examples of the importance of following right dharma. The core of the story involves two cousin branches of the Kuru clan, each claiming rulership over the kingdom. The Kauravas are children of the blind king and the Pandavas are children of the last true heir to the throne. The central moral is that the king who is blind has no right to rule others because he is blind. In this case, the blindness is not just physical; more importantly, he lacks spiritual wisdom, indicating his inner blindness. Though the blind king has received spiritual teachings and has performed many of his regent duties responsibly, he decides to pass on rulership to his direct heirs rather than to his nephews, the rightful heirs. Blind kings have no dharma to be kings, and by unrightfully usurping rulership for his heirs, he abandons his dharma completely. This leads to a vast war that destroys parts of the Earth and the lives of most of the blind king's subjects he had sworn to protect and help prosper. The epic tells many stories of the other characters, including those who fail to follow their dharma, and those who do faithfully follow their dharma. The storyline is extremely complicated; in fact, it is as complicated as determining and following our own individual dharma amid the dynamic unfolding events of life. The sheer volume and epic detail of the stories make the Mahabharata an excellent source for exploring a wide variety of cases of what it means to ignore or follow your dharma.

The Syamantaka Chintamani

Next, let us consider a story thread from the Mahabharata that involves one of the wish-fulfilling gems. This particular gem is known as the *syamantaka mani* and was originally possessed by Surya, the sun god. The gem produces eight *bharas,* or about 170 pounds, of gold every day for the bearer. It is an oddly precise detail but is described both in the *Vishnu Purana* and *Srimad Bhagavatam.* Additionally, the syamantaka mani radiates an energy field that brings about the peace, prosperity, and welfare of all who dwell in the realm. The gold is produced daily no matter who possesses the gem, but benefit to the commonwealth does not occur if the rightful leader does not wield the gem for the greater benefit of others. Further, to the extent that the gem-bearer has self-centered or malicious intent, the gem magnifies the negativity the owner projects into the world. That negativity affects and obstructs the bearer as much as it injures the larger collective extending throughout the entire ecosystem.

The main story revolves around the avatar Shri Krishna, who is the incarnation of Vishnu, the aspect of God that preserves creation. Computer gaming has highjacked the word "avatar," so we need to recall its Vedic meaning. From time to time, creation on Earth descends into disorder to the brink of utter dissolution. At those historic moments, Vishnu becomes an avatar, meaning Vishnu incarnates into physical form to restore dharma to the Earth. These incarnations are an infinite series of avatars of Vishnu, but two sources provide a list of ten and another of twenty-two of Vishnu's major incarnations. Both of these lists end with Krishna, Buddha, and the next future incarnation, Kalki.* Later, in chapter 4, we will discuss the latter two because they also each connect with wish-fulfilling gems. For the

---

*From a Buddhist perspective, Buddha would not be considered an avatar of Vishnu. From a Hindu perspective, Buddha is sometimes listed but not in the tradition of Puranic literature, much of which predated the historical Buddha, Siddhartha Gautama. The Wisdom Library website provides avatar lists both including and excluding Buddha; search under *dasavatara.*

moment, we will focus on Krishna and the story of the wish-fulfilling gem known as the syamantaka mani.

At the start of the Mahabharata, Krishna is presented as the son of Vasudeva and Devaki, and grandson of Ugrasena, a great king of many clans. Krishna is a wise and kind king of his city state of Dwaraka. It is only over the long course of the epic that we experience him more and more as Vishnu's avatar, with omniscience and all the qualities God would show in human form. Krishna is related by birth to both factions of the Kuru ruler families, the Kauravas and Pandavas. The story of the syamantaka mani occurs before open warfare has erupted, at a time when both sides of the Kurus are in touch with one another, but great unease and tensions are developing. Krishna, as the wise king and trusted relative, is the revered and infinitely patient mediator of the Kuru crisis. Within Krishna's realm are nobles of branch clans. One such Yadava clan noble who gained possession of the syamantaka was Satrajit.

Satrajit was a leader of the Yadava clan and a devotee of Surya, the sun god. As he walked and prayed by the ocean shore one day, he encountered Surya appearing dazzlingly bright and fiery. Surya, wearing the syamantaka, gave it to Satrajit as acknowledgment of his great devotion. When Satrajit returned to Dwaraka wearing the syamantaka gem, those who beheld his dazzling appearance mistook him for Surya himself. Even from a distance, Krishna knew that it was Satrajit and not Surya who approached the city. When they met, Krishna did not ask Satrajit to give the powerful gem over to him even though he was king of the city-state and avatar of Vishnu; instead, knowing that the gem was to benefit many, Krishna asked him to give it to Ugrasena, the king of all the clans. Satrajit refused to cede the gem to anyone, despite the good it might do for all. Instead, he kept it selfishly, which eventually led to three deaths amid a morass of gossip and intrigue.

Briefly, Satrajit's brother, Prasena, borrowed the syamantaka mani to wear while he strolled in a nearby forest. He was attacked by a lion and killed. The lion who took the brilliant gem in turn was killed by Jambavan, a bear king who took the gem home to his den. When Prasena did not return to the city, people began to gossip, spreading the rumor that Krishna was jealous of not possessing the gem and probably had killed Prasena for it. To restore the gem to its current owner and to clear his name, Krishna led a search party into the forest. They encountered the bodily remains of Prasena and the dead lion, vindicating Krishna in front of Dwaraka's citizenry.

Krishna pressed on to find the gem, telling the party to wait for his return at the entrance to a cave, the den of Jambavan who had killed the lion. After twelve days, the waiting party left to report what happened back home, but they also speculated that Krishna was trying to recover the gem for himself. Instead, Krishna was locked in a twenty-eight-day, non-stop fight with Jambavan, who was reputed to be the strongest being alive. When Jambavan realized he was losing, he reasoned that he must be fighting a supernatural force. Finally recognizing Krishna, Jambavan surrendered, ceded the gem, and then gave his daughter in marriage to Krishna as atonement for his errors of anger, greed, and not recognizing the very avatar to whom he was especially devoted.

When Krishna returned to Dwaraka, he returned the syamantaka to Satrajit and requested that he now give the gem to Ugrasena, the high king, to benefit all. Satrajit refused, but feeling guilty, he later gave three of his daughters in marriage to Krishna in atonement for gossip and greed, and to create a closer family connection. Satrajit also offered the syamantaka to Krishna, who refused possession and returned it Satrajit. Soon Krishna was called in emergency to the city of Hastinapura to deal with a tragedy. After Krishna left Dwaraka, conspirators who wanted the gem for themselves planned and executed the murder of Satrajit. Satyabhama, daughter of Satrajit and newly married to Krishna, traveled to Hastinapura to urge Krishna to return home immediately and avenge her father's murder. Krishna, obligated by dharma to avenge his father-in-law's murder, tracked down the assailant who had fled the city and killed him, but was unable to recover the gem because the other conspirators had taken the syamantaka. When Krishna returned to Dwaraka, he found the gem, yet refused the pleas of the fickle citizenry to keep it for himself. He adjudicated the claims and obligations to the gem but allowed a conspirator thief to keep the syamantaka as long as it remained in the capital city of Dwaraka to benefit all citizens. In this way, Krishna worked wisely with human greed, cleared his name, and gained the greatest benefit of the syamantaka mani possible in that moment.

The syamantaka story highlights the problem of possessing a wish-fulfilling gem and acting from selfish intentions. On the surface, it seems that the gem was cursed because ownership brought about the deaths of Prasena, the lion, Satrajit, and his murderer. The syamantaka was brilliant and a gift of the sun god, so how could it have been cursed? Indeed, there was no curse; rather Surya gave the gem as an honor to Satrajit for his religious devotion. When the time came for him to make a moral choice, Satrajit preferred his personal benefit more than universal benefit. On deeper examination, self-serving attachment proved to bring about the chain of calamities. It began with Satrajit, extended to Prasena, the lion, Jambavan, and Satrajit's murderer. All were blinded and motivated by fulfilling their own self-interests first. The curse attaching to all wish-fulfilling gems comes from character flaws of the holder of the gem, not from the chintamani gem itself.

The *indrajala* also appears in the Mahabharata, but not as the jewel net of Indra, nor as the representation of cosmic order. The *indrajala* was one of the great weapons wielded by Arjuna, the semidivine son of Indra and general of the Pandavas. It truly was a weapon of mass destruction used during the eighteen-day war between the Kauravas and Pandavas. But the odd twist dealing with a gem occurred on the nineteenth day when the five Pandava brothers and Shri Krishna discover that the last and losing Kaurava commander, Aswatthama, is standing over the beheaded corpses of the children of the Pandava brothers. In his rage, Aswatthama breached two rules of battle engagement that defined the honor of a warrior: first, he attacked an unarmed warrior who was not actively engaged in battle, and second, he fought after dusk. Both rules were bloodily broken. Aswatthama, son of Drona, was born with a jewel embedded as his third eye, which gave him many powers including instantaneous and continuous healing. Shri Krishna cursed him to live alone, wandering for three thousand years away from all human companionship. The third eye jewel was cut from Aswatthama's head and Shri Krishna gave it to Yudhisthira, in recognition of the fact that he was now the undisputed king.[5] The gem also conferred great powers to King Yudhisthira, who as the semidivine son of the god Dharma was the most truthful, pious, and virtuous, as well as eldest, of the royal Pandava brothers.

Buddhist Jewel Net of Indra

Last, consider the net of Indra from a Buddhist viewpoint as presented in the *Avatamsaka,* or *Flower Garland, Sutra.* This instruction in cosmology and yoga was more widely studied in China and Japan as the *Hua Yen* or *Kegon Sutra.* The *indrajala,* or net of Indra, as described in the sutra is very similar to the presentation in the *Atharva Veda.* There is a different emphasis of meaning, however. At every junction of this infinite net, there is a faceted jewel that reflects every other jewel. The net has no beginning and no end, neither in space nor time. The entire net and every gem node are cosmic ecology.[6] Individually and collectively the *indrajala* self-arises, self-sustains, and self-evolves. In Buddhist philosophy, the jewel net illustrates the idea of interdependence and intercausality. This is reflected in an odd but very common exchange in Japanese. Someone may ask: *Genki desu ka?* or "How is your health?" The unusual, almost automatic reply is *Okagesama de genki desu!* Very hard to translate, and harder yet for an English speaker to grasp, the answer means: "Thanks to you (your inquiry, your concern), I am very healthy!" This seems to make no sense, especially if this is the very first time you may have met someone. Their answer reflects the jewel net mindset. My good health is caused by your kind interest in me. My good health may also be caused by my inheritance of long-life genetics and careful practice of a healthy lifestyle. All the causes of my good health are arising at this very moment and, as an ensemble, co-create and co-cause my health. The entire cosmos experienced as the *indrajala* co-causes and co-creates itself moment by moment.

This last bit of philosophy is beyond open-ended, but it may open a profound contemplation about the nature of the chintamani for all of us. Gathering the speculations so far: there are many chintamanis and they respond to the narrowness or breadth of intention the gem holder projects. The chintamanis are everywhere around us—from distant in the galaxies to near at hand. They focus and increase the play of intention. Chintamanis may co-create negative or positive results in the world we inhabit. Chintamanis are at once an essential fabric and a means of the evolution of the cosmos, its life, and consciousness. What we have yet to explore is how to discover and work with chintamanis to co-create beneficial quantum shifts in the inner and outer realms. Below is a scroll by Kano Korenobu (1753–1808) showing Hotei (*Budai* in Chinese), the laughing Buddha who has returned to everyday life to benefit others. His massive sack contains gifts of good fortune for others. He is amused by the chintamani, which others might struggle to possess for its promise of wealth and power. His joy and engaged detachment are exactly the qualities needed to use the chintamani wisely.

Figure 2.1. Hotei sitting on his sack of gifts watching the chintamani spin.
From the Collection of Don Kimon Lightner. Photo by Don Lightner.

3

Jewels Everywhere East

Chintamanis in the Art and Technology of Enlightenment (Bodhisattvas)

May all beings be liberated from the great ocean of existence
And be carried to the jewel island
In the majestic ship of virtues
Through the force of the wind of resolve.

KHAMTRUL GARJE, *THE JEWEL LADDER*

WE BEGIN WITH A CHINTAMANI ACCOUNT from tantric Buddhism dating from the early ninth century CE, the time of Tibet's King Trisong Detsen and the legendary Guru Padmasambhava. King Indrabodhi (also called Indrabhuti) ruled Oddiyana, a location many scholars think was the Swat River Valley of northeastern Pakistan. Oddiyana has as many alternate names as languages in the Himalayas, and is also called the land of the *dakinis*. Like Shambhala, it appears enmeshed in both geographical and mythical dimensions. This chintamani narrative is from Yeshe Tsogyal, a consort of Padmasambhava and a queen of Tibet. She begins the Guru's biography with the quest, reception, and compassionate use of the chintamani.

King Indrabodhi and the Chintamani

King Indrabodhi ruled Oddiyana from a jeweled throne surrounded by 108 queens from the capital city called Glowing Jewels.[1] Having no son for an heir, he bade his court priests to perform a ceremonial offering to create favorable conditions to produce a son and heir. He made a vow of great generosity to seal the ceremony and made good his vow by opening his treasury to all in need. Over the years, even the great wealth of Oddiyana became exhausted. The king could no longer keep his vow, and yet he still had no son for an heir. To continue his generosity, he contemplated how to attain the chintamani. In the middle of the ocean on an island fortress dwelt the naga king's daughter known as Lovely Maiden. It was she who possessed the gem, limitless in granting needs and wants. It was she who would give the gem to a Bodhisattva practicing great generosity for the sake of dharma.

King Indrabodhi prepared an ocean-going vessel under the command of a captain who had successfully brought home many jewels on numerous expeditions. Contrary to the wishes of his ministers and subjects, they raised the four sails. The ship was carried into open ocean and in the right direction by the intention of great generosity. When they landed on an island of precious gems, the king and captain continued onward and alone in a smaller boat. They passed mountain islands of silver and lapis lazuli before seeing one of gold. The captain counseled the king about how to proceed once they arrived on the gold island. The king would go alone, find the castle made of precious gems, guarded by seven encircling lakes and tall walls. He would have to pass areas of poisonous snakes, a feat only possible for a Bodhisattva, but he had to keep his mind fixed on *bodhichitta,* the intention of great generosity. Passing the lakes and snakes, he would come to a walled fortress made of iron and precious substances. He needed to use a *vajra* (indestructible diamond) knocker to announce his presence and ask the naga girl gatekeeper for entry.

One hundred deva maidens would appear before the gate would open, with countless gifts of precious stones. The king was not to converse with the deva maidens nor accept their gifts, but was to knock and ask for entry again. Only then would the beautiful, blue-hued naga princess

Lovely Maiden appear. The king needed to ask the princess to listen to his story before asking her for the great gem. She then would present the king with the gem that fulfills all wishes. The king was to accept the gem, wrap it in his sleeve, then leave immediately. The king followed all the captain's instructions exactly, walking calmly past the snakes to the entry gate, knocking as directed, and ignoring the voices and gem offerings of the deva maidens who appeared. Lovely Maiden opened the gate and heard his story. Recognizing him as a Bodhisattva, she took the blue chintamani gem radiating five colors of light from her hair and presented it to the king to benefit all sentient beings. In an instant he had returned to the captain's position on the shore, and in another instant, they had returned to the main ship. Before setting sail for home, the captain separated precious gems from semiprecious gems, giving the lesser ones to the retinue to create balance so the weight of the jewels would not sink the boat while returning.

Sailing home, the vessel came upon an island that contained a great, multicolored lotus with a boy of eight years seated in the center holding a vajra and lotus—it was beautiful to behold. All were struck with wonder as the king asked the boy:

> Little boy child, who is your father and who is your mother?
> What is your caste and what is your country?
> What food do you live on and what is your purpose?

In reply to these questions, the boy said:

> My father is the wisdom of spontaneous awareness.
> My mother is the Ever-Excellent Lady, the space of all things.
> I belong to the caste of indivisible space and awareness.
> I take the unborn *dharmadhatu* as my homeland.
> I sustain myself by consuming the concepts of duality.
> My purpose is the act of killing disturbing emotions.[2]

King Indrabodhi decided to make this miraculous boy his son and future king of Oddiyana and spoke this intention to his retinue.

Upon returning home, the ministers and subjects of Oddiyana were overjoyed and prepared an elaborate welcoming celebration. The king took the precious gem in his hands and made this wish openly: "If this precious gem that I have found is an unmistaken wish-fulfilling jewel, may my little boy child be seated upon a huge throne made of the seven precious substances and decorated with a parasol of costly gems."[3] As soon as the king's words were uttered, the boy was seated upon the throne exactly as invoked. The boy was empowered as prince and given the name King Padma Vajra. Then the king said: "If this precious gem is the unmistaken and priceless wish-fulfilling jewel, may all the empty treasuries from where I formerly distributed alms become as full as they once were!"[4] Instantly, the treasuries were full again. As a great drum was sounded the king announced: "I, King Indrabodhi, proclaim that the fulfillment of all needs and wants will rain down by the grace of my wish-fulfilling jewel. Come and receive whatever you wish for and whatever you may need!"[5] Thus, the chintamani was found, the invocations of King Indrabodhi were fulfilled as spoken, and the boy who arose spontaneously from a miraculous lotus was enthroned as royal heir of Oddiyana.

Essential Buddhist Context

Namo Ratna Trayaya! Hail Triple Gem! Thus begins many long Buddhist mantras called *dharanis*. The three jewels here refer to Buddha, dharma, and sangha, which are known also as the three refuges at the very heart of Buddhist practice. What we are about to encounter is the further unfolding of the chintamani in concept, imagery, and art as at once the goal, means, and recognition of the awakened state of enlightenment. We are about to see that the chintamani appears everywhere in the outer world while completely pervading the inner experience of consciousness. Another way to say this is that the chintamani is an essential quality of existence and of mind. Let's examine this more thoroughly.

Buddhism begins in recent history with Gautama Siddhartha, the north Indian, or present-day Nepalese, prince of the Shakya clan who attained the awakened awareness of enlightenment. After his realization, he was called Buddha, or awakened one. He demonstrated that a human could indeed practice a disciplined mystic and yogic spiritual path to cut through the fog of false perceptions in order to awaken and sustain an enlightened mind. The first jewel then is both the human teacher called Buddha, as well as the condition of original mind exuding the combined qualities of compassion, clarity, wisdom, and joy referred to as enlightenment. The second jewel, dharma, we discussed in chapter 2 in a Vedic context. In Buddhism, dharma especially refers to all the teachings of philosophy as well as instructions on yogic methods that, when practiced with determination, energy, and skill, will undoubtedly lead a practitioner to realize enlightenment. The third jewel, the sangha, refers to the assembly of those who seriously and assiduously engage the practice of enlightenment. The sangha is made up of skilled gurus, teachers, and good companions walking the path of awakening.

Why are the three refuges referred to as jewels? Certainly there is the quality of great preciousness about them; they are as rare and priceless as a gem. More to the point, the three refuges offer a proven exit from the endless cycles of confusion and suffering, especially past this present lifetime. The three refuges also offer recovery and remembering of the ever-present, prime understanding of the jewel of enlightenment. To make a movie reference, the sure way out of the world *Matrix* starts not with a red pill, but with the mind gem. The three jewels, three refuges, draw attention to relying upon a truly valuable way to resolve the core questions of life and death. At first, a person determined to follow the path of awakening relies on enlightenment, the teachings to reach it, and companions who seriously practice it as outside supports. As progress on the path unfolds, outer reliance is replaced by inner certainty, until our realization is complete. Without relying on the three gems, we wander aimlessly through time and space, believing mistakenly that we are in extreme poverty when instead we possess the chintamani.

Siddhartha, the most recent historical Buddha, taught a mystic psychology of practices yoking mind and body to reveal the enlightened mind. His initial teaching was presented as a physician would present assessments to a worried patient. It answers four healing questions:

1. What is the identity and nature of the disease?
2. What is the cause of the disease?

3. Is the disease curable?
4. If curable, what specific prescriptions will restore health?

Buddha's answers about humankind's existential spiritual disease were formulated in his first teaching called the four noble truths:

1. The disease is pervasive physical, emotional, and mental suffering.
2. The cause is insatiable, chronic craving that attaches us to the wheel of life.
3. There is a cure that can disengage us from suffering.
4. The disengaging cure is the noble eightfold path.

Jumping through hundreds of books of explanation and across 2,500 years of practice in an instant, here are Buddhist chintamani basics:

1. Through history, beings have continued to awaken partially or profoundly to become Bodhisattvas or Buddhas.
2. There are eighty-four thousand paths to enlightenment. Each person's path depends on what karma they need to unravel to fully disengage from their suffering.
3. The chintamani is a metaphor for, a means to, and realization of enlightenment.
4. Full awakening is about completely wielding the chintamani with compassion, wisdom, and skill.

Chintamani Symbols and Art

Buddhas and Bodhisattvas are depicted in sculpture and paintings as spiritual victors. Buddhist art instructs through symbols. As we explore Buddhist aspects of the chintamani, we will consider jewel symbols of various Buddhas and Bodhisattvas as well as mantras and practices that transform distorted perception into enlightened view. The jewel theme is so extensive that we present only a limited sample here, but enough to suggest a fuller scope. Buddhas are considered innumerable through time because it is the destiny of every sentient being to awaken fully. Realized Buddhas are world teachers of a great age. Once their bodies die, they move beyond the perception of all but the most evolved humans. In their place are Bodhisattvas who are awakened beings at various stages of profound enlightenment. They each have taken a vow to remain in the cycle of incarnation until all beings awaken. Bodhisattvas remain perceptible to capable humans.

All Buddhas and Bodhisattvas have the same wisdom mind, but each is unique in how they vow to benefit beings. Each emphasizes a different aspect of compassion to alleviate suffering—whether of sickness, poverty, war, or from any other of innumerable obstacles. The symbols they are portrayed holding or that are arrayed around them show how they can help sentient beings over and above teaching the core wisdom path to enlightenment. For instance, the Medicine Buddha also imparts profound healing. If you are struggling to stay healthy or are a healer yourself, this aspect of enlightenment is of extra personal benefit. You may be drawn to the life vows and skills of any Bodhisattva or Buddha as well as to their wisdom. In the last chapter, we describe practices in which you will visualize a particular Buddha or Bodhisattva as well as the chintamani. As you read through the following archetypal descriptions, perhaps one will resonate more closely to your own needs and aspirations. Your preexisting natural affinity will intensify the practices in chapter 12 to create powerful, personal transformation.

Medicine Buddha

Bhaisajya-guru is the short name of the Medicine or Healing Buddha. His full, formal title is Bhaisajya-guru-vaidurya-prabha-raja, most often translated as Medicine Master, King of Lapis Lazuli Light. Curing all diseases, Bhaisajya-guru heals the root disease of suffering from which all physical, emotional, and mental illnesses arise. Bhaisajya-guru is depicted as deep blue in color, seated in meditation, and dressed as a monk (figure 3.1 on the following page). With his left hand he holds a carved jewel bowl full of amrita, nectar of immortality, in his lap, while his right hand makes the mudra of generosity holding the healing myrobalan plant. In many images, he has a diamond shape on each palm. In front of him, which is common to images of many Buddhas and Bodhisattvas, is at least one pile of wish-fulfilling gems. While chanting his mantra, we visualize Bhaisajya-guru radiating blue

Figure 3.1. Medicine Buddha holding a bowl of amrita and healing myrobalan.
In his auras are wish-fulfilling gems in the *magatama* (bent gem) shape.
Completely surrounding the Medicine Buddha's palace is a
perimeter of twenty-six chintamanis.

Photo by J. Govert

light and rainbow light to heal us, our circle, and all those beings who are suffering from illness now. As the visualization unfolds, we scan for golden light above and at the edge of Bhaisajya-guru's spherical aura. Light shining through a blue gem produces a blue radiance. A blue gem also acting as a prism disperses white light into the visible color spectrum. The entire visualization practice of Bhaisajya-guru and other Buddhas and Bodhisattvas is an encounter with a living gem radiating light, love, and life force to restore health, ease, peace, purpose, and liberation.

We might view each Buddha and Bodhisattva in terms of a particular gem that imparts added effects including and beyond the general qualities of enlightenment. As an example, the Healing Buddha has a deep blue-sky body. Which gem is similar in resonance to the Healing Buddha's radiance? In Sanskrit, the gem is identified as *vaidurya,* in Chinese and Japanese it is translated as *liuli* and *ruri.* Scholars render the Healing Buddha's gem most often as lapis lazuli, the dark blue stone with swirls and flashes of pyrite that looks like gold or silver stars spiraling in the deep indigo night sky. Other scholars and gurus translate *vaidurya* as quartz crystal, glass, beryl, emerald, and sapphire.[6] Sanskrit dictionaries translate *vaidurya* as beryl or cat's eye gem.[7] Whichever specific gem we use in visualization or meditation practice, whether Buddhist or not, will influence the character of that spiritual practice. We explore this more fully in later chapters.

The Five Dhyani Buddhas

There is a group of Buddhas called the five *Dhyanis* or *Jinas. Dhyani* refers to meditating Buddhas while *Jina* refers to victorious Buddhas. One of this group is called Ratnasambhava, whose name means "Completely Jewel Arisen." He appears yellow-gold in color, presides over the ratna, or jewel, family, and provides the key to transform afflictions of greed and pride into the wisdom of equanimity. Seated in meditation, his left hand is open and up-facing in his lap while his right hand is in the mudra of generosity. In front of him is a pile of gems of all colors. His family includes his female Buddha consort, Vajradhatvishvari ("She Who Can Extinguish Pride"). Ratnasambhava is also associated with a number of ratna family Bodhisattvas including Kshitigarbha, Akashagarbha, and Samantabhadra. Practitioners who are too attached to Earth or too greedy can benefit from the ratna family. Everyone whose selfish karma is strong needs ratna family wisdom to transform their me-first greed into generosity and equanimity. Examples we discussed in the introduction and chapter 2 from Hindu myth also warn of the corrupting power of greed that intensifies when close to the chintamani. Ratnasambhava, the conqueror of pride and greed, bears the chintamani as an emblem and seal of his enlightened nature. The enlightened activity of the ratna family is to increase longevity, the worth of character, and material prosperity. Figure 3.2 depicts the five Buddhas and appendix 1 presents all five Buddha families and their correspondences with colors, wisdoms, and actions.

Avalokiteshvara

Perhaps most popular across all Asia is the Bodhisattva of compassion known variously as Avalokiteshvara, Chenrezig, Kuan Yin, or Kanzeon. Depicted as male in India, Nepal, Mongolia, and Tibet, and female in China, Korea, Japan, and Vietnam, the Bodhisattva's name in each language translates as "He/She Who Hears the Suffering of All Beings" and is a manifestation of the *padma,* or lotus, family. Buddhas and Bodhisattvas appear in many forms to connect the blessings of compassion and wisdom to the spectrum of all beings. In one form, Kuan Yin holds the wish-fulfilling gem symbolic of her enlightened ability to benefit all sentient beings. Another appearance is Kuan Yin as "Chintamani Chakravartin" or "Kuan Yin Who Wields the Wish-Fulfilling Gem and Dharma Wheel." Of all Buddhist mantras, one of the most important for developing compassion is the short Sanskrit mantra of Avalokiteshvara: *Aum Mani Padme Hung!* translated as "Hail the Lotus Jewel." The sound of the mantra is meant to vibrate at the crown chakra and at the heart chakra. The jewel in the lotus refers to the crown chakra but is chanted not solely for the verbal meaning but also to generate resonant energy to open and activate both the heart and crown centers, and importantly, the inner chintamani. (See figure 3.3, page 60.)

Kshitigarbha

A very obvious visual of a Bodhisattva image bearing the chintamani is Kshitigarbha, known as Jizo in Japan and Dizang in China. Jizo is depicted `a traveling monk, both seated in meditation or standing, with a pilgrim's

Figure 3.2. The Five Dhyani Buddhas with chintamani fire gems
in front of White Buddha.

Figure 3.3. Four-armed Avalokiteshvara holding
the chintamani at his heart.

staff held in his right hand and the chintamani in the left. Sometimes the chintamani is held at the throat chakra level (figure 3.4 on the following page), but more often it is held in Jizo's left hand, palm up, in the meditation mudra. The gem is depicted as an orb, or turnip shape, with flames rising from the gem. Jizo is a Bodhisattva of the ratna, or jewel, family. There is no consensus about what the exact gem may be. In paintings, the chintamani can look like a clear orb or have a golden hue, but it is depicted with flames, especially in images from Dunhuang.[8] There are some Dunhuang images of Dizang's gem shown as a luminous pearl.[9] Unlike the case of the Healing Buddha, we haven't found discussion that reveals the specific earth gem the chintamani resembles for Kshitigarbha. One translation of Kshitigarbha is "Earth Store." This Bodhisattva appeared in earlier Buddhist writings from a class of Bodhisattvas that have arisen from Earth herself. There is a legendary belief that Kshitigarbha has the ability to gather treasures such as gold, silver, lapis lazuli, mother of pearl, pearl, and red pearl.[10] According to the *Sutra of the Past Vows of Earth Store Bodhisattva,* Jizo takes a number of vows, as do all Bodhisattvas, including to attend to beings whose negative karma has caused their rebirth in the hell worlds.[11] The point for our discussion is that the chintamani's compassionate power can be wielded successfully even from the depths of the greatest possible suffering in the universe.

Akashagarbha

The next Bodhisattva with a prominent chintamani connection is Akashagarbha, who is also considered a part of the ratna, or jewel, family. The similarity in the names of Kshitigarbha and Akashagarbha creates a comparison. Kshitigarbha (or Jizo) is also translated as "Earth Matrix" and Akashagarbha as "Sky Matrix" Bodhisattva. Akashagarbha's short mantra is *Aum Vajra Ratna Aum Trah Svaha!*[12] The mantra does not convey much linguistic meaning. The main words relating to the chintamani are *vajra ratna,* which could mean "lightning/thunder jewel" or "diamond jewel." The other words are sounds that bring about resonant transformation. Here the jewel reference is quite direct. The *Nishpannayogavali* (The Garland of Perfection Yogas) describes a mandala of Akashagarbha in which he showers gems from his right hand while holding the chintamani in his

Figure 3.4. Kshitigarbha (Jizo) with a clear orb chintamani held at the throat chakra level in his left hand. *Kshitigarbha*, late fourteenth century, gold and color on silk, Metropolitan Museum of Art.

left.[13] A Chinese sutra compares the compassion of Avalokiteshvara with Akashagarbha and asserts that they should appear similarly. Akashagarbha is seated in the lotus posture holding the wish-fulfilling chintamani in his hand (figure 3.5).[14]

There is a second mantra associated with Akashagarbha known in Japan's Shingon sect as the Morning Star Mantra. The transmitter of the modern Reiki practice was Dr. Mikao Usui. Before his breakthrough understanding of Reiki, Dr. Usui had practiced an extended retreat at Mount Kurama near Kyoto specifically doing focused recitation of the Morning Star Mantra. Since the morning star is Venus, if we are looking for Akashagarbha's specific

Figure 3.5. Akashagarbha holding a flaming chintamani while sitting in a clear orb. *Kokūzō Bosatsu (Ākāshagarbha Bodhisattva)*, twelfth century, color on silk, Tokyo National Museum, Tokyo.

earth gem with chintamani qualities, we can consider diamond because of Venus' association with it. So we have two different clues to indicate diamond: vajra and Venus.

Tara

Tara is a devi or goddess in tantric Hinduism, but here we consider Tara as a Bodhisattva. There are a number of colors attributed to different forms of Tara—including green, white, red, yellow, or blue—that relate to the five Buddha families. There are also more formal names. Green Tara is the foundational Tara, whose connection to the chintamani is apparent in her imagery and in some forms in which she holds the chintamani in her hand.[15] Tara is seated in meditation with one leg crossed and one leg down, ready to respond to the calls of those who are suffering. She wears no clothes on her upper body but does wear silks on her lower body. Although mostly naked to remind us of the unadorned nature of mind as it is, Tara is adorned in jewels with a gem and flower crown, necklaces, earrings, armlets, bracelets, and anklets. These are not gems of self-adornment but jewels of compassion, wisdom, and readiness to benefit others. There is also a form of White Tara as the protectress, Chintamani Chakra Tara or Wish-Fulfilling Wheel Tara, but below is presented the more common image of White Tara (figure 3.6). Tara in most forms wears and is surrounded by all five colored jewels. While radiating a green glow and white light, she also radiates rainbow light. Thangka painters depict Tara as well as many Buddhas and Bodhisattvas with the five colors of gems embedded in their auras, which reflect and refract light further. Although three-dimensional physical jewels are shown, the important symbolism is that the enlightened ones radiate the essence of the chintamani through the light of their realizations. We might speculate whether Buddhas and Bodhisattvas absorb chintamani energy completely into their consciousnesses or if the chintamani is their conscious energy.

Samantabhadra

Samantabhadra is one of the eight great Bodhisattvas (figure 3.7, page 66). Of that group, half hold the chintamani as an emblem of enlightenment and wield it to benefit beings, including Avalokiteshvara, Kshitigarbha,

Figure 3.6. White Tara frequently serves as a guide to Shambhala.
She is shown surrounded by jewels in her aura
with a flaming chintamani in front of her.

Akashagarbha, and Samantabhadra. There are many images that show the same Buddha or Bodhisattva in different aspects. In the *Nishpannayogavali,* Samantabhadra is described in a mandala as golden in color with a cluster of gems in his right hand. More generally, Samantabhadra is shown as wearing a crown, dressed in royal attire, with his left hand in the mudra of generosity while holding the chintamani. When Samantabhadra appears in an image of all the eight great Bodhisattvas, his emblems are lotus flowers with a jewel, a vajra and one hand in the generosity mudra, and the other in the mudra of deliberation.[16]

Figure 3.7. Samantabhadra, the Bodhisattva, adorned with gems and crowned with gems and lotuses.

Wealth Deities, Jambhala, and White Mahakala

In Hinduism and Buddhism there are a number of wealth deities. These gods and goddesses represent an inner archetype of mastering abundance that emerges from mastering generosity. In Buddhism, the wealth deities are Bodhisattvas who have taken vows to remove the suffering of abject poverty to which so many are subject. In this sense, they are somewhat like the legendary Robin Hood. Wealth Bodhisattvas promote abundance to bring about the conditions in which people have enough leisure and opportunity to practice dharma that leads to enlightenment. Wealth Bodhisattvas in a larger perspective also protect people from the obstructions and calamities that collapse livelihood and stability. As expected, wealth Bodhisattvas are depicted with an abundance of gems. Whether seated or standing, they are shown with piles of gems surrounding them in the palace at the center of their mandalas. Yellow Jambhala is one of the wealth Bodhisattvas considered to be an emanation of Ratnasambhava (figure 3.8 on the following page). He is usually seated in a royal ease posture, like Tara, ready to respond to the distress of sentient beings. In his right hand he holds the chintamani and in his left he holds an unusual mongoose that continually spews gems from its mouth. This gem-spewing mongoose also appears in depictions of the Hindu and Buddhist wealth deity Kubera.

White Mahakala is also a wealth Bodhisattva, usually depicted standing. Unlike other wealth deities who are semi-wrathful, White Mahakala is a wrathful manifestation of Avalokiteshvara, surrounded by a sphere of flames. Like other wealth Bodhisattvas, he is adorned in exquisite silk clothing with many gems set in precious jewelry. There are also gems of the five colors throughout his aura. One of the White Mahakala practices is entitled "The Method of Practice of the Fast-Acting Lord of Pristine Awareness, Jewel King of Power."* White Mahakala is actually identified as the dynamic expression of the chintamani, which he holds in one of his middle six arms among other implements. He is surrounded by hosts of *dakinis* (enlightened female "sky-goers") who help him retrieve all wealth, including all the wealth

---

*"The Method of Practice of the Fast-Acting Lord of Pristine Awareness, Jewel King of Power" is a specific practice sadhana in the Shangpa Kagyu lineage brought to the West by Kalu Rinpoche.

Figure 3.8. Yellow Jambhala with a pile of fire chintamanis and piles of other gems at his feet. He is holding a white mongoose spewing gems in his left hand. Detail from *Jambhala*, Sichuan University Museum, Sichuan, China.

of gods and men. Immediately, the Gem King distributes all that wealth in all its forms to sentient beings in need. He is called the Wish-Fulfilling Gem.

Orgyen Khandro Norlha

Another wealth bringer is Guru Padmasambhava, known in Tibet as the second Buddha (figure 3.9 on the following page). Padmasambhava's name is close to Ratnasambhava's but means "Completely Lotus Born." Padmasambhava is not of the jewel family, but of the *padma,* or lotus, family that magnetizes power for compassionate purposes. Guru Rinpoche (Precious Guru), as Padmasambhava is also known in Tibet, manifests in many forms. One form especially connected to the chintamani is known as Orgyen Khandro Norlha. The narrative that opened this chapter emphasizes the almost simultaneous conflux of the chintamani and Padmasambhava as the lotus-born child into the court of King Indrabodhi. Orgyen is Tibetan for Oddiyana, Indrabodhi's kingdom. Khandro Norlha means "Powerful Sky-goer, Deva of Riches," and he manifests the activity of all the wealth gods and wealth Bodhisattvas. Because of this, Khandro Norlha not only brings abundance to individuals and families but, equally importantly, brings ease and increase to entire economies. Padmasambhava in this form is seated in the posture of royal ease, holding the chintamani in his right hand and a mongoose that spits forth gems in his left. A pile of large gems of the five colors is at his feet. Feeling Orgyen Khandro Norlha's presence, visualizing his mandala palace, and practicing his mantra creates much closer affinity with the chintamani gem and chintamani consciousness.

Chakravartin

A *chakravartin* is a universal monarch, an example of which is the benevolent world King of Shambhala. *Chakravartin* means "wheel-turner," referring to the wheel of dharma, and indicates one who can command, activate, and sustain worldly power and spiritual harmony on a great scale. The meditational deity at the heart of the Shambhala mandala is Kalachakra, who is associated with the wheel of great accomplishment. As emblems and implements of royalty, a *chakravartin* possesses seven gems (*saptaratna*) representing superior qualities and rightful capability: precious wheel, precious gem, precious queen, precious minister, precious elephant, precious horse, and precious general.[17] The precious gem is the chintamani, through which a

Figure 3.9. Detail of a Thangka showing Padmasambhava adorned with jewels. This and other Thangkas are painted with pigments made from ground gemstones.

Photo by J. Govert

chakravartin brings universal benefit to all in the realm. The precious chintamani jewel has the following eight properties:

First, it shines in the night. Just as the harvest moon gives a clear light in the Autumn, so the jewel shines for a hundred *yojana** in the dark night. If, in daytime, one suffers from heat, a bright light comes from it and overcomes the heat.

Second, if one is travelling without water and suffers from thirst, a great river that possess the eight qualities appears and quenches all thirst.

Third, whatever the *chakravartin* thinks of arises out of the jewel.

Fourth, from each its eight parts, or members (*yanlag*), at the right time (*dei tshe*), light of various colors radiates, such as light of blue and yellow and white and red and crimson (*btsod-kha*) color.

Fifth, wherever the jewel is, for about a hundred *yojana* round, there is no sickness. The mind remains always in a state of equanimity. As with karmic actions, none of his wishes go without result.

Sixth, it prevents evil nagas from causing terrible rainfall.

Seventh, sadness, abysses, solitary regions, trees, ponds, gardens, lotuses, forests, and parks are [in a positive sense] perfected.

Eighth, nobody experiences untimely death [or] becomes an animal.† [To none] is harm done by animals. Not even the disharmonious harm each other, as for example, the snake and the mongoose.[18]

Thus, the chintamani fulfills all the positive intentions of a *chakravartin*. The chintamani is often shown tied to the saddle of the precious horse, which is a further symbol of the wind-horse that spreads auspicious blessings in all directions.

---

*A *yojana* is a Vedic unit of distance equal to one twelve-millionth of the distance from sun to Earth, or about eight miles.

†This means that upon the death of a human, he or she will not be reincarnated as an animal.

Chintamani Imagery in Buddhism

The chintamani is most often found in the realms of the devas or *nagas* (serpents or dragons) and is not usually in the hands of humans. The wish-fulfilling gem may appear in five different colors. The shape is more like a turnip or pear. Besides being shown as a single gem, the chintamani is also pictured arranged in sets of gems of more elongated or compressed shapes surrounded by flame aureoles.[19] A single gem or a pile of gems on fire represent no ordinary jewels but, rather, the chintamani itself. A chintamani, as we discussed, may be held in the hand of a Bodhisattva, but also may be wrapped in the topknot hair of a Buddha or Bodhisattva.[20] Chintamanis may also be piled in front of a seated or standing enlightened being.

Figure 3.10. Bodhisattva holding the chintamani depicted as a triple gem on fire. Detail from *Attributes of rDo-rje "Jigs-byed (Vajrabhairava, "The Fear-inspiring One")* in a Tibetan "rgyan tshogs" banner.

Wellcome Library, London

Dzogchen

Of practices in Tibetan Vajrayana Buddhism and Bon, Dzogchen, the Great Perfection teachings, are one of the most advanced systems for realization. Yogic practices in Vajrayana are usually introduced with an empowerment that authorizes a student to practice. Empowerments employ many rituals and symbols and can range from quite simple to extremely elaborate. Dzogchen rituals very often employ crystals to transmit the energy to engage, understand, and create momentum to accomplish the yogic practices. Traditionally, in explaining the Dzogchen teachings of its basis, method, and result, crystals are an important medium and metaphor.[21] The basis of nature of the individual and the universe are illustrated first by a mirror, which only reflects what is near (and the reflection is illusory). Whatever color appears in front of a mirror, that color is reflected. Polished or faceted crystals partly act as mirrors, as some of the light energy that strikes the surface reflects back. Also, when light strikes a crystal, some energy illuminates the interior where an object outside the crystal seems projected inside. Again, when sunlight strikes a crystal, a third effect occurs as white light is refracted into a rainbow spectrum of colors that appear inside and are also bent out at an angle. Sunlight on crystals create these three simultaneous effects. That is the nature and energy of the universe. When the mind becomes confused by the various apparitions, and confusing projections, reflections, and refractions are accepted as reality, that is ignorance. When the mind recognizes the changing displays of light as the primal play of energy, that is enlightenment. The crystal of Great Perfection Dzogchen is the heart of the chintamani light show.

Chintamani in China and Japan

As any philosophy or practice moves across countries, the ideas from one culture are translated when they cross the border into the next. The same was true of the chintamani as it moved farther east from India. The words in Chinese and Japanese share the same written characters that early translators used to convey the meaning of chintamani but are pronounced differently. In Chinese the characters are pronounced *ruyibaozhu* and in Japanese, *nyoihōju.*[22] Figure 3.11 depicts the four traditional, as opposed to simplified, written Chinese characters that translators used to convey the nuances of Sanskrit chintamani.

Kanji, or Chinese characters, are made up of radicals, or components of other written symbol words. The first word, *nyo,* has two parts, a woman on the left side and a mouth on the right. It means "equal," "be like," "thus," or "just as."[23] The second word, *i,* also has two parts. Above is the idea of sound or vibration; below is the picture of heart/mind.[24] Together they imply that words come from the heart to express resonant intent. The third kanji, *ho,* is complex in structure. In different spoken contexts, *ho* by itself means treasure or something precious.[25] The uppermost part is a roof, implying a storehouse. Next, below and to the left is the character for emperor, while next to it is the radical for an earthen water jar, signifying a collection

Figure 3.11. Shodo of *Nyoihōju,* the wish-fulfilling precious jewel
Calligraphy by J. Govert

place. Finally, at the bottom is the radical for seashell, which was valuable and at one time a medium of exchange. Putting it together, the whole character conveys the meaning of collected and stored valuables that are imperial possessions. The last character, *ju,* means "jewel."[26] The kanji has two parts. On the left is the radical for emperor again, while the right has the character for vermillion red. Vermillion is the characteristic color of cinnabar sculptures owned by the rulers of China. Cinnabar is also associated with Daoist alchemists hinting at a mystical and transformational connection. Simply, *ju* refers to a reddish pearl or more generally to a precious, mystical gem. These are the added echoes of meaning chintamani resonated when the transmitted Indian tradition engaged with similar themes arising from within Chinese and other East Asian civilizations.

4

Shambhala, Kalachakra, and the Chintamani

Hidden Realms and the Evolution of Higher Consciousness Cultures

Hail to Buddha as Kalachakra and Consort, in nature
Indestructible compassion and wisdom of emptiness
Made manifest in a form radiant with the marks and signs of
  perfection,
Like an entrancing painting of an exquisite rainbow.
I call out to you, and to all lineage masters past and present.

LOBZANG CHOKYI GYALTSEN,
THE PRACTICE OF KALACHAKRA

RAINBOWS ARE APT IMAGES FOR THE CHINTAMANI, for Shambhala, and for spiritual mastery. A brilliantly colored rainbow can arc across an entire horizon, dwarfing the natural and manmade scenery underneath. It draws our attention to a greater view and inspires us. In many cultures, including Tibetan, rainbows are auspicious omens of impending blessings. Sunlight refracted through mists of rain projects the whole color spectrum just like crystals do. Rainbows are also illusory as they arise, fade, then disappear into the background of a clear or cloudy sky. After they are gone, we doubt what we saw. When they first appear, we are certain of their reality and delighted by the display of light colors. Shambhala is like rainbows in this way, testing the certainty of our cherished perceptions. The hidden realm of Shambhala in Asian tradition is the spiritual center on Earth for wise and advanced beings who guide the evolution of mankind through the mists of time. In Sanskrit, Shambhala means a place of peace, tranquility, and happiness; while the Tibetan translation, *dejung,* emphasizes the source of arising happiness. Shrouded in myth, legend, and common experience, a Shambhala-like land is described similarly across various cultures. Sometimes we perceive the reality of Shambhala and sometimes we perceive its illusion. When we set out to examine Shambhala, we do discover that it is a vivid archetype that resonates strongly from within. Let us next examine the play of light that presents Shambhala to the senses, mind, and spirit more closely.

There are two parallel paths to Shambhala that present a method to prove the experience of Shambhala as illusory or authentic. One is the internal journey of spiritual development. This path has been described in the last century by the channeled Theosophical teachings of Helena Blavatsky, Helena Roerich, and Alice Bailey. Older Shambhala teachings that well precede the Theosophical movement derive from a root tantra describing the Kalachakra as the Wheel of Time in the Vajrayana tradition of Tibetan Buddhism. There are many other spiritual traditions that present the way to Shambhala under that name or under another, but the Vajrayana teachings present a very organized yoga system. The outer path is to search as a pilgrim on the literal road to the place of enlightenment. In chapter 1, we followed the Roerichs on their pilgrimage to locate the physical manifestation of Shambhala, which, as we discovered, was tedious, perilous, and yet a glorious expedition across vast tracts of Asia.

Chintamani and the Search for Shambhala

We will end this chapter's considerations with a revelation about the chintamani. But in order to make sense of this new information, we must return to weave in the context of the Roerichs' adventure from chapter 1 and begin again. The Roerichs were in possession of a chintamani of which Helena was guardian. She used the gem to channel information to guide the quest to the hidden kingdom of Shambhala during two long and dangerous expeditions.

We have the evocative paintings of Nicholas Roerich as well as writings both by him and Helena as descriptions of the purpose, play, and results of their expeditionary efforts on behalf of world peace. What is so important about Shambhala that they risked their family's lives to find it? Is it merely a hopeful myth, or does it have vital substance about actual history that serves as a light guiding the positive evolution of human civilization and consciousness?

The Roerichs used a chintamani to guide their outer search. There is also a parallel inner search for Shambhala guided by a more ethereal chintamani and a Buddha known as Kalachakra, the "Time Wheel Awakened One." There are extensive yogic practices known collectively as the Kalachakra tantra. At the center of these yogas is Kalachakra and his consort, Kalachakri, both fully awakened Buddhas from an earlier age. The goal of Kalachakra yoga is enlightenment, which collapses karma and linear time and opens the continuing experience of bliss, compassion, emptiness, and wisdom. Like the Buddhas and Bodhisattvas discussed in chapter 3, there are many images of Kalachakra and Kalachakri. They appear in one tradition as two-armed and two-legged and in another with multiple faces, arms, hands, and legs with their bodies depicted in five different colors. In both traditions, Kalachakra and Kalachakri are in sexual embrace to emphasize the bliss of enlightened awareness (figure 4.1). In the two-armed version, Kalachakra has a chintamani entwined in his hair, and both partners are adorned in many jewels. In the multiple-armed version, both partners are adorned with many jewels, wear crowns with a central chintamani, and each holds a chintamani in one of their hands. A crown chintamani represents enlightenment attained, radiated, and celebrated from the highest chakra, indicating that the chintamani is the result. A handheld chintamani indicates that it is a means and key to enlightenment and the kingdom of Shambhala. The chintamani is at once a guide on the journey as well as the intended destination.

There are two other images of the Kalachakra as the Wheel of Time. The first is a mandala (figure 4.2, page 80) that is a symbolic map of where to find the two *yidams,* Kalachakra and Kalachakri.* The mandala is a

---

Yidams, or alternately *ishtadevatas,* express the indwelling divine self-nature externally experienced as a Buddha, Bodhisattva, or deva. Yidams are chosen deities for visualization and mantra recitation.

Figure 4.1. Kalachakra and Kalachakri each hold a chintamani,
and Kalachakra has a chintamani at his crown.

colorful, two-dimensional, symbolic representation of a three-dimensional palace that has four access gates on the lower level. On the top level at the very center of the mandala is where Kalachakra and Kalachakri can be found in the middle of more than thirty-five million Buddhas, Bodhisattvas, protectors, and deities.[1] The mandala spins through all the cycles of time. At the center, where you find Kalachakra and Kalachakri, you also find your true self at the still point where there is no revolving

Figure 4.2. The Kalachakra mandala surrounded
by the letter sounds of the Sanskrit alphabet. This Thangka was
painted with pigments of ground minerals and gems.

Photo by Kaleigh Brown

and no time. Because the central couple each hold chintamanis, you will also find the chintamani there, out of time in the enlightened realms at the center. A second image is the visual symbol of the ten Kalachakra mantra syllables woven skillfully into a unified image (figure 10.1, page 239), which we will discuss in chapter 10.

Guides to Shambhala

Along the Roerich pilgrimage route, perhaps the most important goal beside Shambhala itself was Tashi Lhumpo Monastery in Shigatse, the second largest city in Tibet. The monastery is the seat of the Tashi or Panchen Lama, who has been the second most recognized spiritual authority within the Gelugpa order of Tibetan Buddhism after the Dalai Lama. Most importantly, the Panchen Lama was regarded widely as a foremost authority on Shambhala and as a main lineage holder of the Kalachakra tradition, reputed to know secrets about Shambhala not fully understood by other highly advanced Kalachakra yogis.* The Roerichs were seeking a personal audience with the Ninth Panchen Lama (figure 4.3 on the following page) to gain intimate and unerring instruction on the correct path to Shambhala.[2] In addition to his personal knowledge of Shambhala, the Ninth Panchen Lama understood a primary text of one of his previous incarnations. The Sixth Panchen Lama, Lobsang Palden Yeshe (1738–1780), wrote a guidebook in 1775 on how to find Shambhala entitled *Shambhalai Lamyig*.[3] This and other guidebooks provide instructions blending inner and outer pilgrimages into a single path. It gives directional instructions with descriptions of how the waystations appear. It then describes what practices are necessary to surpass obstacles presented at each step, which are simultaneous manifestations of entangled inner and outer landscapes.

---

*The Roerichs were involved in 1909 with a Buryat Lama, Agvan Dorzhiev, to build a Kalachakra Temple in St. Petersburg. Lama Agvan Dorzhiev was a former tutor and an official envoy of the Thirteenth Dalai Lama to Czar Nicolas II, and was also a Kalachakra adept and close personal disciple of the Ninth Panchen Lama. This established a strong personal connection for the Roerichs to meet and learn from the Ninth Panchen Lama.

Figure 4.3. The Ninth Panchen Lama,
Lobsang Thubten Choki Nyima (1883–1937).

Photo taken in 1907 by Sven Hedin, *Trans-Himalaya*, 1922.

Affinity with Shambhala

To find Shambhala, we first need affinity. The affinity can show itself as contagious enthusiasm for a wide range of Shambhala topics, an eagerness to learn more no matter how skeptical we may be. The guidebooks point out that affinity is demonstrated by having dreams about the kingdom of Shambhala—whether mere glimpses, being there, or seeking the path there. The vividness and frequency of these dreams show the intensity of the quest. Affinity is also established and nourished by contemplation of the Kalachakra texts and practices, and by study of Shambhala topics through cultural lore and philosophic inquiry. Affinity is formed for this life and future lives by participating in an empowerment ceremony that provides a strong, inner introductory connection through a guru and future adept. Chanting a Kalachakra approach mantra also establishes resonance.* Studying the related Kalachakra texts, and receiving and then actually practicing the outer, inner, and secret yogas, strengthens the connection. The Kalachakra yogas are considered highest yoga tantra and difficult to obtain without previous study or practice. The current Fourteenth Dalai Lama, however, has made it one of his lifetime goals to connect the unprepared general public directly with Shambhala. To that end, he has provided the Kalachakra initiation thirty-four times worldwide to audiences multi-thousands in size. The Kalachakra initiation creates the affinity to be reborn into Shambhala at the conclusion of this life. To discover why this is important to the Dalai Lama, let us review Tibetan Buddhist tradition about Shambhala.

Buddhist Shambhala

Teaching of the Kalachakra in the present era took place at Dhanyakataka stupa† in India by the historical Buddha at the request of King Suchandra. Suchandra emerged from the hidden kingdom of Shambhala seeking teachings to accomplish enlightenment while tending his regal duties. Thus, the

---

*One approach mantra is *Aum Guru Shri Kalachakra Ye!*

†A *stupa*, a Buddhist architectural monument, generally used to house relics, resonates with the human chakra system to bring enlightenment to Earth and to bless the land.

Kalachakra was taught in 900 BCE, according to some Tibetan sources, near the end of Buddha's life.* The eighth successor to Suchandra, Yashas, an incarnation of Manjushri, simplified the Kalachakra teachings into the *Laghutantra* text and united the kingdom of Shambhala into a single spiritual practice. For this, he became known as the first Kalki King. Whereas previously, various other Hindu dharmas were taught and practiced, during his reign, all the inhabitants of Shambhala came to practice the Kalachakra path. The next Kalki King, Pundarika, composed a commentary on the root tantra entitled *Vimalaprabha,* or *Ornament of Stainless Light.* The Dalai Lamas are believed to be continuing reincarnations of King Pundarika. By the tenth century CE, the Kalachakra teachings were not well practiced in Buddhist lands anymore, only in Shambhala. Master Jamyang Dorje of Kashmir had a vision of Manjushri instructing him to follow a northward path where he encountered the eleventh Kalki King of Shambhala, who initiated him and transmitted the entire Kalachakra texts and teachings. Later, Jamyang Dorje journeyed to Shambhala where he perfected and accomplished all the Kalachakra learning and yogas. Upon returning, he taught and transmitted the Kalachakra again to northern India and later became known as Kalachakrapada the Elder.

The Kalachakra teaching is about uncoupling our mind and energies from the wheel of time, a stream flowing from the past, through the present, and into the future. The linearity of time and flow of cause and effect is an illusion. The cause-effect chain is elsewhere described as karma, which simply is the result creators experience from their creations. The ability to operate both inside and outside the karmic wheel of time is another definition of enlightenment. Looked at this way, Shambhala is a field simultaneously in and out of conventional, Earth-bound perception of time. Recognizing that Shambhala lies outside our perceptions of time and space helps explain often contradictory reports and personal experiences of where, how, and what Shambhala appears to be.

As Shambhala is outside the Wheel of Time, it is not surprising that the Kalachakra teachings make future predictions. A long-term prediction in both Vedic and Kalachakra astrology are the cycles of yugas, vast

---

*This dating of the reigns of Suchandra and subsequent Shambhala dharma kings is at odds with other chronologies of the life of Buddha.

time periods reckoned not so much in years, but in planetary precession cycles of 25,920 years. According to Vedic tradition, the current Kali cycle, or dark age, began on the midnight meridian of Ujjain, India, on February 18, 3102 BCE.[4] The Kali yuga is about the continual increase of ego-driven ignorance and conflict at the expense of wisdom and peace. The average human lifespan is also predicted to decline along with the quality of life for all on planet Earth. This is where the prophecy of Shambhala resonates with the world's current collective awareness. The degradation of the environment, animals, and humans clearly has increased despite the majority who want the opposite, a much more harmonious world. There is an obvious growing tension between a world leadership who pursue control of greater forces of power while conditions for general welfare, peace, and harmony are ignored. The resolution of this clash is predicted to occur in the reign of Rudra Chakrin, the twenty-fifth and final Kalki King, around 2400 CE, when the lords of Earth with their armies pursue absolute power to breach Shambhala. Rudra Chakrin, the "Wrathful Wheel Turner," will be able to subdue this chaotic onslaught to bring about a long era of meaningful peace and dawn of a renewed golden age.

What and where is Shambhala, the place of peace? There is another Shambhala guidebook included in the *Tengyur,* the official compendium of Tibetan Buddhist commentary texts.* This guide uses many older Sanskrit place names that the Sixth Panchen Lama adopted in his *Shambhalai Lamyig* guide to keep the search obscure for the insincere.[5] Edwin Bernbaum, in his *The Way to Shambhala: Search for the Mythical Kingdom Beyond the Himalayas,* provides a condensed translation of the *Tengyur* guide with comparisons to the Panchen Lama's guide.[6] The Sixth Panchen Lama directs the search to begin at Bodh Gaya, the site in India where the Buddha attained enlightenment. There is much more detail about the type and level of accomplishment of necessary spiritual practices than there are of explicit travel directions. Nonetheless, the Shambhala guidebooks do provide some references for travel in a three-dimensional coordinate system. The quester must travel ever northward beyond the Ganges River, beyond Lhasa, where Shambhala can be found north of Tibet, between Mongolia

---

*The direct teachings of the Buddha are the collected sutras, or *Kangyur* in Tibetan.

and the North Pole. Physics considers time a fourth dimension for which the Kalachakra texts provide a spiritual technology intended to navigate beyond the limitations of space and time dimensions. Shambhala, as a higher dimensional reality, is perhaps embedded in the Earth's field or tangent to Earth. Any serious searcher for Shambhala must be prepared to pass through and beyond the third and fourth dimensions to find its truth.

Beyuls

There are several templates in Vedic and Buddhist cosmologies to explain what Shambhala is, or at least what it resembles. Padmasambhava, sometimes called the Second Buddha, helped establish Tantric Buddhism in Tibet after arriving in the year of the Iron Tiger, 810 CE. During his time in the Himalayas, he identified 108 future hidden lands or *beyuls* to protect people during periods of chaos and danger. They are islands of spiritual presence and practice during eras of moral, social, and environmental decay. The beyuls are cloaked in local ecology and indexed to open by time cycle. They are indexed to be opened by an enlightened master who has both the karmic affinity and conscious awareness to open a particular beyul. Tulshuk Lingpa led a group of sincere practitioners toward Beyul Demashong on Mt. Kanchenjunga (figure 4.4) in order to open it during the Cuban missile crisis of 1962.* The attempt was tragically unsuccessful and buried both Tulshuk Rinpoche and the approach to the beyul in an avalanche.[7]

Opening or accessing a beyul is not certain even when it is the right time, right place, right master, and right karma. It also requires a field of the right collective consciousness. Another beyul example is in an area called Pema Kod at the juncture of a number of Himalayan border countries. India and China have each annexed a portion of Pema Kod, which is a province in southern Tibet, east of Bhutan and north of the Indian province of

---

*Tulshuk Lingpa Rinpoche (1916–1962), whose name means "Crazy Treasure Revealer," literally followed in the footsteps of his guru, Domang Tulku, who also tried to open the same Beyul Demashong in the 1920s but died trying. Tulshuk Lingpa was a crazy wisdom yogi known for his eccentric behavior and for a number of miracles, brilliant teachings, and profound practice.

Figure 4.4. Mount Kanchenjunga on the
Sikkim and Nepal border.

Arunachal Pradesh. Dudjom Rinpoche, one of the foremost recent Tibetan
Buddhist masters (1904–1987), was born in Pema Kod and helped engineer
the transfer of many Tibetans, and Buddhist and cultural treasures, into the
safety of Sikkim in 1959 during the Chinese communists' violent seizure of
Tibet. Thereafter, Sikkim became a place for renewed and enthusiastic practice of Tibetan Buddhism.

Buddha Fields

Another Shambhala template are Pure Lands, also known as Buddha fields.
These are places better described as extradimensional. Whereas beyuls are
nested in Earth's field, Buddha fields or Buddha realms are accessible from
Earth, but there is no information describing where they exist. Buddha
fields are usually established as the result of the vow of a Buddha or great
Bodhisattva to provide a place conducive to spiritual practice and conscious

evolution. As such, they are created by intention. They are free from the obstacles of suffering, worldly debt, familial obligation, and karmic confusion. Instead, there is strong spiritual guidance present and the opportunity to advance one's spiritual realization so that only one more Earth incarnation is necessary before attaining *anuttara samyak sambodhi,* highest perfect awakening. Examples of Buddha fields and their usual, yet spongy English translations are: the Western Paradise or Pure Land of Bliss of Amitabha Buddha (*Sukhavati* or *Dewachen*), the Copper Colored Mountain of Padmasambhava (*Zandokpalri*), and the Eastern Land of Medicine Buddha, Master of Sapphire Radiance Healing (*Vaiduryanirbhasa*). The reason why the Fourteenth Dalai Lama would want to initiate people into the Kalachakra teachings and connect them directly with Shambhala is twofold. Anyone dying in the next four hundred years is likely to reincarnate into a world of greater degeneration and suffering. Being born into the Shambhala Pure Land at death provides an alternate path to avoid the probability of greater suffering, but more importantly it exponentially accelerates spiritual evolution in order to bring about ultimate personal and worldly happiness.

Lokas

The next Shambhala template is the understanding of *lokas*. Related to the English word "locations," a *loka* refers to any place that can be described by a coordinate system of physical dimensions, time, density of matter, and subtlety of consciousness. Many ancient cultures picture the universe as a world tree or world mountain. Buddhist and Vedic cosmology use the imagery of Mount Meru or Sumeru as an ascending hierarchy (figure 4.5). At the base of Mount Meru are the seven most materially dense realms often thought of as the hell worlds. The beings who dwell there are the least free and suffer the most, as they are extremely self-absorbed with little concern for any other being. These beings are in the *lokas* called *kama dhatu* or the desire realms. The lower the *loka* the greater are the manifestations of negative desires. The Earth, including the realm of most of the gods, form the upper tiers of the desire worlds. There are also realms of form (*rupa dhatu*) and formlessness (*arupa dhatu*) above. The Vedic cosmology discusses seven upper *lokas* that include Earth and six more planes of increasingly

Figure 4.5. The central temple buildings of Angkor Wat representing Mount Meru and surrounding continents.

greater subtlety and purity above. In the perspective of the *lokas*, beings in lower *lokas* do not have the full ability to perceive beings in upper *lokas*. Shambhala, as a less dense world, is difficult for ordinary Earth humans to perceive clearly. Ignorance and confusion of emotions and mind therefore cloak the ability of any being to perceive Shambhala clearly. The spiritual practices discussed in the guidebooks are intended to purify the gross senses to recover greater innate abilities to perceive Shambhala and to resonate body and mind in unitary frequency.

The Seven Rishi Council

Shambhala resonates as the council of seven sages (*saptarishis*) from Vedic mythology. These sages are present for each long cycle of cosmic evolution. They are neither humans nor devas but are greater beings in that they are identified as mediators for the continuing evolution of the yugas, or planetary cycles. They are great light beings who temper the incoming and outgoing energies and consciousness that radiate change to Earth and harmonize Earth's subsequent responses. The *rishis* were considered more as a group in earlier Vedic literature rather than as seven individuals. Later, the names of individual *rishis* were separately enumerated and associated with the seven stars of the Big Dipper. The position the *saptarishis* define is the still point at the North Pole and the daily pivotal revolution of the heavens around their center among the stars. Shambhala also has a role in guiding the evolution of mankind and of Earth from denser materiality to the subtler expressions of spiritual intelligence as awakened consciousness.

Theosophical Shambhala

In the late nineteenth and early twentieth centuries, the Theosophical movement and offshoot philosophical schools identified the *saptarishis* with the Great White Brotherhood, which they understood as a guiding council of great beings nurturing the growth of consciousness and culture on Earth over the ages. The Great White Brotherhood, referring to light beings not Caucasians, was considered the core hierarchy of spiritual masters from Shambhala. Much of the knowledge from the Theosophical schools was received via channeled information from various ascended masters, such as Master Morya, who was in contact with Helena Roerich. Madame Blavatsky's two major books, *Isis Unveiled* (1877) and the *Secret Doctrine* (1888), were the initial, public presentations of the Theosophical movement. They contained numerous quotes from an ancient text Blavatsky called the *Book of Dzyan,* which she claimed was an ancient Tibetan text.[8] Since Shambhala is an important topic in her two books, we are left with some questions. Was she in possession of the Kalachakra commentary *Ornament of Stainless Light?* Or is *Dzyan* another channeled, invented, or unknown ancient work? In 1919, Alice Bailey received channeled information from the Tibetan also referred to as Master Djwal Khul or simply D. K., which she published in seventeen books written between 1919 and her death in 1949. Among the many topics discussed is the existence and purpose of "Shamballa and the Hierarchy of Masters." The larger question is: How much authentic left-hand

and right-hand* information from the ancient Egyptian and Greek mystery schools was released through Theosophical movement teachers, groups, and publications? Their perspectives often recast Hindu and Buddhist traditions in a European cultural context and blended these with traditions of the Western Mystery Schools. Theosophical perspectives on Shambhala are often opaque but reinforce many Vedic and Buddhist themes.

Agarttha and Shadow Worlds

In 1886, Marquis Alexandre Saint-Yves d'Alveydre published *The Kingdom of Agarttha: A Journey into the Hollow of the Earth*. He introduced the idea that humans living on Earth's surface are only a portion of planetary inhabitants. Those living deep in the Earth are descendants of a great civilization that choose to remain unknown to surface dwellers. The deep civilization is Agarttha and its language, Vattanian.[9] Saint-Yves d'Alveydre was a student of Sanskrit and offered the meaning of Agarttha as "inaccessible to violence and inaccessible to Anarchy."[10] Agarttha also may be a close linguistic jumble of *aryavartha* or *aryavarta,* referring to the Aryans' homeland. The early Vedic interpretation of *arya* is "noble," describing a high degree of spiritual realization. Later connotations of *aryavarta* are as the region in which the Aryan culture bearers lived, south of the Himalayan and north of the Vindya mountain ranges. Later European esoteric writers continued exploring the subterranean Agartthan theme of a great civilization, technologically and culturally evolved but purposefully elusive. Agarttha's almost palpable presence as a super-culture was bound to blend with other prevailing visions of Shambhala at the beginning of the twentieth century.

This all took a very dark turn with the Nazis. The Vril society sent expeditions from Germany to Tibet from 1926 to 1942 to persuade

---

*The left- and right-hand paths denote contrasting ways to practice self-cultivation. Left-hand can refer either to unconventional types of practices or to black magic that employs higher knowledge primarily for self-benefit. Right-hand refers to white magic or use of higher energy and wisdom for compassionate benefit avoiding harm to others.

"Cave Communities" of dark practitioners of the occult to support and lend power to Nazi causes.[11] They identified two shadow traditions and sought adepts of "Agarthi and Schamballah" to live in and work their black magic for the German Reich.[12] The Agarthi black magicians agreed to join the German war effort under Heinrich Himmler as part of the *Ahnenrerbe*, or Nazi Occult Bureau, that grew to forty-nine branches.[13] The black magicians of Schamballah refused the offer because they had already been working secretly with lodges in England and America.[14] With the Nazis, we encounter a credible, palpable, and horrifically offensive attempt in very recent history to subvert the golden age of Shambhala from manifesting. The fact that the power-obsessed lords of Earth are actively on the attack proves the Shambhala prophecy that the battle of good triumphing over evil is both true and approaching impending resolution.

Forgotten Civilizations

Shambhala may also derive from diverse cultural memories of lost continents mixed with lost civilizations. Most of these memories can be regarded as nostalgia for times thought to be better, unless, of course, the civilizations that have passed were actually equal to or greater than our present ones. Archaeologists have been challenging Plato's story, asserting that the Atlantis narrative was myth or metaphor, but not history. If Atlantis (or the Incas, Gobekli Tepi, Kumari Kandam, Zhang Zhung, predynastic Egypt, or any of the many others) was greater than present civilizations yet failed anyway, we cannot tell the tale of actual history as one glorious ascent. Whether the cataclysms that engulfed past great civilizations were self-engineered or arose naturally, the result was a precipitous collapse technologically, culturally, and spiritually. Civilization did not restart itself from *tabula rasa* trial and error. Behind reestablishment and reeducation after each failed civilization is Shambhala, technologically, culturally, and spiritually. Other living remnants of past civilizations may also have survived and acted over time in parallel to Shambhala, but they may or may not have worked with compassion for the welfare of all.

Vedic Shambhala

India's Vedic culture provides another perspective on Shambhala. Within the Vedas, there are three aspects of God: as Creator, or Brahmin; as Sustainer, or Vishnu; and as Destroyer, or Shiva. Over the span of yugas, life, culture, and spiritual awareness rise and fall. When degeneration has become too negative, Vishnu has incarnated as a human to reinspire and recalibrate civilization to harmonize with the opportunities of a new age. From a Hindu view, Krishna and Buddha are considered the most recent avatars of Vishnu. The next, tenth, and last predicted Vishnu avatar in this cycle is Kalki, who will be born in northern India in the village of Shambhala.[15] He will ride a white horse as his symbol of power and command. Just as predicted of Rudra Chakrin, Kalki will defeat army hordes in service to leaders of the Kali Yuga, which will usher in a golden age of prosperity, peace, and spiritual evolution. The avatars of Vishnu have a personal role in maintaining the cyclic evolution of the web of life, assuring it manifests with greater conscious awareness as it ascends in subtlety, dharma, harmony, and benevolence. Shambhala, in the background of Earth's history, exercises the same role as the avatars of Vishnu, waging an ongoing campaign to guide life on Earth away from competitive dominance-power and toward collective benefit throughout all the realms of Mount Meru. Whether through Vishnu, Bodhisattvas, or the Shambhala collective, spiritual evolution is not random, rather it is intended ascent.

Details of managing Earth's evolution are found in three of the greatest Asian epics: the Indian epics Ramayana and Mahabharata, and the Tibetan/Mongolian epic of *Gesar of Ling*. The two great Indian epics recount the lives of two successive avatars of Vishnu. The earlier epic, the Ramayana, relates the deeds and accomplishments of Rama, while the later, the Mahabharata, narrates the history of Shri Krishna. These are the longest epics written and recited on Earth. The Ramayana, at twenty-seven thousand verse *slokas*, is about the size of the *Iliad* and *Odyssey* combined. The Mahabharata is one hundred thousand verse *slokas* long, while the epic of *Gesar of Ling* is ten times larger than the Mahabharata at over one million verses. What these three epics show in extensive detail is the level of difficulty that even an avatar of God has in directing the events of individuals, families, and kingdoms to neutralize their karma and fulfill their spiritual destinies. We are going to draw attention to a few points that will weave a broader understanding of Shambhala as reflected in the Mahabharata and *Gesar of Ling*. The following description of Shambhala from the Mahabharata is older than the one referenced above from the *Kalki Purana* by about 2,300 years:

> And commissioned by Time, a Brahmana of the name of Kalki will take his birth. And he will glorify Vishnu and possess great energy, great intelligence, and great prowess. And he will take his birth in a town of the name of Shambhala in an auspicious Brahmana family.* And vehicles and weapons, and warriors and arms, and coats of mail will be at his disposal as soon as he will think of them. And he will be the king of kings, and ever victorious with the strength of virtue. And he will restore order and peace in this world crowded with creatures and contradictory in its course. And that blazing Brahmana of mighty intellect, having appeared, will destroy all things. And he will be the Destroyer of all, and will inaugurate a new Yuga. And surrounded by the Brahmanas, that Brahmana will exterminate all the *mlecchas*† wherever those low and despicable persons may take refuge.[16]

Epic Shambhala

The Mahabharata epic describes Krishna's home city of Dwaraka on the ocean in Gujarat, northwest India. The Pandavas, who are protagonists in the Mahabharata because they nobly uphold dharma, watch from afar as the ocean covers over the last of the golden towers of Dwaraka under the swell of successive waves. This scene has been regarded by Western academics as a myth like Troy. In 1870, however, Heinrich Schlieman began excavations that eventually provided evidence of the actual site of the Trojan city in the *Iliad*. So, too, Dr. S. R. Rao and an archaeological team from the Indian National Institute of Oceanography have spent twenty years examining

---

*A Brahmana family refers to a family lineage of the Brahmin or highest Hindu caste distinguished by the primary duty to practice Vedic rituals and teach Vedic wisdom.
†*Mlecchas* is Sanskrit for barbarians.

underwater ruins up to a half mile offshore from the present Dwaraka.[17] Dr. Rao believes the structures and artifacts his team have uncovered and examined prove that strata of these ruins are likely to be Krishna's lost city. This verification is moving the great epics from the mists of myth as lost and misunderstood civilizations of lore into a sharper historical focus as their unremembered cities and truly great events are rediscovered. The epics document details of the incredible range of intervention that higher- and lower-level beings are and have been exercising to direct the unfolding of life on Earth in opposition to one other. The epics are the actual and symbolic revelation of the process of Shambhala.

The Earth home of any avatar is a manifestation of Shambhala for an era because it is the local physical center for the work of that avatar to guide humanity back onto a more spiritual and positive trajectory. An avatar's mission is an expression of the continuing mission of Shambhala. The Vedic and Tibetan Buddhist descriptions of evolutionary guidance of humanity are differently expressed but have many shared themes. Vishnu is the constant consciousness for maintaining and adjusting the ongoing upward expression of life. Shambhala is also a constant presence that sends forth many envoys and teachers for the same evolutionary purpose. Avatars reintroduce the meaning of dharma or natural truth. The kings of Shambhala are gurus who rule a philosopher's state. Their main purpose is to teach, practice, and demonstrate the truth of enlightened realization. The Mahabharata chronicles the last great complex of Earth interventions. The *Gesar of Ling* epic chronicles how the once and future king will intervene again to guide Earth from a perilous and very pressing demonic dominance.

Gesar of Ling, the Once and Future King

Apart from Virgil's *Aeneid,* epics are not authored by a single person. In fact, writing epics down in words and symbols is a late stage of composition. Epics, first and foremost, are long songs of cosmic struggle and victory. They are performed as recitations or dance with music, or as theater with actors, costumes, props, and sets. This makes the sheer length of the *Gesar of Ling* epic mind-boggling. Wandering minstrels and theater groups still perform this epic drama in the villages, festivals, and cities of Mongolia and Tibet. No performer knows the entire set of verses by heart, and the epic cannot be performed completely in a single season. The verses that arise are the direct inspiration of the epic muse that performers of the *Gesar* epic have expressed spontaneously, and then have come to repeat faithfully. The *Gesar of Ling* epic has sprung from the collective mind, and because of the immense information channeled by so many independent minstrels, we need to pay very close attention to its message, which involves Shambhala and the defeat of the control of world demons to initiate a golden age of peace.

Padmasambhava, the second Buddha, takes the role of a Vishnu avatar. He guides and engineers everything from the birth of Gesar to the birth of all the protagonists and antagonists from the realms of devas, nagas, and humans that will interact in the epic. Gesar (figure 4.6) is chosen as the only being who has the karma and ability to defeat the dark forces. In the Mahabharata, Krishna guided and engineered the events while also participating in the divine drama. Also like the Mahabharata, planetary war is inevitable between the forces of good and evil. During the eighteen-day

Figure 4.6. Gesar of Ling, the epic hero of the age of peace.
Nicholas Roerich, *King Gesar*, 1941, Nicholas Roerich Museum, NY.

war of the Mahabharata, weapons of mass destruction were unleashed that devastated whole peoples and regions. J. Robert Oppenheimer, director of the Manhattan Project, which produced the nuclear bombs dropped on Hiroshima and Nagasaki, implied the Mahabharata weapons to be a previous use of atomic weaponry on Earth.[18] In contrast, Gesar of Ling wins by illusion, stealth, and strategy. Gesar Khan causes as few casualties as possible even though he eventually commands armies that easily could overwhelm and devastate the armies of his enemies with greater force. By not engaging overwhelming force, and with Padmasambhava's reliable out-of-time view, Gesar avoids setting in motion future causes for retribution and destroys instead the seeds of subsequent cycles of cosmic warfare. Gesar acts more like a wizard than a king at times. The setting for the epic is the kingdom of Ling, which traditionally has been identified with the eastern Tibetan province of Kham.[19]

Like King Arthur Pendragon of Welsh and English legend, Gesar is the once and future king. The scale of warfare that Gesar Khan commanded does not match recent Asian history, yet the tale is told as if it is completed. One tradition is that Gesar was born in 1027 CE, which is the same year as the introduction of the Kalachakra tantra and the initial year of the Kalachakra calendar. The first publication of the *Gesar* epic was a Mongolian text commissioned by Manchu Emperor Kangxi in 1716, which is likely not the oldest copy, but there are no earlier written versions yet discovered. While verses of the Gesar epic were arising in the mind-streams of many Central Asian minstrels, musicians, artists, and actors, Tibetan Buddhist masters of the Kagyu and Nyingma schools were receiving revelations of Gesar *termas* or spontaneous treasure teachings. In these *termas*, Gesar Khan is predicted as the reincarnation of Rudra Chakrin, the last Kalki King of Shambhala. The final battle resolving the Shambhala breach and the dharma-ending age is therefore ultimately led by King Gesar. As new Kalachakra-related treasure teachings arise, sincere practitioners of those teachings create stronger affinities with Shambhala in this and future lifetimes.

Our last topic involves another way to create deeper affinity with the Shambhala by using the inner chintamani. In the introduction, we saw how the fourteen ratnas, and particularly the blue sapphire-like kaustubham, emerged from the churning of the milk ocean. This chintamani gem could only be possessed by Vishnu, who would use it for all creation, especially to return balance to the fallen ages. In chapter 2, we discussed that in the Mahabharata, Krishna, an avatar of Vishnu, retrieved and managed to give the syamantaka, the ruby-like chintamani jewel, to a resident of Dwaraka. From very early in creation, a chintamani has always been near when great evolutionary events have occurred. Two epithets of Gesar Khan are Mani Raja, "Jewel King," and Yishin Norbu, "Wish-Fulfilling Gem." His identification with the chintamani transcends mere possession of one. Gesar is the chintamani; his personal spiritual transformation over successive reincarnations has led him to manifest the inherent qualities of the chintamani. His enlightened presence, body, energy, and mind no longer require him to have an outer chintamani in order to wield the chintamani. Rather than the physical, outward manifestation of the chintamani creating access to Shambhala, Gesar's practice of the Kalachakra yogas creates deep affinity with Shambhala while transforming the mind of the yogini and yogi into the chintamani.

A sign of realizing the chintamani as a mind gem is the development and display of the *jalus,* or rainbow body. Tibet has recorded a number of stories of great yogic practitioners who have transformed their physical bodies at death into rainbow light. Usually, as death draws near, masters will advise their disciples to lock them in a room or a tent for about a week while the master meditates alone inside. Disciples practice outside the room during that week and often observe rainbow lights appearing and surrounding the room. In the most successful cases, when the disciples reenter the room at the appointed time, all they find are the hair, nails, and clothes of the master. Transformation into a light body at death is demonstration of the rainbow body and chintamani mind.*

---

*For an examination of the rainbow body phenomena that is introductory but thorough for Westerners and Christians, refer to *Rainbow Body and Resurrection* by Father Francis Tiso, which examines the rainbow body transformation stories of Khenpo A Cho. He compares Tibetan rainbow body attainment to the phenomenon of Christian resurrection. See bibliography.

5

Power Crystals across Cultures

Crown Jewels, the Grail, and the Right to Rule

I met a traveler from an antique land
Who said: Two vast and trunkless legs of stone
Stand in the desert . . . Near them, on the sand,
Half sunk, a shattered visage lies, whose frown,
And wrinkled lip, and sneer of cold command,
Tell that its sculptor well those passions read
Which yet survive, stamped on these lifeless things,
The hand that mocked them, and the heart that fed:
And on the pedestal these words appear:
"My name is Ozymandias, king of kings:
Look on my works, ye Mighty and despair!"
Nothing beside remains. Round the decay
Of that colossal wreck, boundless and bare
The lone and level sands stretch far away.

PERCY BYSSHE SHELLEY, "OZYMANDIAS"

IN OUR CULTURAL EXAMINATION OF THE CHINTAMANI, we now explore how gems of human empire have projected power in the kingdoms of history. The jewels possessed by rajas and ranis, emperors and empresses, and kings and queens are the best, biggest, and most valuable found on the planet. On a wealth level, empire-scale gems illustrate the unimaginable abundance of rulers and their realms. On that level, they function as emblems of power, but rulership by divine right is also asserted by possession of imperial gems. The symbolic power of imperial gems is great, but what we are about to consider is whether there are other powers inherent in or channeled through empire-scale gems that render worldly control to those who wield the chintamani irrespective of royal bloodline. In chapter 7 we will investigate the scientific side of crystal power more deeply, whereas here we explore crystal power expressed in the world of government, politics, and rulership, tracing the chintamani through history and across cultures.

Worldwide Chintamani Art Motifs

Along with the wealth of goods and power that flowed along the great Silk Road routes, art motifs appeared in trading cultures east to west. One of these motifs is the chintamani that decorated a wide range of media. Julianna Lees studied and cataloged over three hundred images of chintamani-influenced art found from China to France and England, dating from 600 BCE to the twentieth century.[1] The chintamani decorates manuscripts, textiles, carpets, sculptures, metalwork, church masonry, frescoes, ivories, enamels, netsuke, household items, miniatures, and weaponry. Lees and other art historians have identified the chintamani decorative theme as consisting of three dots forming a triangle. We have cited the example of the Roerich peace pact banner from chapter 1, and later in this chapter we will consider Japanese chintamani clan crests (figure 5.4, page 107).

A direct adaptation of the Sanskrit word, the Ottoman *çintamani,* or *çintemani,* refers to a well-recognized theme in fifteenth to sixteenth century textiles and tiles from the region (figures 5.1 and 5.2). Asian examples of this theme contain three circles instead of the three-dot representation found primarily in Europe. We choose this example because it explicitly demonstrates that the art pattern is connected to the chintamani of Hindu and Buddhist origins. Turkey is at the crossroads of Europe and Asia and in a position to transmit art themes both eastward and westward. Did the three-dot triangle chintamani motif arise spontaneously as an archetypal design? Did it arise primarily in the east and move west, or arise in the west and move east?

There is evidence that the theme moved in both directions along the silk trade routes. The chintamani as art and narrative is well known and well defined in Asia from India to Japan, but much less so throughout Europe. If the three-dot motif found in the Levant, Arabia, Persia, and Europe is indeed the Ottoman *çintamani* theme, it proves that the predominant flow is east to west. The same motif has been found in the Etruscan culture as early as the sixth century BCE and in the Thrace in the third to fourth centuries BCE.

Figure 5.1. Ottoman
çintamani kaftan design.

Figure 5.2. Ottoman *çintamani* tile pattern.

There are many examples of medieval chintamani motifs present in Europe, including illustrations from the *Book of Kells* and the *Book of Macdurnan* in the eighth and ninth centuries CE. Much of the three-dot motif graces religious figures, and the dots are found on altar fronts, frescoes, church stone sculptures, and books illustrated by hand (figure 8.16, page 197). Lees notes that in her research, the chintamani motifs can be associated with the Trinity, but are more particularly associated with Christ, Blessed Mother Mary, saints, angels, Biblical personages, and prominent patrons indicating high status.[2] Asian chintamani associations of jewels and preciousness transferred directly into Western art as symbols of power and value. If the chintamani theme was associated only with wealthy and ruling-class Europeans, that would indicate the gem that manifests earthly power. Most medieval European chintamani symbols, however, decorate Christ and holy persons, emphasizing the activity of the chintamani more as religious and compassionate.

China:
Dragons and the Chintamani Fire Pearl

In China, the mother civilization of East Asia, mythical flying dragons are shown chasing or clasping a great, blazing pearl in their extended claws. Chinese emperors of succeeding dynasties considered themselves descendants of the dragon. Following the symbolism of the dragon's flight, an emperor who possessed the chintamani of power claimed the right and might to rule the empire under the mandate of heaven. The dragon is a culturally complicated symbol depicted on seven-thousand-year-old *yangshao* pottery that display very early dragon images.* Another complicated symbol is the fiery pearl the dragon chases or holds (figure 5.3 on the following page). The character for pearl (珠), as we discussed in chapter 3, is composed of two symbols: a gem on the left side opposite vermillion red on the right side. Cinnabar, a mercury sulfide mineral, is identified with vermillion red. In China, cinnabar was commonly used to create high-end sculptural art, but more importantly to our inquiry was also an alchemical ingredient in secret formulae for longevity and self-transformation. The dragon in flight clutching a flaming chintamani in its claw signifies dynamic and dangerous worldly power as well as mastery of otherworldly powers. It shows absolute control of the physical, energetic, and spiritual dimensions of life.

Jade, the Stone of Heaven

We cannot consider China and the chintamani without exploring jade. The word for jade, *yu* (玉) in Chinese, can also refer to jewels in general. When the character for jade attaches as part of another character (hanzi

---

*Yangshao was a neolithic culture (5000 to 3000 BCE) located along the Yellow River.

Figure 5.3. Dragon confronting the fire pearl.

in Chinese, kanji in Japanese), the resulting character meaning often refers directly to gems or the idea of preciousness and value. In other words, jade is the primary jewel of the East. Jade has a dual reach—as do all chintamanis, having both earthly power and spiritual accomplishment components. In Daoist mythology, the ruler of the gods who inherited creation was the Jade Emperor, Yu Huang (玉皇). He retired from rulership and spent roughly the next 226 million years in self-cultivation, after which he underwent an additional 3,200 trials of approximately three million years each. At the end of his retreat, he defeated a demon who had cultivated himself for three thousand trials, each also of three million years duration. The demon, in a war to conquer the universe, defeated many gods and immortals; nonetheless, the Jade Emperor prevailed because of his greater power and virtue cultivated with discipline over a longer time.

From the point of view of self-cultivation of character and spirit, Kongfuzi (Confucius) adds a revered and oft-quoted praise of jade from the classic *Liji,* or *Book of Rites.* In the forty-eighth chapter, Kongfuzi is questioned:

"Allow me to ask the reason why the superior man sets a high value on jade, and but little on soapstone. Is it because jade is rare and the soapstone plentiful?" Confucius replied: "It is not because the soapstone is plentiful that he thinks but little of it, and because jade is rare that he sets a high value on it. Anciently, superior men found the likeness of all excellent qualities in jade. Soft, smooth, and glossy, it appeared to them like benevolence; fine, compact, and strong, —like intelligence; angular, but not sharp and cutting, —like righteousness; hanging down (in beads) as if it would fall to the ground, —like (the humility of) propriety; when struck, yielding a note, clear and prolonged, yet terminating abruptly, —like music; its flaws not concealing its beauty, nor its beauty concealing its flaws, —like loyalty; with an internal radiance issuing from it on every side, —like good faith; bright as a brilliant rainbow, —like heaven; exquisite and mysterious, appearing in the hills and streams, —like the earth; standing out conspicuous in the symbols of rank, —like virtue; esteemed by all under the sky, —like the path of truth and duty. As is said in the ode,

> 'Such my lord's car. He rises in my mind.
> Lovely and bland, like jade of the richest kind.'

This is why the superior man esteems it so highly.[3]

This passage is significant. Kongfuzi was the source of one of the three most influential philosophical schools in China, as even to this day Daoism, Buddhism, and Confucianism remain influential. Kongfuzi studied and systematized the values, learning, and writings of ancient culture from before his time, which was around 500 BCE. Kongfuzi revered the true value of jade from earlier dynasties, especially the Zhou dynasty (1046 BCE–256 BCE). Kongfuzi was a preeminent sage of Chinese civilization urging all who strive to become superior women or men to use jade to develop their benevolence and humanity (*ren,* 仁). In the long history of Chinese civilization, jade's use for self-cultivation can be taken as metaphorical advice, as Kongfuzi described above, or it can be taken literally, as in wearing jade to purify illness, negative feeling, and imbalanced thinking. Furthermore, jade ground into a fine powder in an alchemical formula was ingested to facilitate longevity and spiritual transformation. The jade chin-tamani of the Chinese is another means of self-development to rule oneself and to rule others beneficially or greedily.

The more popular Chinese historical thread is the quest to acquire the chintamani to gain great and ultimate wealth and power. Adrian Levy and Cathy Scott-Clark have written a well-researched book detailing this power obsession with jade especially from the mid-eighteenth century to the present in *Stone of Heaven: The Secret History of Imperial Green Jade*. In their book, they detail the green jade (*fei cui*) obsession of one of China's great Emperors, Qianlong, who ruled for sixty years from 1735 to 1796.[4] Qianlong began a costly war to conquer the western barbarians in northern Burma in whose lands the *fei cui* jade mines were located, surrounded by almost impassable terrain. Levy and Scott-Clark narrate a centuries-long story of greed, war, death, disease, and misery surrounding the efforts to excavate and exclusively possess these imperial pedigree gems. On the dark side of the chintamani are the measures the great immoral power seekers are willing to take to gain global power.

Japan's Imperial Regalia: Mirror, Gem, and Sword

According to the ancient chronicles of Japan, the *Kojiki* and *Nihongi*, ruler-ship in Japan was bestowed by the elder *kami* (神, gods, spirits) through the sun goddess, Amaterasu-no-omikami, to her first human ancestor, Emperor Jimmu.[5] He was invested with three imperial regalia from the gods: a mirror, sword, and jewel. The imperial jewel is an unusual shape called a *magatama*, or bent gem.[6] There is even a special word and kanji, *tomoe* (巴), that signi-fies a comma-like design describing more accurately the form of the imperial gem.[7] Figure 5.4 shows a few Japanese family crests that depict *magatama* themes around the comma gem design. This particular design is not just divine inspiration. Before the migration of the Yamato people of whom Jimmu became Emperor around 300 CE, the Jomon, Yayoi, and Kofun peoples previously occupied Japan.[8] Comma-like artifacts made earlier of earthen materials, then later of jade, were discovered in burial mounds and other archaeological sites of these peoples.* The original imperial *magatama* gem, mirror, and sword have been hidden from public display, so we are left to speculate rather than examine physical evidence. After all, the imperial regalia bring worldly power to the hands of the reigning dynasty, represented by the recently ascended Emperor Naruhito and Empress Masako of the Imperial House of Japan, who have not been eager to share the power of the Chrysanthemum Throne. Another indirect connection from our discussion in chapter 3 is that the *magatama* shape of gems depicted in the aura field of some Buddhas and Bodhisattvas, even outside Japan, are not always shown in the turnip gem shape, but rather in the *tomoe,* comma form.

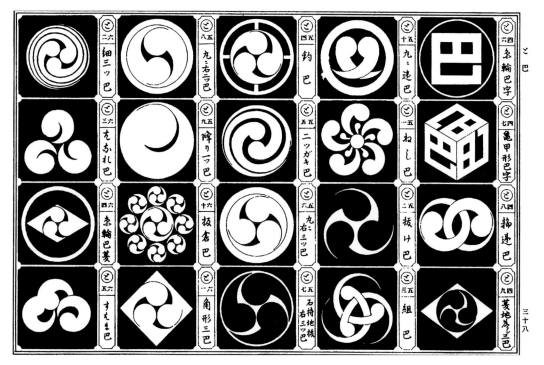

Figure 5.4. Japanese crests with the comma design
of the Imperial *magatama* jewel.
Japanese Design Motifs, Dover Publications, 1972.

---

*Yayoi period (300 BCE–300 CE).

America:
Archaeology and Crystals

Ancient cultures in North and South America incorporated precious gems, minerals, and metals into their spiritual ceremony. In the American Southwest, ancient Pueblo tribes built kivas, circular rooms in the earth, where they held communal ceremonies. These underground rooms served as portals to the underworld and were linked to transformation and communication with the spiritual dimension. At the ceremonial center of many of these kiva sites, archaeologists have found gems and semiprecious minerals. At a site we visited in Arizona, Besh-Ba-Gowah Pueblo, the hole in the kiva, called a *sipapu,* a symbolic earth navel, allowed spirits to pass from middle earth to this world. The *sipapu* at one time was filled with turquoise and sealed with a large quartz crystal, demonstrating that crystals were used as ceremonial objects to open a portal to the spiritual dimension. Crystals were placed inside the *sipapu* at other sites as well, including the Pueblo Bonita kiva in Chaco Canyon in New Mexico where both quartz and turquoise were found. At a large kiva located at an ancestral Hopi site, Homolovi, diamond quartz crystals from Payson, Arizona, were placed in the *sipapu.* Payson diamond quartz is a special form of double-terminated quartz similar to Herkimer diamond quartz. While we were visiting the Taos Pueblo in northern New Mexico, a native told us a story about how some tribes have a rare shaman called a "rock talker." At the pyramid Temple of the Feathered Serpent in the ancient city Teotihuacan, precious objects were found in an underground passage, specifically hundreds of orbs covered in a shiny pyrite metal, small pools of liquid mercury, masks with inset gems, mineral powders of pyrite, magnetite, and hematite, sheets of mica, quartz crystal, and other precious objects. Statuary made of jade adorned with gems was also discovered. The passageway under the pyramid was used by the natives to communicate with the creators of the Universe.[9] The Cherokee have a myth about a great horned serpent named Uktena with a powerful shining stone called Ulunsuti ("transparent") in its forehead. For those who captured the Ulunsuti stone, it had the ability to bring fortune and help its user see the future, but it would bring misfortune if improperly used.

Peru: Incan Stone Technology

The Incan megalithic civilization is one of the quintessential stone cultures of the world. When you stand in front of the three undulating tiers of megalithic walls built on the steep overlook of Cusco, Peru, perched just two kilometers from the main city square, you are overcome with awe. The massive three-dimensional puzzle shapes of unique limestone boulders cut and fit together five meters high, two-and-a-half meters wide, and four hundred meters long presents a palpably unfathomable scale. The fortress of Sacsayhuaman confronts your mind; it confronts the monumental blindness of any claim that this could be the work of a people with rudimentary technology. Whoever built the many megalithic sites all over Ecuador, Peru, and Bolivia employed superior technology. They chose to project their mastery of power in stone architecture and their mastery of culture in transformative crystals and gold.

We limit our discussion to two examples found at the hidden mountain settlement of Machu Picchu fifty miles northwest of Cusco where author Johndennis explored. The expedition guides included several disciples of an Incan spiritual master with whom the group met for several days. Among the many distinctive architectural mysteries is the Roca Sagrada, or Sacred Rock. Located at the northern end of the site, the Roca Sagrada is set on a pedestal of chiseled stone near the Huayna Picchu trail. The boulder resembles a mountain shape about twelve feet tall at the center and about eighteen feet long, but less than two feet thick. The Incan guides told us that there are seven sites in Machu Picchu that are places of spiritual initiation and testing. Of these, Incans were instructed by those who originally constructed the city how to use only the first four sites. The Roca Sagrada is the first test. Each in our group followed the procedure the Incan disciples outlined. First was to sit meditatively with your back to the great stone. When ready, you were directed to stand on the pedestal with arms and legs extended, making an "X." Face to the stone, you were to inch along until you observed a flash of light with eyes closed. At that spot, a message would appear by sound, vision, or thought. Once you thoroughly received the message, you were to move to the pedestal's end, then step back on the earth. Later, when describing this stone to a Tibetan master, he psychically viewed inside the stone and described that on the interior a large blue gem radiated light and information even though the Roca Sagrada apart from size appears to be ordinary.

The Incan guides also described the purpose of rooms in the main temple that had a series of niches in identical trapezoidal shapes. According to the living oral tradition, the niches in these rooms once were fitted with various crystals. Near each niche was a stone rod that protruded and could be turned right or left or moved in and out. The rods were described as tuning devices for any or all of the crystals. Each crystal was quite large and custom carved to fit the niche and the same type of crystal placed in each niche, or a group of various crystals picked especially for the situation. Photos taken at Machu Picchu illustrate these crystal niches, tuning rods, and rooms (figures 5.5 and 5.6).

According to the Incan guides, the rooms used crystal technology for improving human capacity in a number of possible ways. The room might be arranged for healing or increasing longevity, and the crystals would vary according to the disease and the person's underlying physiology and energy

Figure 5.5. Control rod for tuning a crystal placed in
the niche to the right located at Machu Picchu, Peru.

Photo by J. Govert

Figure 5.6. Crystal niches and rods in a
megalithic wall located at Machu Picchu, Peru.
Photo by J. Govert

constitution. The room might be arranged to augment a person's memory, perception, insight, compassion, or wisdom. The room could also be arranged to initiate disciples to the next level of spiritual accomplishment and prepare them for the next learning stage. These niche crystals would be magnificently impressive to encounter. Even more impressive is the technological knowledge and skill needed to produce and integrate the Incan crystals into a spectacular healing architecture. Here we encounter a more ancient chintamani, a subspecies of the fire crystals of Atlantis, but dedicated to wise and peaceful uses for the conscious elevation of humankind.

The Chintamani as the Grail

Is there a connection between the chintamani and the Holy Grail? Marinus van der Sluijs contends that the Grail narrative, as it appears in von Eschenbach and Albrecht, is a close parallel to and derives from the chintamani story of King Indrabodhi and Padmasambhava, which we related at the beginning of chapter 3.[10] In the first half of his study, Van der Sluijs compares the Indrabodhi chintamani narrative detail for detail with early grail accounts. The second half of the same article explores how historical authors may have transmitted the chintamani story directly to Europe. The research of Van der Sluijs combined with the three-dot chintamani art motif material provided by Julianna Lees and Jaroslav Folda support the contention that the grail is a Western version of the chintamani.[11] The Mongolian Empire and Yuan emperors of China in the twelfth and thirteenth centuries formed an alliance with the Crusader kingdoms in the Holy Land, encompassing trade and military cooperation. This established direct cultural exchange between Asia and Europe, including the chintamani tradition.[12] The Mongol emperors adopted Tibetan Tantrayana Buddhism in the thirteenth century and officially sponsored the leader of the Sakya sect as their proxy temporal ruler as well, making Tibetan Buddhism part of the Asian and European cultural exchange.

In medieval Europe, minnesingers and troubadours narrated enduring romances of the Holy Grail cycle. The connection of the chintamani and the grail does not occur directly in all grail literature but does occur in *Parzival* written by Wolfram von Eschenbach in 1211. Trevrizent, a hermit and brother of the Grail King, describes the grail to his nephew, Parzival: "many brave knights dwell with the Grail at Munsalvaesche [the Grail Castle] . . . They live from a stone of the purest kind. If you do not know it, it shall here be named to you. It is called *lapist exillis.*"[13] By the eleventh century, the Romance languages were emerging as spoken developments of "vulgar" or common Latin. Vulgar Latin was much less formal and grammatically precise than written literary Latin. Wolfram's Latin is neither literary nor classical. Wolfram's word, *lapist,* seems intended as *lapis* meaning stone, not a cup, nor a bloodline, as the grail is more commonly depicted. The adjective, *exillis* is more problematic because *exilis* in literary Latin means small, thin, or poor, which is clearly not a grand revelation of the true nature of the grail. Many have rendered *lapis exillis* as the Philosopher's Stone. The translators of the *Parzival* edition quoted above, H. Mustard and C. Passage, speculate on other intended meanings of *lapist exillis*: *lapis ex caelis,* or "stone from heaven"; *lapsit ex caelis,* "it fell from heaven"; or *lapis lapsus ex caelis,* "a stone fallen from heaven."[14] These interpretations suggest the grail is a meteorite, was created by meteor impact such as a tektite glass like moldavite, or was brought from outer space.

In the French Pyrenees, we discover actual medieval "grail castles" that bear witness to the former presence of the Holy Grail. Strong traditions blend the powerful *lapis exillis* into the conflux of history, alchemy, astrology, and local landscape. It is difficult to pinpoint what exactly this stone is, but its legends closely associate it with the Knights Templar, Cathars, and grail romances.

In the intersection between myth and recorded history, there is an incident of particular interest that places the grail as a chintamani-like stone at the center of a conflict between spiritual and temporal power. The Albigensian or Cathar crusade was called by Pope Innocent III in 1209 and was the second crusade directed against Christians.* The crusade was called after the Lateran Council of 1179 declared the Cathars of the Languedoc to be heretics, which set in motion their wholesale massacre, as well as the murders of other regional political rivals of the French crown in southern France. The Cathar crusade was a twenty-year military campaign initiated by a brutal massacre in Beziers leading to the fall of Carcassonne in 1209. It ended in a final military siege in 1244 at Montsegur, a grail castle in the Pyrenees. This was the Cathars' last stronghold but was difficult to besiege as the castle sat atop a towering limestone cliff. After several failed attempts, the crusaders took custody of the castle mount in 1244. The Montsegur siege has an interesting grail connection. The Cathars were thought to possess the grail, an object, relic, or stone also referred to as the *mani*. The Cathars were careful to maintain custody of the treasure so that it would not fall into the hands of the "evil ones" whom they regarded as the repressive powers of the Catholic Church and French crown. It is rumored that the *mani* was held in Montsegur for safekeeping during the thirty-five-year crusade.

Otto Rahn, an archaeological researcher who was hired by the Nazis to locate the Holy Grail, wrote a book about his own quest for the grail that led him to examine Cathar spiritual practices.[15] He linked the grail romances of Wolfram von Eschenbach with the Cathars and saw a strong correspondence in the grail myth with the history of the Cathars. In the grail legend, Munsalvaesche, the grail castle, is really Montsegur, and the Holy Grail is the

---

*The earlier Fourth Crusade was against Byzantine Christians in 1202–1204.

mani, a stone that feeds the knights spiritually. Linguistically, the word *mani* is of special interest due to its similarity with the word *chintamani.* The grail knights were well-traveled and had sojourned to India where such a term could have been adopted and transmitted to southern France where Gnostic thinking had been transmitted. A widely accepted theory is that the *mani* referred to Manichaeism and specifically related to its prophet, Mani. However, it has been countered that there is no proof that the Cathars even knew about Manichaeism. The *mani* is described more as an object rather than a set of esoteric teachings, especially the way it was smuggled out of a castle.

There was a spiritual holy day ritual called the *manisola* practiced by the Cathars. Because the crusaders destroyed all Cathar literature, just like the *mani* itself, little is known about the mysterious *manisola.* Otto Rahn reports that this may have been a religious practice held four times a year during the solstices and equinoxes that involved the *mani.* The word *manisola* may be the joining of two Nordic words that represent the names of the Norse god of the sun (Sola) and the god of the moon (Mani). It has also been reported that the original edifice of Montsegur Castle was a temple aligned with the summer solstice. Perhaps the sacred *mani* was a stone that was the focus of a light ceremony held by the Cathars four times a year. At the center of a sacred ceremony, the *mani* stone may have been the holder and transmitter of light that was activated by the intention of the participants who called in the Paraclete, or Holy Spirit, that lit up the stone, which in turn activated the light within the Cathar Perfecti ("perfect ones"). It is no coincidence that the Cathars negotiated an additional two weeks for praying and fasting as a part of the surrender conditions after Montsegur fell to the crusaders on March 1, 1244. They negotiated the terms of surrender on March 2 and physically surrendered on March 16. The vernal equinox occurred that year in the early morning hours of March 13. The extra two weeks allowed them another opportunity to use the *mani* stone for their last vernal equinox ritual. There were several Cathars that converted and received the consolamentum* during the two-week period. Notably it was recorded in a list of those who were executed that many had received the

---

*The consolamentum was an initiation ritual sealing conversion and commitment to the Cathar way of life.

consolamentum and were converted to Catharism on March 13, 1244, the exact date of the vernal equinox.[16] After the ceremony of the new initiates receiving the Holy Spirit through the *mani* stone, which in turn activated their own spirit, the Cathars would have three days to devise a plan to smuggle the *mani* out of the castle walls, perhaps even using their own surrender as a ruse. Rahn reports that four knights scaled down the steep cliffs of Montsegur undetected and fled with "the treasure of the Cathars" so that it could not be captured by the crusaders and placed in the crown of their king, who the Cathars regarded as Lucifer. It is possible that the *mani* could have been taken to one of the other two Cathar castle mounts that had not fallen, Puilaurens or Queribus. Either way, the *mani* fades from recorded history that day. On Montsegur, approximately 220 Cathars were burnt alive on March 16, 1244, including the new converts.

While exploring grail castles in southern France, author Hara observed light emitting through castle fortress windows and slits in Chateau de Puilaurens at sunset. Montsegur had a similar architecture to Puilaurens, including small windows with very narrow window slits.* It is possible that the four knights fleeing from Montsegur may have found refuge at Puilaurens, which would have been the closest stronghold still standing after the fall of Montsegur. The focused light through the narrow window slits at sunset was golden, brilliant, and even grail-like (figures 5.7 and 5.8 on the following page). An object, such as a *mani* stone, at the center of such intensified light, during an equinox, could be the quantum holder of both solar and lunar light that could be focused, radiated, and transmitted with intention in spiritual ceremonies—truly a form of spiritual technology.

Intensification of solar rays through light beaming through window slits may have been an important design of a *manisola* ceremony during an equinox, and may have been utilized to activate the *mani* stone. This same type of technology may be used at other archaeological sites around the world to create a similar light display. Robert Temple has recorded an interesting light phenomenon in a temple in Karnak, Egypt, involving light emitting through slits. In the morning, the light would transmit through a small window with

---

*The narrow window slits were used for militaristic purposes, but they may have had other uses, including focusing and intensifying light sources.

Figure 5.7. Chateau de Puilaurens in Southern France.
Photo by H. Hara

Figure 5.8. Light at sunset transmitting through a window slit at Chateau de Puilaurens.
Photo by H. Hara

four slits and produced a light display on the opposing wall where it appeared that the Pharaoh depicted on the wall was making a living "light offering" from an incense tray to an Egyptian god.[17] Robert Temple noted many other light phenomena in Egyptian temples and reported on their spiritual significance. An important part of Temple's discovery is that light itself was being used as an offering in Karnak.

Considering çintamani art themes present in crusader Europe, the Cathars' mani is more likely to be a chintamani gem than an obscure reference lost to history. The çintamani motif was a common theme present in art of the Crusades as described by Professor Folda.[18] The manisola ritual is also more likely to have included an actual revered jewel or a gem symbol as central to the Cathar ceremony. The Cathars were active for perhaps a century before the appearance of Eschenbach's grail romance, but their destruction in 1244 followed the publication of Parzival by a generation. The esoteric philosophy and religion of the Cathars overlapped the grail and chintamani traditions not only in time but in spiritual focus as well. The Cathars may have been an anchor of the chintamani tradition in the West. It is not just a plot twist when Eschenbach's grail kingdom withdraws to the East as Cathar culture is exterminated. The successor of Anfortas as grail king passed to Prester John, son of Parzival's half-brother, Feirefiz. Prester John moved the grail kingdom east, perhaps to India, from where his father, Feirefiz, had come, and back into the heartland of the chintamani.

Atlantis:
Crystals of Fire and Power

Unexpected chintamani connections are entangled in the semi-mythical mists of the lost continent of Atlantis. Plato's detailed description of Atlantis, recorded in his Timaeus and Critias Dialogues, is discounted because it contradicts the academic narrative that our current civilization is the highest cultural expression so far existent on Earth. There is a growing body of verifiable evidence for highly evolved social and technical achievements of pre-Sumerian civilizations from many disciplines, including underwater archaeology.[19] Plato reports that Atlantis itself was inundated after earthquakes and cataclysms. Using his timeline, Atlantis last disappeared beneath the waves in the era of great worldwide melting at the end of the last Ice Age about 11,600 years ago. The question is not whether there is evidence of Atlantis, but what progress or regress mankind made during that epoch. As a human race, the Atlantis memory rings of truth even when we do not care to recall all the details.

At this point, we enter the arena of speculation to trace not how the gods interacted with the chintamani, but rather how humans interacted with it. We present a few broad themes of the Atlantis story as the glue for our speculation. First, Atlantis was scientifically advanced beyond our current culture and had spectacular technology that worked both with the physical world and the spiritual or more subtle world of energies entangled in consciousness. Second, Atlantean society was split on how to engage the technology it possessed. One faction emphasized projecting unlimited power to control the physical and subtle aspects of life, whereas the other sought ethical limits in using the technological power at their disposal. The latter faction emphasized employing the technology at hand for accelerating the development of spiritual consciousness. Third, the destructions of Atlantis were caused over a long period because of the unchecked experimentation, development, and application of the darker technological agenda. This is a familiar dilemma in our era, with the primary emphasis on developing weapons that can cause catastrophic destruction, rather than providing technology to uplift the world's web of life. Fourth, the technology of Atlantis was centered around what Edgar Cayce in his Atlantis psychic readings called the "tuoai" stones or fire crystals. Fifth and last, Atlantean knowledge and fragments of the fire crystals were deposited in hidden caches and libraries around the Earth, in the succeeding advanced civilizations of the Egyptians, Incas, and Mayas to cite a few.[20] Each of these great civilizations began with advanced technology, yet over the course of their history lost their understanding and abilities to accomplish what they formerly had achieved. The Great Pyramid of Giza stands as the most conspicuous single example of this degeneration of knowledge and technology because, even now, we cannot replicate its advanced engineering, nor understand its full purpose, let alone exceed it.

If there were fire crystals central to the power and development of Atlantis, Edgar Cayce suggests that the chintamani-like tuoai crystals became the basis of planetary technology. Crystal technology in the form of memory matrix in computer hardware has emerged as important to technological development in our era. We will explore this dimension of the science and technology of gems, crystals, and the chintamani in chapter 7. The opposing factions of Atlantean civilization struggled whether to use advanced crystal technology for the repression or evolution of the human species. This is the crux of the quest to possess and wield the chintamani. The Atlantis story, like the Roerich story and the myth of the battle of devas and asuras, presents the same archetypal struggle. Will the chintamani power destroy the basis of life through intentional or inadvertent ignorance, or will it infuse wisdom, peace, and brilliance into the whole web of life through the same core technological power? The fire crystal chintamani was at the heart of the destruction, not only of an advanced civilization, but also of the very earth on which it stood. Much worse, wielding the fire chintamani for a struggle of power caused a sudden dark-age degradation of global human culture from which collectively we have yet to recover.

Cross-Cultural Chintamani Symbol

As we began this chapter, even when we intended to discuss the earthly power of the chintamani, we ended up discussing both the worldly and spiritual power of the chintamani because both are so entangled. It is as if we were discussing yin without reference to yang while considering the yin-yang circular diagram. In the image on the following page (figure 5.9), observe the yin and yang sides of the symbol and recognize the two, intertwined, nestled *magatama* or bent gem shapes. This symbolism infers that the dark and light chintamani effects are interdependent. Depending on the intention and character of the wielder of the chintamani, darker or lighter effects are invoked into the active play of life.

We have noted many cultures across Eurasia and the Americas with plentiful examples of chintamani art motifs. Each local decorative appearance suggests a set of deeper connections to the chintamani. Beyond the highly visible symbols of imperial gems, both tangible and intangible, there are also crystal technologies at play. In later chapters, we investigate how

Figure 5.9. The Taiji symbolizing the interlocking,
interdependent nature of yin and yang.

much of this technology is inherent in crystals, and how much technology
can be embedded. The cross-cultural range of legends and discoverable evidence from those civilizations allow us to argue that there has been very
advanced crystal technology throughout history. These technologies have
been and are being applied to elevate or degrade the evolution of Earth.

6
Gems and Stones of Renown

Superlative Jewels and Stones Intertwined
in the Web of History

And Jacob went out from Beer-sheba, and went toward Haran.
And he lighted upon a certain place, and tarried there all night,
because the sun was set; and he took of the stones of that place, and
put them for his pillows, and lay down in that place to sleep. And
he dreamed, and behold a ladder set up on the earth, and the top
of it reached to heaven: and behold the angels of God ascending
and descending on it.

GENESIS 28:10–12

WE HAVE APPROACHED THE USE OF CRYSTALS from both mythical and cultural standpoints, focusing on the chintamani stone and its qualities to enlighten or empower humans. There are theories that there is one all-powerful chintamani and many have sought it out as a magical talisman, although it has eluded discovery. There are legends that pieces of the chintamani, located in Shambhala, were chipped off and King Solomon wore a piece of the chintamani in his signet ring, which allowed him access to supernatural powers. Roerich reports that Solomon, Tamerlane, Akbar, and other world leaders possessed a piece of the chintamani stone.[1] As we outlined in chapter 1, Roerich was also in possession of a piece of the chintamani and he reportedly returned it to its home in Shambhala during one of

121

his expeditions. Frank Joseph traces the chintamani in ancient history and purports Moses stole the chintamani from the Egyptian pharaoh, which was the central stone powering the Great Pyramid. Moses subsequently placed the chintamani inside the Ark of the Covenant, which gave the Ark its special powers.[2] Unless one is in possession of the stone, there is not a definitive way to prove its tangible existence. Yet because there are so many stories about the chintamani and other power stones, both ancient and modern, it is equally difficult to disprove its existence. It is likely this stone exists between two worlds, both material and spiritual. Much like the end of the rainbow, it is visible and seems within reach, but illusory and difficult to pinpoint in time and space. Those who are attuned through spiritual practice can access the stone through an alternative sense and, in that connection, potentially influence their own evolution and earthly outcomes.

In the last chapter, we explored crystals from a broader cultural perspective. In this chapter, we explore tangible earth gems and crystals as a subspecies of the mythical chintamani to discover ways we can align with gems to activate and empower our energy, mind, and spirituality. Certain gemstones, such as diamonds, emeralds, rubies, sapphires, and pearls, have been famous since ancient times. Yet rarely do many in Western cultures stop to consider why we are collectively obsessed with gemstones. In this chapter, we explore famous gemstones and some of the reasons for their fame, which extends into the ancient practices of astrology, alchemy, and energy medicine. We begin with one of the world's most famous diamonds: a diamond associated with the ancient syamantaka stone.

The Mountain of Light

Legend has it that the person who owns the Koh-i-Noor owns the world. In Indian lore, the Koh-i-Noor is believed to be the syamantaka gem (see chapter 1 about chintamani origins). The Koh-i-Noor has been a part of Indian history for so long, its origins are shrouded in the mists of ancient myth. Prior to its faceting, it was 793 carats, making it one of the largest diamonds ever discovered. While its clarity and size undoubtedly contributed to its near mythical status, the sordid history surrounding the Koh-i-Noor is strikingly similar to the greed and violence depicted in the syamantaka story.

In more recent times, the Koh-i-Noor has a turbulent history with ownership not only changing physical hands but empires as well. It was successively owned by the Indian, Mughal, Persian, Afghanistani, and Sikh empires before the British Empire took possession of the Koh-i-Noor in the nineteenth century. It was owned by the rajas of Malwa until the 1300s, after which the Emperor of Delhi took possession in 1304. In 1306, a Hindu manuscript recorded a curse on the diamond: "He who owns this diamond will own the world, but will also know its misfortunes. Only God, or a woman, can wear it with impunity." From 1339, for three hundred years, the diamond was in the city of Samarkand, part of a kingdom along the Silk Road that has long since vanished. Its ownership was unclear at this period. Emperor Babur received the diamond from Sultan Ibrahim Lodi around 1526. It was then called Babur's Stone, and appraisers estimated its value at "two and half days' food for the whole world."[3] Babur established the Mughal dynasty, and his descendants owned the stone, including Shah Jahan who built the Taj Mahal and the Peacock Throne—where the Koh-i-Noor and the Timur Ruby were both inlaid into the legendary throne alongside hundreds of other gemstones. Although now dismantled, dispersed, and mostly missing, the Peacock Throne is one of the most fabulous thrones ever built. It was purposely designed to emulate the opulence and glory of King Solomon's throne. It was reported the Koh-i-Noor was inlaid into the ceiling of the jewel-encrusted throne.

The Persian general, Nadir Shah, took possession of the Peacock Throne and the Koh-i-Noor diamond after a violent military conquest and looting of Delhi in 1739. Nadir was the first to coin the name Koh-i-Noor, which translates to "mountain of light," and he wore it proudly in an armband, believing it gave him power during battle. In 1747 he was betrayed and killed by his own guards. His general, Ahmad Shah, took possession of the Koh-i-Noor. A descendent of Shah returned the diamond to India in 1813, gifting it to the founder of the Sikh Empire, Ranjit Singh. After a bloody conflict with the British following the decisive Battle of Gujrat in 1849, Britain annexed the Sikh Empire and the Koh-i-Noor was effectively confiscated by the British East Indian Company through the Treaty of Lahore. When the diamond was transported to England, cholera broke out on the ship and the keeper of the diamond temporarily lost the jewel.

Despite its turbulent journey, the stone found its way to Queen Victoria in 1850. When the famous diamond was placed on display in the Great Exhibition of 1851, its organic cutting style (typical of diamonds from the Middle East at that time) was disappointing to many viewing the large stone. To visually enhance the diamond's appearance, Prince Albert commissioned the diamond's recutting to its present 105.6 carats. It is reported Victoria disliked wearing the stone and left instructions that the Koh-i-Noor should only be worn by a female queen, suggesting she believed in the ancient curse.[4] Initially, Victoria wore the diamond in a brooch before it was inlaid in a crown and worn by Queen Alexandra, the wife of King Edward VII, the successor of Victoria (figure 6.1). The diamond was transferred successively to queen consorts including Mary of Teck and Elizabeth (the Queen Mother and mother of Queen Elizabeth II). The Koh-i-Noor is currently a part of the British Crown Jewels and the diamond is set in what is referred to as Queen Mary's (grandmother to Elizabeth II) crown, presently on display in the Tower of London. Although not worn by male monarchs, it is hard to dispute the influence and power the queen consorts have had on the royal family, outliving their monarch husbands, and strongly influencing heirs to the throne.

Despite its multigenerational ownership by the British Crown, the diamond remains controversial as several countries claim ownership, demanding England return the stone, including India, Iran, Pakistan, and Afghanistan. England maintains that even if they did return the diamond, it would be impossible to determine whom they would return it to and for what cause, especially since previous owners also stole the gem. England further defends itself by claiming it was legally obtained under the conditions of the Treaty of Lahore. So it begs the question, as we found in the myth of the syamantaka: Who is the rightful ruler and bearer of the Koh-i-Noor?

Interestingly, this stone, which has a large, broad culet* at the center, resembles something of a black hole when viewed directly. Perhaps the stone's current facets enhance a quality that can potentize a wrathful energy. As diamonds are considered stones of power and can amplify radiant energy and intent, looking at the diamond and reflecting on how it has a dark center

---

*A culet is a flat face forming the base of a faceted gem.

Figure 6.1. Queen Alexandra wearing the Koh-i-Noor
in her coronation crown (August 9, 1902).

like a black hole may cause the diamond to embody those attributes and reflect them back to the wearer or observer. Like the many thousands of tourists who have visited the Tower of London, the author Hara has visited the Crown Jewels a few times over the years and observed how the exhibit has changed. The current Jewel House in the Tower of London offers access to twenty thousand visitors per day, including a moving walkway that does not allow visitors to study the jewels for long. Placards were placed alongside the larger diamonds with historic information reporting curses associated with the diamonds. Hara particularly remembers the curse discussed on the placard next to St. Mary's Crown (which has the Koh-i-Noor diamond set at its center) and its curse on males who wear or possess the stone (figure 6.2). At the time, she felt this was ominous and remembers the Koh-i-Noor and its associated curse more than any other diamond curse in the exhibit. She recalls thinking how energetically negative it was to trigger dark thoughts in the minds of thousands of tourists per day around jewels that have the power to amplify and radiate energy. While perhaps less tangibly intense due to their smaller size, conflict diamonds from Africa bring up the same negative associations as the larger and more famous diamonds, with miners working in horrific conditions while depleting the Earth of its resources.

Figure 6.2. The Koh-i-Noor in the front cross of Queen Mary's Crown.

Photo by Cyril Davenport in *The Crown Jewels of England* by G. Younghusband and C. Davenport, 1919.

The Curse of the Hope Diamond

Aside from the chintamani, there are a few precious jewels famous not only for their rarity, exceptional size, and uncommon beauty but also for their energetic or magical properties. Undoubtedly, one of the most famous gemstones in the world is the Hope Diamond. At 45.52 carats and valued at $350 million, the Hope is the largest faceted blue diamond in the world. Currently on display in Washington, D.C., it is one of the most frequented exhibits at the Smithsonian Institute, attracting approximately seven million people a year and has, over its time at the Smithsonian, been visited by over a hundred million people. The gemstone occupies its own room in the gem and mineral collection at the Smithsonian. Is this a possible indication of the power of its energetic field—both in its need for space from other minerals and crystals as well as its magnetic powers to attract visitors?

The Hope Diamond is not only famous because it is the largest blue diamond in the world but because of its professed powers to "curse" or create unlucky conditions to those who hold or own the diamond. Although darker in nature, stories surrounding the Hope Diamond are paralleled by myths around the chintamani stone. The Hope Diamond has a convoluted narrative of passing into the hands of powerful and wealthy people. An unsubstantiated tale has the diamond stolen out of the eye of a statute from a Hindu temple, thus perpetuating a curse on those who possessed the diamond without sacred right. This parallels chintamani stories about the right to ownership and rulership. The Hope Diamond curse presents us with an opportunity to explore the area between myth and reality and the energetic use of tangible power gems.

In spite of the curse, this most famous of blue diamonds is curiously called "The Hope" after the Hope family who were its owners for over sixty years (1839–1901). In the 1600s, French gem dealer Jean-Baptiste Tavernier purchased an exceptionally large blue diamond from the same Indian mines where the famous Koh-i-Noor diamond was found. Tavernier presented and sold the diamond to Louis XIV, who commissioned the rough diamond to be faceted into what was later called the Tavernier, French Blue, or Le Bijou du Roi (The King's Jewel). The diamond was a focal point among the French crown jewels. Novel gemstone-cutting techniques were applied to the French Blue, revolutionizing diamond-cutting technology. The diamond was cut to an exceptionally high standard and weighed 67 carats from its original 112 carats as a raw diamond. It remained in the French crown jewels until it disappeared during the French Revolution and was not seen again, at least not in the guise of the French Blue.

Much of what we know about the history of the Hope Diamond was verified by the Smithsonian Institute in 2009 when a team of scientists investigated its gem cutting, provenance, history, and chemistry. The Smithsonian discovered historical diamond cutting diagrams of the French Blue and compared these to the modern Hope Diamond, later announcing that the Hope was indeed the lost French Blue. After it was stolen from France, the blue diamond was recut to its current shape and size to disguise its identity. Unfortunately, it was cut down to 45.52 using inferior cutting techniques. What happened to the Hope Diamond after it disappeared from France and resurfaced later in London is open to conjecture, but its possible story is reported by Richard Kurin,[5] who gives an account of the French Blue's history among the powerful elite in Europe while it was missing after the French Revolution.

The Hope Diamond acquired its infamous reputation in the twentieth century when its owners were falling victim to misfortune and delivery carriers were meeting tragic deaths when simply in possession of the diamond for a few hours. These stories have become urban legends, and some sources say these stories are simply not true. It was in the possession of the French Crown during the French Revolution and, incidentally, the French Revolution was partially triggered by an event called "The Affair of the Diamond Necklace." The incident involved Marie Antoinette's unpopular and controversial involvement in the purchase of a necklace set with 647 diamonds, some of which were quite large (figure 6.3).

The Smithsonian Institute did not limit its investigation to provenance alone, but also carried out chemistry examinations. As explored more fully in chapter 7, quartz crystal has piezoelectrical properties that occur in quartz, topaz, and tourmaline crystals, and also in blue diamonds. The blue color in diamonds is caused by boron atoms in the lattice of the carbon diamond crystal. The presence of boron gives diamonds piezoelectrical properties. When testing the Hope Diamond, high concentrations of boron atoms were present in the gemstone, creating its intense sapphire-blue color (figure 6.4 on the

Figure 6.3. Marie Antoinette wearing a large blue gemstone pin that resembles the French Blue, the original Hope Diamond. *Portrait of Marie Antoinette*, after 1775 in Musée Antoine-Lécuyer, Saint Quentin, France.

following page). When worn, the energy and heat generated by the human body may serve to activate piezoelectricity inherent in the Hope Diamond. The Smithsonian also carried out ultraviolet and phosphorescence testing on the Hope and found that under phosphorescence, the diamond glows bright red, a quality not present in the diamonds surrounding the Hope in its necklace setting. While explanations have been offered as to the reason the diamond reacts in this way, other scientists have said that "phosphorescence in blue diamonds is not well understood."[6]

Figure 6.4. The Hope Diamond.

HH: *I visited the Hope Diamond on display at the Smithsonian Institute. Having studied the energetic properties of crystals and the practice of Reiki, I visited the stone with the notion that the Hope Diamond was amplifying radiant energy through its natural refraction. My intention was to visit the Hope Diamond and radiate a peaceful, loving vibration using Reiki techniques to disprove the notion that the diamond is cursed. The blue diamond rests on*

a rotating stand in a glass case, stopping for a few seconds at each turn. At first I found the turntable in the glass case irritating, but it turned out to be a workable solution to the problem of meditating with the diamond and without interfering with the many visitors who were also observing. After tuning into the stone, I felt pulled into the diamond and its rich blue color. I have worked with many crystals throughout my life, but I was surprised by the tangible power of the gemstone and how quickly I tuned into it. I noticed the diamond tuned into me and pulled me into it. In an intuitive visionary state, I noticed that beyond the deep blue of the diamond, it radiated an intense red color.

Early in my meditation, I sent peaceful, loving vibrations into the gemstone. I sensed the vibrations were not influencing the stone and seemed to be bouncing off of it energetically. I intensified my intention, but eventually I stopped because I was perplexed by the energy dynamics. When I was silent, the gemstone spoke inside me. It said very curtly that I was not there to influence the stone with positive energy but, rather, I was there to receive energy and purification from the stone. I was surprised by the message and by the sentient presence in the stone. At once, I felt like I was in a trance state and noticed waves of energy washing through me as though I were being cleansed. I think if I had willed myself to move, I could have, but I felt entranced and not motivated to move. I stood perfectly still and lost track of time while the stone cleansed me with energetic waves. There was a merging of energies, and I did not feel like the glass of the case between us affected the energetic potency of the stone on my field at all. The length of time in front of the case and my trance state was such that Smithsonian security guards came alongside me twice, but I did not move at all when they came up to me. While I noticed them with peripheral vision, I did not respond to the guards. Eventually, the stone's energy subsided, and I gradually returned to a "normal" state. I was at the Smithsonian with a colleague who observed the interaction and reported later that I stood in front of the case for over twenty minutes while attracting the attention of the guards who watched me the entire time. He also commented that it seemed like I was inside the glass case with the diamond, but he could not explain why he felt that way.

Energetically, I felt different after the interaction. It was a humbling experience, because I had approached the diamond with the intention that I would influence the stone using a sort of "mind over matter" approach.

The stone's power and purity deflected that intention and instead cleared my field. In spite of my knowledge of crystal energy, I realized I was dealing with a powerful energy that I did not fully understand. After the experience, I became a little obsessed with the Hope Diamond and later learned how the stone turns an intense red after exposure to phosphorescent lighting. I started having dreams about the blue stone, including a dream where I was standing in front of a mirror wearing the Hope Diamond. There have been times since that experience when the Hope Diamond has appeared in dreams, meditations, and visions, and I feel as though the energy of the diamond is inside me and I can connect with it.

The Hope Diamond influenced the story of one of the most popular movies ever made. James Cameron's *Titanic* (1997) had at the core of its plot a large blue diamond called the "Heart of the Ocean," which the heroine, Rose, throws into the Atlantic Ocean at the end of the film. The greed and obsession of the characters in the film around the diamond creates a sort of "curse," and the viewer wonders if the negative energy around the blue diamond caused the *Titanic* to sink. The real Hope Diamond was never on the *Titanic,* but the obsession and greedy frenzy around the diamond was accurately portrayed in the film. As diamonds have historically been associated with power, it may be advisable that those who own diamonds wear them with positive and spiritually pure purposes. Diamonds such as the Hope, Cullinan, Koh-i-Noor, and others may be best used for enlightenment for large groups, nations, or the world, not necessarily in the possession of greedy or selfish monarchs who are not using their influence or intention with integrity. There has been a recurring theme in researching the chintamani that those who own a stone of power need to also possess the spiritual authority, worthiness, and right to rule, but diamonds also possess unique scientific properties that help to bridge the connection between the science and spiritual technology of crystals.

The Pearl of Allah

The Pearl of Allah (also known as the Pearl of Lao Tzu) is one of the largest natural pearls ever found, discovered through a tragic accident. One of its owners, Wilburn Dowell Cobb,[7] tells the story that in 1934 a native diver in the Philippines was searching for conch shells and accidentally caught his hand in the sudden clamp of a giant man-eating Tridacna clam shell, drowning as he struggled to free himself. Retrieving the drowned diver required taking the giant clam up to the surface. In freeing the hand of the deceased diver, a monstrous-sized pearl was discovered in the clam shell. At fourteen pounds, it is one of the largest pearls in the world. This pearl is famous for its size alone, but its intriguing story continues. A complex monetary negotiation ensued around selling the pearl. One of the negotiators was able to save the life of a family member who was ill, which would not have been possible if the giant pearl had not been discovered through the accidental death of the native diver. The discovery of the pearl is at once associated with sacrifice, misfortune, and accident, but also with abundance, wealth, renewal, healing, and life. The result was the pearl took the life of the diver, but then supplied the means to save the life of another. This true story sounds more like a legend of a magical talisman or gemstone.

Other large pearls from history include Queen Cleopatra's earrings. At the time, her pearls were considered the largest and finest in the world. Indulgent and impulsive by nature, Cleopatra challenged Marc Antony, her lover, about which of them could have the most expensive banquet. Not to be outdone, Cleopatra dropped one of her large pearl earrings in vinegar wine. The priceless pearl dissolved in the vinegar and Cleopatra drank the mixture, winning the competition. This drink, while strange, did not harm Cleopatra because pearls are made of calcium carbonate, which aids digestion. Pearls, which are connected astrologically to the moon, water, and the ocean, are considered nurturing stones and are a type of bioorganic gem because they are formed inside oyster shells originating in the sea. Cleopatra's remaining pearl earring later adorned the statute of sea-born Venus in Rome's Pantheon. The whereabouts of the pearl earring is now lost in history. Other Roman statues from the first and second centuries show Venus with one pearl earring, which could be alluding to Cleopatra's famous pearl (figure 6.5 on the following page).

The Stone of Destiny

We move to a unique entry among earth chintamanis, the Stone of Scone. Currently on display at the top of Edinburgh Castle, the Stone of Scone is

Figure 6.5. *Head of Venus*, c. 100 CE, bronze with gold and pearl, 73.AB.24,
The J. Paul Getty Museum, Villa Collection, Malibu, California.
Courtesy of the Getty's Open Content Program

a visually unimpressive block of sandstone. The humble stone seems out of place sitting alongside the Scottish crown jewels. It weighs 335 pounds and measures approximately 26 × 16 × 11 inches with metal rings bored into its sides to help in transporting. This unassuming rock is the coronation stone for the monarchs of the British Empire. National identity is tied to the stone, with the British and the Scots disputing ownership of the Stone of Scone for centuries. The stone is first recorded among the high kings of Ireland and was originally called the Lia Fáil. It sat atop the Hill of Tara in County Meath, where the ancient kings of Ireland were crowned. It was later taken to the Isle of Iona where the Pict kings, who united Ireland and Scotland, were anointed and crowned on the stone.

Ancient myths encircle the stone like a shroud of mist, and it has a compelling origin story. The Stone of Scone is reputedly Jacob's stone pillow. In the Biblical book of Genesis, the patriarch Jacob slept on a stone while he dreamed of a ladder connecting heaven and earth with angels ascending and descending the ladder. According to the description in the Bible, prior to his dream, Jacob collected a group of stones and slept inside what could have been a stone grid. When Jacob awoke, he was awed by his dream experience of the ladder to heaven and stated, "'Surely the Lord is in this place; and I knew it not.' And he was afraid, and said, 'How dreadful is this place! This is none other but the house of God, and this is the gate of heaven.'"[8] It seems there was a connection between the energy of the stones and the place, which may have helped prompt the extraordinary vision that Jacob experienced.* He may have created a stone circle with the stones indigenous to the area to enhance the natural earth energy and opened an energetic portal that he accessed while sleeping. Stone circles as old as Stonehenge existed in Israel, so Jacob may have been familiar with this type of ancient stone technology.† Jacob stood the stone near his head upright as a pillar and anointed it saying: "And this stone, which I have set for a pillar, shall be God's house."[9] A translation from the original Hebrew text refers to Jacob's pillar as "sandstone."[10]

While Jacob set the stone up as a memorial, or perhaps as a center stone, in that place which he renamed Bethel, it is purported that the Children of Israel treasured the stone as a sacred relic of their patriarch, perhaps retrieving it from Bethel hundreds of years after Jacob passed away. An anointing ceremony for Israelite monarchs involving a pillar continued as an Old Testament tradition. During the Babylonian captivity, the prophet Jeremiah and two princesses from the royal house of Judah fled to Egypt. According to legend, Jeremiah carried Jacob's pillar with him. Although Jeremiah's recorded

---

*In the British Isles and among the Druids, supernatural places of power are known as "thin places" where the veil between the seen and unseen world is more accessible.
†One of the oldest stone circles in the world (over five thousand years old) is Rujm el-Hiri located in Israel near the Sea of Galilee.

history stops in Egypt, there is a legend that he and the princesses traveled from Egypt to Ireland where one of the princesses married an Irish king and Jacob's stone thereafter became the Irish Stone of Destiny, the Lia Fáil, upon which the Irish kings were anointed and crowned on the Hill of Tara.

Having looked into the Stone of Scone's history, we are not in the position to prove or disprove the stories surrounding this humble block of sandstone, nor can we make definitive statements about its energetic properties other than in our visits to Edinburgh Castle, a popular tourist destination. Although we spent more time standing in front of the stone than the average tourist, we did not notice any special energy radiating from it. However, the stone's energy is drawn more from its symbolism as a religio-spiritual relic in the coronation ceremony. A mythos has developed around the coronation stone, and that intentional energy is more important than the sandstone in which the stone is formed. When the monarch is anointed and crowned on the Stone of Scone, the sacred right to rule is conferred in a similar vein to King Arthur pulling the sword from the stone. Reenacting this powerful myth has continued into the twentieth century with the crowning and anointing of Queen Elizabeth II sitting in King Edward's chair atop the Stone of Scone in Westminster Abbey in 1953 (figure 6.6). The Archbishop anointed the monarch, who was seated above the Stone of Scone, with consecrated holy oil while proclaiming: "Be thy Head anointed with holy oil: as kings, priests, and prophets were anointed: And as Solomon was anointed king by Zadok the priest and Nathan the prophet, so be thou anointed, blessed, and consecrated Queen over the Peoples, whom the Lord thy God hath given thee to rule and govern, In the name of the Father, and of the Son, and of the Holy Ghost. Amen."[11] The language used in the anointing process atop the Stone of Scone, like the myths surrounding the stone itself, is tied to the ancient Israelite kings.

The British returned the controversial stone to Scotland in 1996 on the condition that when crowning the next monarch, the British could borrow the stone and place it under King Edward's Chair in Westminster Abbey in the coronation ceremony. There are alternate theories that the Stone of Scone currently on display in Edinburgh Castle is not authentic. According to this theory, the coronation stone King Edward I forcefully took from Scotland at the Palace of Scone in 1296 was a fake, while the real stone

Figure 6.6. King Edward's Coronation Chair with Stone of Scone, Westminster Abbey, ca. 1875–1885.

Cornell University Library

was hidden somewhere in Scotland. Nevertheless, the currently accepted stone was stolen from Westminster Abbey by a group of Scottish nationalists in 1950. It was eventually returned to its place under the coronation chair in Westminster Abbey on February 26, 1952, coincidentally following the death of King George VI on February 6, 1952. After the monarch's death, there would have been an urgent need to locate the coronation stone. Elizabeth II was not officially crowned on the Stone of Scone until 1953.

Was the delay caused by an attempt to authenticate the rediscovered stone or perhaps find the real Stone of Scone? There is speculation that the stone that was returned was a copy and that Elizabeth was not crowned on the real Stone of Destiny. However, if the stone King Edward I took in 1296 was not authentic, then none of the British kings have been the rightful heirs to the throne in the same way that those who could not pull the sword from the stone could not be king. Theories place the real coronation stone on the Isle of Iona as St. Columba's stone pillow (figure 6.7), but it is also said that the Stone of Destiny is hidden in a cave in the Isle of Skye off the western shores of Scotland.[12]

The amazing part of the Stone of Destiny is not its composition or the possible energy it could generate—it is a candidate for a chintamani stone because of what it represents. It is impossible to prove that any version of the Stone of Destiny is the genuine stone Jacob used as a pillow thousands of years ago; but proving that it was Jacob's pillar is not the point. To fully understand the Stone of Destiny, we need to return to Jacob's story from the Bible and examine the conversation between Jacob and God during the

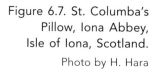

Figure 6.7. St. Columba's Pillow, Iona Abbey, Isle of Iona, Scotland.
Photo by H. Hara

"stairway to heaven" dream. Above the stairway reaching into heaven stood Jehovah promising the land to Jacob and his seed in the four directions, blessing all future generations, and promising not to forsake Jacob. Jacob awoke awed and frightened. He set up the stone that "he had put at his head" as a pillar, anointed it with oil, and vowed that if God kept his promise to keep Jacob clothed and fed during his journey to return to his father's house from exile, "this sandstone which I have placed as a pillar shall become the house of God."[13] Other translations refer to the stone as a "memorial pillar." The stone becomes a "contract bound in stone" between Jacob and God that extends into future generations. A monarch crowned and anointed on the stone inherits the protections that God offered to Jacob. The vows taken and the commission received by the monarch are sanctified by the original agreement between the patriarch and God. There is a manifest blessing involved if future generations remember the contract. There are many ancient memorial stones throughout the British Isles called Pictish stones. These stones are used to record the generations of families who own areas of land and are used as boundary markers. Essentially, the stones act as generational memorial pillars. The importance of Jacob's pillar or the Stone of Destiny is entwined with divine birthright and the remembrance of ancestral covenants as guideposts of destiny.

Stones from Heaven

Here we investigate stones from heaven, both meteorites and meteoritic impact glass, as well as a particularly famous meteoritic stone: the Kaaba. These peculiar stones are especially important because the Roerichs believed the chintamani in their possession was either a meteorite or a tektite (meteor impact glass). Supposedly, the Roerichs saw a Sanskrit message etched onto their chintamani, which though usually invisible was rendered visible when the holder meditated. The secret message indicates the stone's star-born origins: "Through the desert I come—I bring the Chalice covered with the Shield. Within it is a treasure—the Gift of Orion."*[14] Nicholas Roerich indicates the three belt stars of Orion are the chintamani's source. These three

---

*This was published by Helena Roerich under the pseudonym Josephine Saint-Hilare.

stars are 1,200, 1,260, and 2,000 light years distant from Earth. Another possible origin of the chintamani is the star Sirius. At just 8.6 light years away, it is the brightest star in the sky and part of a binary system with the likely inclusion of a third brown dwarf. The mutual orbit of the Sirius star system is fifty years, which is a significant number symbol that we explore further in chapter 7. Robert Temple not only explicates this in detail but also weaves multicultural knowledge of Sirius into a global phenomenon.[15]

The Roerich chintamani may be moldavite, a green glass tektite, which is molten glass created during meteor impact activity. There are various impact glass stones around the world, most of which are black. Moldavite is found in the Moldau River area in the Czech Republic, where there is an ancient meteor impact site. The impact glass in this area is world famous because of its brilliant green color when transmitting light through the stone. It is considered a stone of heaven, not just because it is impact glass but because, according to legend, it was a green stone set in Lucifer's crown, which was shattered by Michael the Archangel's silver sword when Lucifer was cast out of heaven.

Moldavite is a tektite glass made of silica and is harder than ordinary glass due to its higher silicon dioxide content.[16] Microscopic analysis of moldavite reveals an unusual inclusion not found in glass: lechatelierite, a noncrystalline form of silicon dioxide. Microscopic photos of the inclusions show wavy, fibrous, circular, and spiral-like forms.[17] These radical, amorphous, irregular, and eccentric forms may be partially responsible for the unusual metaphysical properties frequently reported by those who work with moldavite (figure 6.8). Among crystal energy enthusiasts, moldavite has a reputation as a stone of transformation because of the tangible energetic rush it transmits. Perhaps the amorphous and spiral inclusions inherent in moldavite aids one to reach an energy state during meditation that taps into the crystal, quantum, and DNA fields.

Moldavite is a popular tektite due to its beautiful shade of vibrant green, especially through transmitted light. There are many other tektites, but most of them are black or brown. Some of them are translucent when backlit while others are opaque. We are not going to discuss all tektites, but a few are worth mentioning within the context of the chintamani. A tektite from Safford, Arizona, saffordite, is also referred to as a chintamani stone. These black

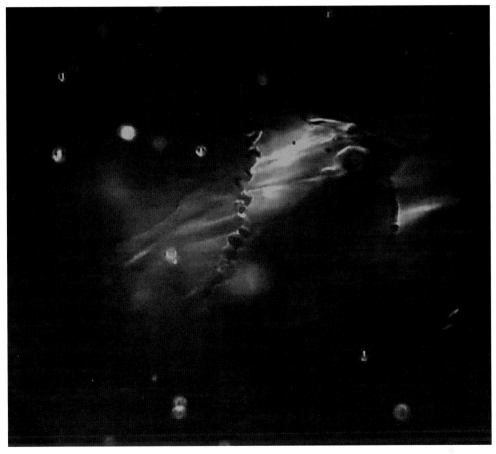

Figure 6.8. Microscopic photograph of moldavite magnified 140X.
The spiral forms are lechatelierite inclusions.
Photo by H. Hara

tektites, which can be translucent or opaque, are mysterious and confound scientific testing. They are often called pseudotektites, as they may be obsidian glass rather than meteor impact glass. Although different from moldavite both in color and energy, they have an attractive and unusual energy. In our intuitive work with the stones, we have found that they interact with meditative states by dissolving desire, which is, curiously, diametrically opposed to the concept of the wish-fulfilling gem. Coincidentally, these tektites are found in a large expanse of desert at the base of Mt. Graham in southeastern Arizona, a sacred site to the San Carlos Apache Tribe. At the mountain's summit, one of the most powerful telescope arrays in the world operates in cooperation with the University of Arizona, the Max Planck Institute for Radio Astronomy (Bonn, Germany), the Vatican, and other universities. The Large Binocular Telescope Near-infrared Utility with Camera and Integral Field Unit for Extragalactic Research (nicknamed "Lucifer") is a part of the telescope array. There have been reports of UFO activity, including light orbs, in and around the mountain range.

Black tektites are found throughout the world, but most come from China and Indonesia. Historically, they have been referred to as the stones of the gods, magic seed stones, the gem of Krishna, and other similar titles.[18] A tektite found on an island off of Indonesia is called agni manitite. In Sanskrit, *agni* translates to "fire" and *mani* means "jewel." Many of these black tektites are translucent, and just like the saffordite, they are considered pseudotektites. Interestingly, Indonesia is also home to a famous active volcano called Mt. Batur located in the Kintamani Mountains in Bali. Kintamani is an Indonesian spelling of chintamani.

Libyan desert glass is a tektite found in the desert in Egypt and Libya. Usually found in shades of yellow, it has a different energetic sense than other tektites. King Tutankhamun was buried wearing a breastplate with a scarab at the center made of yellow Libyan glass. The yellow tektite, like moldavite, has an inclusion called cristobalite, which has the same chemical formula as quartz but with a different crystal structure.[19] The crystal structure is created through several transitions of heating and cooling; phases of the transitions are considered dynamically disordered. The crystal structure of the cristobalite inclusion forms within the amorphous glass tektite, the two integrating in a yin-yang dynamic. We theorize the unusual inclusions found in tektites may be responsible for the intense attraction and interaction experienced by those who work with crystal energy. The inclusions support the metaphysical paradigm of alchemical change and transformation, qualities the tektites are famous for among crystal energy users.

Stones created or altered by lightning strikes are also considered stones from heaven. These peculiar formations involve lightning strikes that change the structure and chemistry of the host earth material. For example, when lightning strikes sand it can form a fused sand-glass funnel referred to as fulgurite, or petrified lightning. Fulgurites can occur anywhere in the world, but most have been found in the Sahara Desert where sand is plentiful. It is reported that fulgurites are used as prayer pipes by indigenous peoples. This practice coincides with the stone being used for intentional purposes such as fulfilling wishes or prayers. The more technical name for fulgurite is lechatelierite, which is the inclusion found in moldavite. The presence of this formation shows extreme forces were involved in its creation.

Tektites are a controversial stone and elude absolute scientific definition, as it is not certain if the material is extraterrestrial in origin or is a byproduct of the extreme forces caused by meteor impact. We turn from meteor impact glass to the core impact stones, meteorites. A complex topic, we will highlight some unusual characteristics about meteorites and introduce a true extraterrestrial gemstone. A rare meteorite called pallasite contains green peridot. These peridots are not the byproduct of the explosion but are, in fact, from space. Testing that compares the mass spectrometry of Earth-based peridot and meteoritic peridot reveals that they have different chemical compositions.[20] It is possible meteorites bearing peridot gems originate from the asteroid belt between Mars and Jupiter and are the remnants of an ancient planet that was destroyed in this solar system.

Because many meteorites are made of iron and nickel, their metallic content have made them historically useful as tools and weapons, but because of their strength and extraterrestrial origins, they have also been fashioned into powerful ceremonial objects. Tibetan *vajra* and *phurba* ritual objects have been made of meteorite and some pyramid capstones from Egypt (called pyramidions) have also been made of meteorite. The ancient Egyptians used meteorite iron in ritual burial implements. They considered meteorites "bones of the star gods"[21] and thought meteorites were responsible for life on Earth.[22] Many ancient goddesses of antiquity had meteorites called *betyls* represent or empower them at shrines, including Cybele in the Temple of Pessinus, the Statue of Artemis in Ephesus, and the Sanctuary of Aphrodite Paphia in Cyprus.[23] The sacred omphalos stone at the Oracle of Delphi may have been a meteorite *betyl* stone. Because meteorites were powerful iron-based materials that fell from the sky, they were considered artifacts of gods from heaven.

Religious and scientific fascination with meteorites has continued into modern times. In 1808, Austrian Count Alois von Beckh Widmanstätten discovered a distinctive pattern of lines on certain iron meteorites when cut and polished (figure 6.9). These lines, which form a part of the crystal structure, are found on several different types of iron meteorites around the world. The lines look like the interior of a sophisticated interlacing network that is so ordered it seems a little unnatural. The Widmanstätten pattern is unique to iron meteorites and is not present in any crystal formed on the Earth, nor can this crystal pattern be replicated in a laboratory. In Japan, the Hiroshima University and the University of Tokyo reported the magnetic qualities of meteorites are different from magnetic properties of earth minerals. In researching and harnessing the unique magnetic qualities from the iron meteorites, Japanese researchers found a "new magnetic domain structure," which originates from tetrataenite, unique to meteorites.[24] The material is being tested for future devices including next-generation magnetic devices and green nanotechnology. Tetrataenite is considered an "equiatomic and highly ordered, non-cubic Fe-Ni alloy mineral that forms in meteorites."[25] It is not found on Earth and is considered to have superb magnetic properties.

Figure 6.9. The Widmanstätten pattern of a Gibeon meteorite.
Photo by Kevin Walsh

Turning to what is arguably the most powerful stone on Earth, the Black Stone of the Kaaba is in a black cube at the center of the Great Mosque of Mecca. Kaaba means "cube" in Arabic. Its power is attested by the fact that the Black Stone attracts more than two million devotees during the annual Hajj, a pilgrimage all Muslims are required to make at least once in their lifetime to the Kaaba. During the Hajj, Muslims circle counterclockwise around the mosque seven times. The Hajj is the world's largest pilgrimage and represents Muslim people's solidarity and devotion to Allah. Videos of this event are mesmerizing, as massive rivers of people flow around the Kaaba. The Muslim devotees point their attention toward the stone in the cubic structure, which represents the House of Allah. Intense devotion combined with millions of devotees in a coordinated movement would undoubtedly generate a tremendous influx of intentional energy.

Not surprisingly, this mysterious black rock has a complex history that originates in myth, like many of the powerful stones we have reviewed. It is widely believed that the Black Stone of the Kaaba was given to Muhammad by the Archangel Gabriel, and Muhammad placed it in Mecca. There are other stories tying the stone to Adam and Eve, Abraham, Ishmael, and even to Rome—where it represented Cybele, an ancient pre-Roman goddess who was considered the mother of all gods. Around 200 BCE, the Romans, fearing the omens surrounding a meteorite shower that had recently occurred and under the recommendation of the Oracle at Delphi, sent representatives to Phrygia to obtain the black meteorite stone from the temple at Pessinus (in modern-day Turkey) and bring it to Rome. As previously mentioned, it was common for black meteorite stones, or *betyls*, to be used in goddess worship in antiquity, which is of interest since meteorites possess unusual magnetic qualities and feminine energy is associated with magnetism.* The Romans not only took the famed black meteorite but also imported the cult of Cybele, who was known as the Magna Mater (Great Mother). The famous Cybele black meteorite was used as the head of the goddess on a statue in Rome but disappeared during the Empire's

---

*There is a theory the black meteorite's representation as Cybele was the ancient origin of the worship of the Black Madonna, whose visage is still present in prominent places in European Catholic cathedrals such as Chartres, France.

decline. It is theorized, although unproven, that it may have reappeared in the form of the Black Stone of the Kaaba.

Although the Kaaba was once a single large stone, the stone appears to be several pieces cemented together and encased in a silver frame located in the eastern corner of the Kaaba shrine. Although there are many theories about the composition of the Kaaba stone, it is not possible to conduct a scientific study, as it is a spiritual ritual object protected by the Muslim community. However, most theories speculate that the black stone is a meteorite. If the Kaaba stone is a meteorite, then the natural magnetic properties of the extraterrestrial rock could align with the circulating energy of its devotees. As the center stone of the throng turning around it, it could be activated by powerful intention and centralize a whirlpool of energy. Perhaps there is significance to housing the mysterious Black Stone in a cube. There could be an interesting juxtaposition of energies involved with the non-cubic meteorite housed in a cubic structure as a male and female balance of energies. The worship of the Kaaba may be a remnant of ancient goddess worship incorporating a *betyl*. Curiously, the oval Black Stone set in its silver frame resembles a birth portal (figure 6.10).

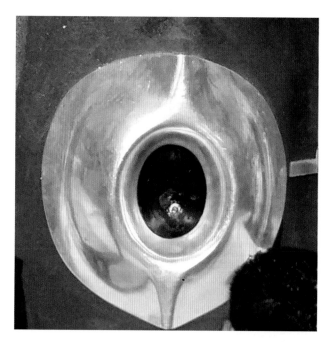

Figure 6.10. The Black Stone of the Kaaba.

Written in Stone

Most have heard of the famous alchemical text written on stone, the Emerald Tablet of Hermes. Although the tablet is missing, there is another famed emerald tablet, the Moghul Emerald. At 217.8 carats, it is one of the largest emeralds in the world. The gemstone is a rectangular mini tablet with carving and lettering on both sides of the 10-centimeter emerald plate (figure 6.11). Dating from 1695 CE, it is an Indian artifact, although the emerald was mined in Colombia. One side bears an Arabic inscription of a Muslim prayer and invocation in Shi'a script, while the reverse is decorated with an ornate flower pattern. The detail work on this small emerald tablet is considered some of the finest engraving in the world. The Mughals perfected the art of stone engraving, even engraved lettering on diamonds such as the Shah Diamond and the Taj Mahal Diamond. The Mughals' engraving skill is a mystery, as it is not known what technology the Mughals utilized to carve such well-defined, detailed engraving into the world's hardest mineral.

Engraving on stone is a fine art and some of the world's most important religious artifacts incorporate engravings on stone. Ancient cultures frequently have stories about powerful or magical manuscripts written on

Figure 6.11. The Mughal Emerald with engraved inscription, 1107 CE.

gemstones, including the Emerald Tablet of Hermes, the Sumerian Tablet of Lapis Lazuli, the Ten Commandments written on sapphire, the Jeweled Tablet of Fate, the Tablet of Destinies, and the Jade Books. Engraving on rocks is found throughout the world on petroglyphs, tombstones, temples, and mani stones. Mani stones have a specific connection to the chintamani, as they are the mantra *Aum Mani Padme Hung!* carved onto stone (figure 6.12; refer to chapter 1 for more on the mani stones).

Figure 6.12. Carved mani stones in the Himalayas.

Magic Stones in Popular Culture

Thus far we have reviewed a few of the most famous gemstones in the world as well as gemstone-related talismanic objects used for alchemical transformation and spiritual technology. While gemstone talismans are popular in Eastern cultures, many do not know why we wear precious gemstones other than for adornment or for their perceived economic status. The influence of gemstones and especially powerful chintamani-like objects is prevalent in myth and fantasy. Our fascination with magic gems and talismans is widely seen in popular culture through fantasy stories, comic books, video games, and film. Some of the most popular films of all time have involved chintamani-like stones and relics. Superman's glowing green kryptonite, originating from his exploded home planet Krypton, bears a remarkable resemblance to moldavite. In the *Lord of the Rings,* the hero, Frodo Baggins, throws a golden ring of power into a volcano because the object is too powerful to remain in Middle Earth. In *Star Wars,* kyber crystals are used to power lightsabers, the mythical laser swords of the Jedi Knights, but they are also collected to power the laser ray of the Death Star that is used to obliterate entire planets. Episodes in the *Star Trek* universe involved the search for dilithium crystals, which powered faster-than-light-speed warp drives. *Harry Potter and the Sorcerer's Stone,* the first story in the series, centers around the famed Philosopher's Stone. In the *Indiana Jones* film series, the hero seeks out powerful relics such as the Ark of the Covenant, crystal skulls, the Holy Grail, and Shiva Lingam stones. In all the films, the villains and Indiana Jones ultimately prove incapable or unworthy to keep the powerful objects.

In the Marvel Cinematic Universe, a long multi-film story arc involves six infinity stones whose power and qualities strongly resemble chintamani stones. Heroes and villains alike seek out the infinity stones, resulting in galactic battles. When gathered together, the six infinity stones act as a wish-fulfilling jewel, granting the bearer of the six stones his or her desires. Unfortunately, whether hero or villain, the wishes of the bearer center on power and destruction over one's perceived enemies or imbalance in the universe. Even the hero bearing the infinity stones does not choose enlightenment or a positive outcome for all sentient beings. Appearing heroic on the screen, in a moment of instinctual reaction during battle, the flawed hero succumbs to the limitations of the ego and chooses a destructive path in a final galactic battle. In the end, no one is truly worthy to wield the powerful infinity stones.

Beyond the superficial Hollywood gloss adulating ego-based heroes, an alternate message can be found as a reaction to modern myths. Rather than emulating the ego-based heroes of popular culture, find the path leading to the balanced use of the chintamani, a path of compassion, patience, humility, and the purity of heart that accompanies a true desire to help sentient beings. Only on the enlightened path can a chintamani stone be of service to the universe. Otherwise, it becomes a dangerous and destructive object in the hands of those who are self-serving and focused on power.

7

Crystal Spiritual Technology

Unexpected Crystal Capabilities Intersecting
Quantum Intention

> *In the center of a jewel palace*
> *On lotus and lion thrones, abide the awakened.*
>
> LOSANG CHOKYI GYALTSEN, *MEDICINE BUDDHA*

SPACE, TIME, INTENTION, MATTER, and consciousness all entangle in crystals. We begin with crystals in the human body. Surprisingly, crystals are part of the human body infrastructure, so we cannot consider them as outer objects without recognizing that they influence our perception from the inside too. Crystals are networked in human biology and physiology, specifically in the ears and pineal gland. Ear crystals are called otoliths (ear stones) or otoconia (ear dust), while crystals in the pineal gland are called myeloconia (brain dust). Otoconia are found in spherical shapes of crystal calcite from 1 to 50 microns in size (1×10^{-6} meter or 1μm). In one branch of the inner ear, these crystals establish balance, while crystals in another branch facilitate hearing. Otoconia have been found in all vertebrate species. These microcrystals help orient our bodies in the vertical and horizontal planes and allow us to sense velocity. These crystals, networked with our biology, create the ability to navigate space.

Researchers at Ben-Gurion University of the Negev found two different types of crystals embedded in the pineal gland: polycrystalline complexes of mulberry-like concretions hundreds of microns in size and well-defined microcrystals up to 20 microns in size. The well-defined calcite crystals have cubic, hexagonal, and cylindrical shapes. Scientists found that there are 100 to 300 calcite microcrystals for each cubic millimeter of the pineal gland, meaning that there are about 13,000 to 38,000 microcrystals embedded in the average human pineal.[1] The primary biological function of the pineal gland is to secrete hormones, especially melatonin, which synchronizes daily circadian rhythms. These crystals, networked with our biology, help us navigate the realm of time. In animals, the pineal gland is the organ of instinct. In humans, the pineal gland at the ajna chakra is identified as the "third eye." According to many mystic traditions, when activated, the pineal opens intuition through a range of psychic perceptive abilities. Most importantly, it opens the experience of the universe as a dynamic, unified whole.

Crystals, and therefore the chintamani, are hard-wired into vertebrate and, more especially, human biology. In this chapter, we consider how crystals specifically express geology, chemical composition, structure, energy charge, memory, attunement, and light. We also consider the idea that the crystal-human interface blurs the separation between subject and object, because as we observe crystals, the crystals reflect a changed version of ourselves. We enter this discussion recognizing that the chintamani is inseparably inside and outside of us. Crystal qualities resonate human qualities.

Crystals are the intriguing apex of the mineral kingdom: so solid, so varied, so structured. At first glance, they don't seem to have ineffable connections to consciousness. In the eighteenth century's scientific view of the clockwork universe, minerals are hierarchically at the bottom of Earth evolution, no matter how fascinating they might appear. However, we no longer examine the universe through that lens now that the quantum world of quarks and Higgs bosons have revealed themselves in theory and have been verified experimentally. In 1928, Werner Heisenberg formulated the Uncertainty Principle about paired properties of subatomic particles, which applies to wave phenomena as well. He found that the experimenter can discover either the position or the velocity of particles, but not both at the same time. You can only know either where the wave is located or how fast it is moving. What you discover depends on what you intend to learn and which aspect of the phenomenon you watch.

In addition to the uncertainty principle influencing experiments, the observer effect also modifies experiments. The observer, even if it is an automated machine, changes something in that observed system. Mindset influences outcome! There is no objective, fully detached observer. The experimenter is an integral part of the experiment. In our inquiry into crystals, we recognize that our preconceptions have limited our discovery process and our discoveries. Every subject of study, including gems, is conditioned by previous perspectives and older perceived limits about the nature of consciousness. Next we explore how the crystal-consciousness connection is much more extensive than gemologists had ever imagined.

Crystal Geometry

Crystals are so archetypically expressive of shape that the very science of determining the molecular geometry of chemical compounds at the atomic level is called crystallography. Crystals have regular and irregular structures. Their growth pattern follows the golden ratio spiral, opening in ever larger arrangements, and can unfold in single, double, or multiple interacting spirals.[2] The most symmetrical three-dimensional structures include crystals with faces of exactly the same two-dimensional shapes. These are the five platonic solids, hearkening back to Plato's time when science, philosophy, and spirit were considered a coherent whole (figure 7.1 on the following page). The five three-dimensional shapes are correlated to the scheme of elements as noted by Plato and amended by Aristotle (see table).

PLATONIC SOLIDS AND STATES OF MATTER				
PLATONIC SOLID	# FACES	FACE SHAPE	ELEMENT	MATTER STATE
Icosahedron	20	Triangle	Water	Water
Dodecahedron	12	Pentagon	Ether	Ionic Plasma
Octahedron	8	Triangle	Air	Gas
Cube	6	Square	Earth	Solid
Tetrahedron	4	Triangle	Fire	Combustive

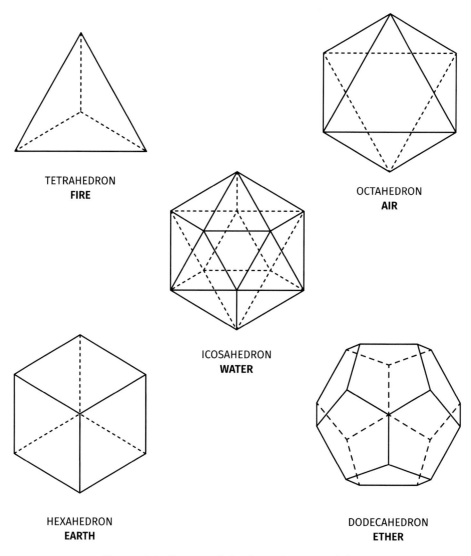

Figure 7.1. Shapes of the five platonic solids.

When modern science looks at Plato's elements, there is a pejorative attitude that the knowledge of the ancients was simple-minded. Instead of viewing ancient element categories as imprecise jumble, regard them in light of the states that matter can take. The ancient elements describe the range of density states that matter can assume: earth is solid, water is liquid, fire is combustive, air is gaseous, and ether is ionic plasma. The platonic solids are all dense structures, but each shape vibrates harmonically with one of the five states of matter across the full range of densities. The principle of wave resonance is at the heart of how crystals connect with and affect all densities of matter. Light and sound have differing frequencies that interact with matter, energy, and mind in a range received from dissonant to resonant waves. Light and sound phenomena can be focused locally or at a grander scale. When synchronized with astronomical-scale light and sound waves, a gem like the chintamani becomes a worldwide or super-galactic-scale resonator.

Platonic shape resonance is directly wired to the human chakra system, which we compare in the table below. There is an inexact correspondence of qualities but enough to suggest that both systems derive from an earlier shared system of knowledge. Chakra means "wheel" in Sanskrit, and each wheel has a set number of spokes. Chakras are alternately symbolized as lotus flowers, each with the same number of petals as spokes. Chakras are energy centers vertically stacked along the spine, integrating local nets of blood vessels, nerves, muscles, hormones, and organs with a type of energy and consciousness. Ascending the spine, each higher chakra houses a more refined and greater form of energy-consciousness. The view of a chakra from the side appears like a double lens, similar to the shape of the Milky Way galaxy bulging in the center and tapering off toward the outer reaches of space.

QUALITIES OF CHAKRAS AND PLATONIC SOLIDS COMPARED					
CHAKRA	**VEDIC SCHEME**	**SPOKES OR PETALS**	**FACE NUMBER**	**PLATONIC SOLID**	**GREEK SCHEME**
Third eye	Sun/Moon	2	N/A	N/A	N/A
Throat	Ether	16	20	Icosahedron	Water
Heart	Air	12	12	Dodecahedron	Ether
Solar plexus	Fire	10	8	Octahedron	Air
Below navel	Water	6	6	Cube	Earth
Spine base	Earth	4	4	Tetrahedron	Fire
Sum	N/A	50	50	N/A	N/A

The Vedic and yogic systems of chakras provide fundamental information used to teach the spiritual science of cultivating consciousness. Learning about the platonic solids is foundational geometrical information used to perfect technology, philosophy, and spiritual growth. There is a curious correlation from the previous table comparing the total number of faces in all five platonic solids to the total number of spokes or petals that exist in the six chakras. The sum in both is not a random result, but the very symbolic number 50. In Chinese numerology, 5 symbolizes earth, while 10 relates to heaven. The sum or multiplication product of earth and heaven numbers, 15 or 50, signifies the entire universe. The ancient Chinese used a 50-yarrow stalk divination method to consult the *I Ching, or Book of Changes,* oracle.[3] The number 50 appears in the Bible as the Jubilee Year, as the full term of ministry of a Levite, and as David's payment of 50 shekels of silver for the threshing-floor to locate Jehovah's altar. Moses received the Ten Commandments 50 days after the Egyptian Exodus, and the Feast of Pentecost was celebrated 50 days after Passover. In Sumerian mythology, there were 50 great Anunnaki gods and 50 companions of Gilgamesh. In Greek mythology, there were 50 Argonauts, 50 Nereids, 50 Danaids, 50 Pallantids, and 50 companions of Hercules.[4]

The symbol groups listed above are not close to a full catalog of 50 in mythology and science. In chapter 6, we discussed chintamani connections to the stars in the Sirius binary system, but we want to reinforce that these stars have a 50-year mutual orbital cycle. The number 50 in these recurring contexts symbolically indicates completed cycles or full measures of time, activity, or connection. This suggests that the geometry of platonic solids and the vertical chakra system are complete in themselves and yet have further correspondence to other whole systems. Finally, 50 features as one of the magic numbers in nuclear physics.[5] Nuclear magic numbers refer to the number of nucleons, either protons or neutrons, at the nucleus of any atomic isotope. Atoms that have magic numbers of 2, 8, 20, 28, 50, 82, or 126 are much more stable than elements with any other atomic nucleon number. The elementary stability of 50 in nuclear physics echoes the integrity of completeness that both mythology and mystic numerology also suggest.

When looking at natural crystal shapes, very few crystals actually take the five platonic solid forms. In fact, while some crystals can be tetrahedrons, cubes, or octahedrons, none form as dodecahedrons or icosahedrons. A few examples of platonic solid minerals are sphalerite and tetrahedrite, both which form as tetrahedrons. Spinel forms as an octahedron, while fluorite (figure 7.2) and iron pyrite (figure 7.3 on the following page) can form either as cubes or octahedrons. The great majority of the approximately 5,500 mineral species have forms that combine two or more different varieties of face shapes.[6] The total field of possible shapes minerals can take are eight basic systems with about 770 variations.[7] Even that is a mathematical oversimplification of all the idealized crystal shapes, yet it nonetheless remains extremely complicated. Nature makes this even more complicated because there are thousands more variations each crystal may take as it grows uniquely over centuries and millennia. Extracting the gem or crystal from the earth often alters its appearance from how it was found. Finally, gems and crystals can be shaped further by tumbling, polishing, and faceting to produce shape effects not found naturally.

Figure 7.2. Fluorite octahedron.
Photo by Kaleigh Brown

Figure 7.3. Pyrite cubic crystals on marlstone matrix
from Navajún, Rioja, Spain.
Photo by Carles Millan

At the root of crystal shape is the underlying molecular structure of the chemicals that comprise any gem or crystal. At the root of chemical structure is the electromagnetic arrangement of electrons, protons, and neutrons at the subatomic level. These energy arrangements and potentials ultimately determine how the elements of any crystal combine in space to manifest shape. This means that shape and energy are reflections of one another and interdependent. The shape will determine how a crystal will absorb, store, and radiate energy and information. Michael Gienger proposed a correlation between crystal shapes and lifestyle types based on eleven years of research.[8] He further explores how various crystals can heal or balance the excesses induced by the eight shape systems: cubic, hexagonal, trigonal (or rhombohedral), tetragonal, orthorhombic, monoclinic, triclinic, and amorphous (figure 7.4).

What is the relevance of gem and crystal shapes for our inquiry into the chintamani? We have proposed a few possibilities so far: (1) there is an infinite gem and mind field that constitutes the chintamani; (2) there are

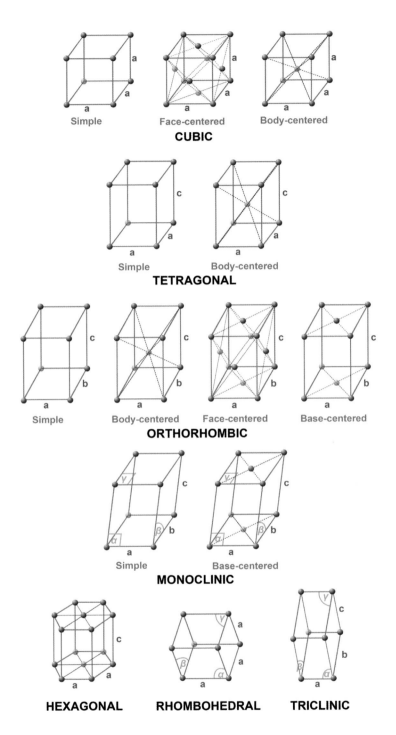

Figure 7.4. Seven crystal system shapes contrasted. The eighth shape, amorphous, is symbolized by a circle and is not shown.

powerful gems on Earth that physically interface with embodied consciousness; or, (3) there are a set of gems that are particularly attuned to resonate with human consciousness. Each of the gems have different shapes with corresponding different resonances to stimulate the evolution of the full range of sentient beings, both human and nonhuman. Each instance of a crystal with its unique shape presents a unique way to manifest that crystal energy into the self-creating universe. So the question about shape becomes: How do we entrain our bodies and minds to the resonance of the gem that is a harmonic of the chintamani? How can we connect with the crystal to direct its latent powers through our own life field for positive results?

Using any crystal to help increase compassion, wisdom, and generosity is a practice question. Though we discuss crystal chintamani practices in more detail in chapters 11 and 12, we will make a few observations here. Three basic, practical, and approximate shapes are cubic, spherical, or wand-like. Cubic shapes hold and conserve consciousness and energy within a stable medium. In turn, they can resonate stillness, rootedness, or concentrated duration. They facilitate connecting with energy or knowledge through a slower, more deliberate process. Whatever the cubic crystal may hold can be accessed, but in a measured, timed-released manner. Spherical shapes radiate the energy or information held by the crystal in all directions. Whatever the spherical crystal holds releases in a wide field and reveals a great perspective. Spherical crystals emit a greater amount of energy and data in a shorter time period than do cubic crystals. Finally, the wand-like crystal is a familiar form that may have sharper or duller points, or one or two pointed ends. Wand-like crystals stream a narrower beam of whatever they hold and can be directed toward a precise location. They operate with focus and the greatest intensity of these three shapes. None of the shapes is superior in itself but rather depends on a compatible connection. Does the person holding the crystal need logical and ordered data, a great perspective, or a focused result? The combination of crystal, intent, and operator need to work together in concert to be effective.

Crystal Mineralogy

Gems and crystals vary by chemical composition, which add to the number of unique combinations, shapes, and colors we encounter in the mineral kingdom. Of the 118 elements in the periodic table, including 94 naturally occurring elements and 24 created under laboratory conditions, only 35 natural elements combine to form minerals. The elemental composition of minerals is divided into eight classes: pure elements, sulfides, halides, oxides, carbonates, sulfates, phosphates, and silicates. Michael Gienger discusses each of these groups in relation to commonly available crystals used for healing a variety of root illnesses.[9] Crystals display an amazing range of light and color due in large part to the combination of elements, not just in a type of mineral, but in the very mix and quantity in local samples of the same mineral. As an example, let's examine the coloring agents in beryl. Adding iron can produce a blue aquamarine, a yellow heliodor, or a green beryl. Adding manganese can produce a pink morganite or a rare red beryl. Adding chromium creates a green emerald.

Gem color has a chemical base, but it also has psychological and spiritual dimensions and uses. There are several color-correspondence models that suggest there is a color resonance with parts and functions of the body and with the mental and spiritual functions of the chakras. One scheme begins with the colors of longer wavelength at the base of the spine and progresses upward in shorter wavelengths toward the head. Red corresponds to the base chakra while indigo and purple corresponds to the brow and crown chakras. In this view, for example, any green crystal may be helpful in healing, opening, or balancing the heart center. Green gems can integrate love, both self-love and selfless love, in our lives. Each person will intuitively resonate with different shades and intensities of green or of any other color. To discover how the color expressions of crystals create intended transformation, we need to follow our intuitions and test them in the field of our life experiences.

Crystals and Energy

Crystals are pyroelectric; when heated or cooled, crystals change vibration and reverse their existing polarity and electrical flow along the crystal's length. While investigating crystal pyroelectricity in 1880, Jacques and Pierre Curie also discovered that crystals are piezoelectric. Piezoelectric is the charge generated by mechanical stress. The prefix *piezo-* is from the

Greek meaning "squeeze" or "press." Not all minerals can be activated by human or mechanical pressure. Of the 32 classes of crystal symmetry, 21 are capable of piezoelectric activation. For instance, only blue diamonds, yet all quartz crystals, tourmalines, and topazes, are piezoelectric. This is why many crystals become energized by being hand-held, rubbed, and warmed. When we energize crystals, crystals mutually energize us. When we program crystals with intention, we mutually program ourselves with the same intent. The field of energy, information, and intention forms a mutual resonance between crystals and humans physically and consciously.

Crystals and Memory

In addition to electromagnetic capability, crystals hold and store information, and hold and transmit intention. Let's take a moment to explore these facets of crystal power. We discuss crystal skulls more fully in chapter 10, but here we present a prevailing theory that authentic crystal skulls have been programmed and store a vast library of human, Earth, and galactic history; very advanced scientific and technological development; and the methodology for accelerated mental and spiritual evolution. The data storage capability of the crystal skulls presumes that a highly advanced technological and spiritual culture did this in the past. Although that level of technology is not well known now, we do have current examples approaching this application of crystal data storage with older 3D and now 5D optical data storage. For example, researchers at the University of South Australia and University of Adelaide are working to perfect the "Superman" memory crystal.[10] Scientists have been able to write information into the lattice of microscopic crystals using femtosecond (10^{-15} second) laser light pulses.[11] The 5D data inscribed is rewritable and can hold a petabyte (1024 terabytes) of information reliably for well over millennia. As comparison, the human brain is estimated to be able to hold 2.5 petabytes of data. Current scientific knowledge has not invented a way to inscribe that amount of data directly and reliably into quartz crystals. Yet. We are asserting, however, that focused human consciousness and energy can input data into crystals and can retrieve that memory without technological interface because gems and crystals themselves are inherent technology already coupled with human consciousness. This line of reasoning is part of the revisioning of the scientific paradigm of psychoenergetics presented by Dr. William Tiller.

Crystals, Quanta, and Intention

We approach crystals and quantum entanglement by examining subatomic particles. Two subatomic particles like photons can become paired with opposite charges, one with up-spin, the other with down-spin. The particles are posited to exist in all possible states until one of them is measured. At that moment, and that moment only, the condition of the other particle is instantaneously determined. The conundrum for quantum physics is that if the paired particles are in close proximity, one here and the other down the block, then the information from one particle can travel to the other within the speed of light, which many physicists point out is the universal speed limit. However, what if one particle of the pair is here and the other is at the star Sirius, which is 8.6 light years distant from Earth? Measuring one particle of the pair instantly affects the other, but the information would have to travel faster than light can travel. This problem disturbed Einstein so much that he characterized it as "spooky action at a distance."* To resolve this impasse, some theorists have posited that there must be particles that can travel faster than light speed. These are called tachyons, but physicists currently lack experimental proof of hypothetical tachyons.

Dr. William Tiller:
New Scientific Paradigm

The contemporary scientific model can calculate quantum mathematics very well, but cannot adequately explain the universe in which matter, energy,

---

*Einstein's famous comment about quantum entanglement is the subject of an award-winning book and website exploring the phenomenon of nonlocality. See George Musser, *Spooky Action at a Distance* (New York: Scientific American/Farrar, Straus and Giroux, 2015) or www.spookyactionbook.com.

and mind coexist. Dr. William Tiller avers that only a science that includes consciousness and matter in interaction will have a chance of describing the universe with greater accuracy: "The **real** message for the world's scientific community . . . is that our present frame of reference for viewing the many phenomena of nature is **not large enough** to encompass a reliable, internally self-consistent description of **all** nature's phenomena."[12] He came to this conclusion through study, theory, and experimental verification, especially of the question of intentionality, which is also at the chintamani core as the wish-fulfilling gem. What Dr. Tiller and his associates experimentally and repeatedly demonstrated is that intentions can and do affect physical processes. They began with the intention of increasing or decreasing the pH of water.[13] They used an intermediary device they invented and named an IIED (Intention Imprinted Electrical Device) to focus the intention. They found statistically significant and replicable results that the pH of water could be changed with intention via an IIED, both of which constituted the main experimental variables. This takes the Heisenberg effect of expectations from the eerie world of particle physics into the everyday, everywhere world of water.

Dr. Tiller and associates formulated a new scientific paradigm. It begins with the three-dimensional world of space in time that has been the object of past scientific inquiry, which he termed D-space. Next, he postulated that there is also a four-dimensional reciprocal R-space. Altogether, seven dimensions can sometimes operate independently or interact in a coupled state. D-space is where positive mass and energy, electric particles, and electric substances operate and travel less than the speed of light. R-space is where negative mass and negative energy information waves operate and travel greater than light speed.[14] Specific intentions are mediated by hypothetical particles called deltrons, which can interact both with D-space and R-space. Intentions have pathways that move from the realms of spirit and thought into the apparent physical universe to affect matter.[15] Crystals are naturally occurring IIEDs that mediate intention to manifest in the physical world. Crystals and gems are instruments to connect multiple dimensions to accomplish specific intentions.

Master Guan-liang Quan: The Science of Intention

Master Guan-liang Quan (1931–2016) was the author Johndennis' root guru. He was involved in a number of controlled scientific experiments to verify that energy, information, and intention flow affect physical matter. In one experiment, while physically located in Seattle, he was tasked to alter measurable characteristics of one of three test tubes each containing the same liquid solution. The test tubes had different colored stoppers and were placed next to one another in a Houston laboratory. He was told to affect only one of the test tube samples while leaving the other two unchanged. The testers identified the target sample either by the test tube's stopper color or by its position (right, middle, or left). After satisfying the investigators that he could produce the intended effects remotely, consistently, and directly, he participated in more experiments. The follow-up experiments introduced extra variations, such as using different solutions and different intended alterations. Though different, the experiments were similar to one another in design and result. It made for a good experimental protocol but contributed to very slow overall progress.

After working with physicists over the course of his life to prove that intentionally directed energy, light, and information can shape material processes on small and large scales, Master Quan grew weary of the snail-like progress toward understanding. He was a trained chemist who translated scientific works from German into Chinese, so he clearly understood how scientific knowledge advances through experiment and theory. Master Quan was also a highly adept practitioner of qigong, Traditional Chinese Medicine, and Tibetan Vajrayana Buddhism in the Nyingma school. Through a practice called *Xian Lung Fa Men,* or Spiral Dragon Dharma System, as well as other advanced practices of Tibetan tantric yoga, Master Quan perfected the art of healing as well as abilities to shape the environment from the state of enlightened mind. He was very interested in revising the materially oriented scientific paradigm to include, as Dr. Tiller and associates have stated, the whole spectrum of natural phenomena, giving recognition to consciousness as center. Master Quan spoke his own axiom often: "Science is Buddhism and Buddhism is science! But all scientists and Buddhists do not understand this yet."

Dr. Marcel Vogel:
Advanced Crystal Science

Another scientist who worked extensively with crystals and intention was Marcel Vogel (1917–1991). He was an IBM engineer for twenty-seven years and an inventor awarded thirty-two patents in phosphor technology, liquid crystal systems, luminescence, and magnetics. His inventions in liquid crystals initiated the field of LCD technology. His work with crystals began as an investigation of the technological potentials for crystals in the field of electronics. Dr. Vogel was also a mystic who studied sentiency and communication in plants, meditation, yoga, and healing. He experimented with the use of crystals in meditation and healing and explored how crystals might direct intention more potently. This led him to create and perfect various types of "Vogel crystals." He knew that lasers are a focused and coherent stream of light capable of much more than diffuse light. Dr. Vogel reasoned that through the use of specifically faceted crystals, intention could be transformed from diffuse to coherent. This inspiration led him to create, or perhaps re-create, crystals in a form of intentional technology similar to Dr. Tiller's IIEDs.

Dr. Vogel tested his uniquely faceted crystals to direct intention coherently for meditation and healing. For these different purposes, he designed differently faceted crystals in basic patterns. Meditation crystals were designed with one pointed end, but with the other flat, in order to be able to direct and accumulate energy and thought. Healing crystals were designed to be doubly terminated, with one end blunter and the other sharper, in order to direct energy from the therapist more precisely to physical areas in need of healing (figure 7.5). In practice, since Dr. Vogel faceted his own crystals, he tuned each crystal first to the frequency of water, and then to the underlying energy resonance of the person who would use the crystal either for meditating or healing. The crystal was the external technology, but it needed to be coupled with the focused intent of the meditator or healer. Dr. Vogel used both imaginal vision and breath to program crystals, and to pulse specific intentions through them. A faceted crystal created focused coherence for any given intention and was able to broadcast that intention in a particular direction. Dr. Vogel concluded that love is our primary responsibility and is

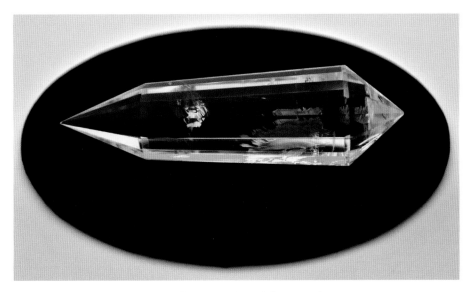

Figure 7.5. Vogel healing crystal faceting by Ray Pinto.
Photo by Kaleigh Brown

the power that maintains the material universe.[16] He envisioned love to be the primary motivator needed as the root of all specific intentions. In his pursuit of the mystical application of crystal technology, Dr. Vogel came to hold a parallel view of the gurus and rishis: quartz crystals must be powered by unlimited compassion.

Dr. Erwin Schrodinger:
DNA and the Aperiodic Crystal

In 1944, Erwin Schrodinger published a book of recent lectures, *What Is Life: The Physical Aspect of the Living Cell.* He speculated as to what bio-logical structure might be able to carry the complex "script-code" of living organisms. Genes were known then, and the DNA molecule was being actively researched and deconstructed. In 1953, Watson and Crick published their findings on the molecular structure of DNA leading to a Nobel Prize in medicine. Schrodinger posited that the carrier of life, "the most essen-tial part of a living cell—the chromosome fibre—may suitably be called *an aperiodic crystal.*"[17] This notion stretches the common dictionary entry that a crystal is transparent and almost colorless quartz. The online Oxford English Dictionary defines crystal as: "A piece of homogeneous solid substance having a natural geometrically regular form with symmetrically arranged plane faces."[18] In chemistry, however, a crystal is considered as any solid of atoms, ions, or molecules arranged in a pattern that is periodic and three-dimensional.[19] Later, with further research and discovery, amorphous crystals (like glass), quasicrystals, aperiodic crystals, time crystals, and virtual algorithmic crystals have expanded our concept of just what a crystal may be. And for us, what might the chintamani be?

What we have been calling crystals are more formally described as periodic crystals, in that they have order and symmetry in three dimensions. After describing periodic crystals as fascinating and complex material structures, Schrodinger compared a periodic to an aperiodic crystal: "The difference in structure is of the same kind as that between an ordinary wallpaper in which the same pattern is repeated again and again in regular periodicity and a masterpiece embroidery, say a Raphael tapestry, which shows no dull repetition, but an elaborate, coherent, meaningful design traced by the great master."[20] Most of the chintamani earth gems and crystals we have discussed are periodic crystals. Quasicrystals, or more formally, quasiperiodic crystals, have an ordered structure that is not periodic because it is only partially symmetrical. Quasicrystals cannot replicate seamlessly in all three dimensions. To our knowledge, no earth chintamani is a quasicrystal. Amorphous crystals are random and have no periodic structure. The Roerich chintamani has been speculated to be the amorphous crystal moldavite. Research into time crystals holds promise in identifying a chintamani occurring in time cycles. In 2012, Dr. Frank Wilczek of MIT, a 2004 Nobel laureate in physics, first proposed that there may be crystals arrayed in a repeating pattern in time instead of a three-dimensional pattern in space.[21] In 2017, two separate materials were experimentally discovered that could act as stable time crystals using processes beginning with ytterbium ions and diamonds. A Harvard research group, directed by Mikhail Lukin, pulsed lasers into defects of diamonds called nitrogen vacancy centers. They observed a change in spin pattern of the nitrogen vacancy centers occurring at timing intervals different from the timed laser pulses. This new timing became a stable periodic pattern. Diamonds can serve as an alternate basis for time crystals and possess the inherent technology to transform into time crystal chintamanis.

According to the International Union of Crystallography, an aperiodic crystal lacks or has weak three-dimensional periodicity.[22] In the short run, it is unable to maintain indefinite symmetry, but in the long run, it may create another scale of symmetry. Schrodinger noted that avoiding endless periodic crystal repetition in favor of the aperiodic creates the means to convey the complex code of life. He reasoned the necessity for more complicated organic molecules "in which every atom, and every group of atoms, plays an individual role, not entirely equivalent to that of many others (as is the case in a periodic structure). We might quite properly call that an aperiodic crystal or solid and express our hypothesis by saying: We believe a gene—or perhaps the whole chromosome fibre—to be an aperiodic solid."[23] Aperiodic crystals, especially DNA, open profound implications as to how they connect and interact with the chintamani.

Dr. Bruce Lipton:
Epigenetics and Reprogramming DNA

A crystal that is periodic can receive, store, and transmit information and intention in a wide or narrow band depending on the synergy of the practitioner and actual crystal. An aperiodic crystal can do the same, but in the case of DNA can also replicate, check for accuracy, and transmit information, and possibly intentions, with dynamic spontaneity in reaction to the environment. Since we can program crystals, we can program our own DNA to function in the direction of our highest intentions. As a researcher in medical genetics, Dr. Bruce Lipton contends exactly this from the viewpoint of epigenetics. Protein interaction can overwrite the expression of any underlying DNA message, meaning that the environment is more important to the result than the underlying code.[24] He also cites that there are quantum mechanisms that influence proteins that ultimately modify DNA expression, namely: "entanglement (wherein one energy source couples and influences another energy source), tunneling (wherein particles pass through physical barriers), and superposition (wherein particles *simultaneously* experience all pathways and then choose the most effective one on which to travel—these particles are effectively in many places at the same time!)."[25] Dr. Lipton identifies subconscious programming as a main influencer of a person's environment and therefore as an important translator of DNA into body, health, and behavior traits. Erasing negative subconscious programming is the first step, followed by conscious reprogramming of a chosen intention.[26] Erasing old programs and replacing them with more positive intentions can be amplified by meditating with gems and crystals, which we discuss in more depth in chapter 11. The resonance of periodic and aperiodic crystals, or the resonance of the chintamani with DNA and intention, is a profound subject that we cannot adequately explain but that we can explore experimentally in our own lives. Consider that DNA and crystals can couple to carry the same programmed intention in a mutually reinforcing energy field.

Tachyolithic Technology

We have explored outer and inner aspects of crystal technology. The outer technology resides inside the crystal and is bound up with all the qualities of mineral chemistry, color, shape, energy state, information storage, as well as crystal transmitting and receiving capabilities. The inner technology resides in humans, found in DNA, myeloconia, chakras, acupuncture meridians, aura, and consciousness, all of which can be focused through intention. In addition, there are inherent and created components of both outer and inner technology. We stated that crystals are inherent technology, but also discovered that inherent crystal technology can be amplified by faceting, and by clearing, and then by re-embedding intentions into crystals. This part of created crystal technology includes a range of techniques for using crystals more effectively for various purposes. Inherent human technology is the open-ended capability of body, energy, and mind to connect with the multiverse. Self-cultivation refers to the created aspects that increase human capability. This includes self-study, moral development, and practices such as compassionate action, prayer, qigong, yoga, mantra, contemplation, and meditation. These practices allow the inherent mental and spiritual qualities of humans to focus intentions more coherently.

In between the technology of crystals and humans is the capability for these two to "couple," to use one of Dr. Tiller's terms. Both technologies engage around intention to move information and aspiration back and forth from the material and spiritual realms, or between D-space and R-space to create envisioned change. Chapter 12 on chintamani practices will develop the inquiry into increasing resonant interaction of human and crystal technologies in ways readers can test directly for themselves. The practices we provide are a manual for discovering and using the wish-fulfilling gem wisely.

Our concluding topic here is a brief contemplation of this book's title and subtitle: *The Chintamani Crystal Matrix: Quantum Intention and the Wish-Fulfilling Gem.* The chintamani is a powerful, multidimensional gem for accomplishing intent whose renown reaches from the mists of myth into the applications of current scientific research. It is at every possible juncture of evolutionary choice. The chintamani is engaged at every node of the matrix of life, in and out of time simultaneously. The chintamani presides over the entangled choices of the paths of power and of love. It is at the nexus of the quantum entanglement of moral intentions. The scale of the chintamani is super galactic and the incalculable distances of its domain rely on faster-than-light actions to resolve states of paired decisions instantly. We introduce the term "tachyolithic" to describe the chintamani as a stone that can interface with information and energy instantaneously and at the speed of thought even at galactic distances. The density of stone in contrast to the deft superluminality of subatomic particles captures the paradox of the chintamani and of crystals in general. Consider the question of not only what the chintamani can accomplish but what the chintamani ought to accomplish in the hands of a spiritually developed being.

8

The Crystal Matrix

*Gems in Engineered Grids to Create
the Harmony of the Spheres*

*Thou hast been in Eden the garden of God; every precious stone
was thy covering, the sardius, topaz, and the diamond, the beryl,
the onyx, and the jasper, the sapphire, the emerald, and the
carbuncle, and gold: the workmanship of thy tabrets and of thy
pipes was prepared in thee in the day that thou wast created.*

*Thou art the anointed cherub that covereth: and I have set thee so:
thou wast upon the holy mountain of God: thou hast walked up
and down in the midst of the stones of fire.*

EZEKIEL 28:13–14

IN WORKING WITH CRYSTALS OR GEMSTONES in grids, we encounter the
concept of alignment. One of the first considerations with respect to gemstones and grids is the purpose and intention of the grid. The purpose dic-
tates both the shape and pattern of the grid as well as the type of crystals
used in the grid. The crystals within the grid are then directed by the practitioner and his or her purpose or intention. Many people think of crystals
either as simply rocks with no energy or as a magic talisman. The truth
exists between the two extremes. Crystal energy is interdependent and
relies on human interaction for activation and focus. This chapter is the

first of a few chapters that set the stage for tangible practice with crystals.

Historically, gemstones have been set into precious metals and grids for spiritual and evolutionary purposes. Jewels have been set in crowns, scepters, and necklaces since time immemorial. While wearing any stones around the neck can be powerful, there are a few legendary necklaces worth noting that seem to have been used for purposes beyond simple adornment. The Egyptian menat necklace of Hathor was used in religious ceremonies and was made of metals, glass, agate, carnelian, lapis lazuli, and turquoise beads.[1] In the Nordic lands, Freyja acquired a magical necklace from the dwarves. The brilliant, golden necklace, called Brisingamen, was strongly associated with the goddess, and assisted her with fertility, magnetism, and invisibility.[2] In Greece, the magic necklace of Harmonia was fashioned in the shape of two snakes and was made of gold and jewels. It was reputed to bring eternal youth and beauty to its wearer, including a curse to all who wore it except Harmonia, the daughter of Aphrodite.[3] In Tibetan and Indian imagery, necklaces and jewelry adorn the gods, goddesses, and other mythical figures. Surrounding the Buddhas and Bodhisattvas are rings of jewels in their auric fields. Tara, a Buddhist Bodhisattva, wears little clothing but is always heavily adorned with necklaces and jewels.

On a larger scale, grids and alignments involving stone circles and similar formations are employed for harnessing earth energy and connecting with star and planetary alignments. Whether working with small gemstones or large granite boulders, humankind has been using stones for empowering purpose, intention, and energy since ancient times. The effectiveness of crystals in a matrix can be compared to a computer program. The program is only as good as the user. As such, when working with crystal grids, the effectiveness is largely dependent upon the focus and alignment of the practitioner with his or her intentions and how well that intention aligns with the stones and grid shape employed.

Astrology and Birthstones

When considering wearing or meditating with gemstones, it is natural to look to astrological birthstones. There are classical gem associations for the twelve astrological signs (see table on the following page). Unfortunately, there is a great deal of confusion about the birthstones, especially in the Western approach to astrology. Certain stones may be assigned zodiac signs based more on gemstone supply and demand in the mineral industry than on any association with astrology. Jewelry and gift stores tend to approach birthstone marketing based on the twelve months of the calendar year rather than the timing of the twelve astrological signs. However, the notion of working with birthstones has its foundation in astrology, so relying on the birth month, instead of the astrological sign, makes the use of birthstones arbitrary. A more meaningful approach uses the birthstones for balance of the elements and energies within astrology.

WESTERN ASTROLOGY SIGNS AND BIRTHSTONES							
HOUSE	SIGN	SYMBOL	DATE	GEMSTONE	COLOR	MODALITY	ELEMENT
1	Aries	♈	Mar 21	Diamond	Clear	Cardinal	Fire
2	Taurus	♉	April 20	Emerald	Green	Fixed	Earth
3	Gemini	♊	May 21	Agate	Multi	Mutable	Air
4	Cancer	♋	June 21	Pearl	White	Cardinal	Water
5	Leo	♌	July 23	Ruby	Red	Fixed	Fire
6	Virgo	♍	Aug 23	Peridot	Green	Mutable	Earth
7	Libra	♎	Sep 23	Sapphire	Blue	Cardinal	Air
8	Scorpio	♏	Oct 23	Opal	Multi	Fixed	Water
9	Sagittarius	♐	Nov 23	Topaz	Orange	Mutable	Fire
10	Capricorn	♑	Dec 22	Garnet	Red	Cardinal	Earth
11	Aquarius	♒	Jan 20	Amethyst	Violet	Fixed	Air
12	Pisces	♓	Feb 19	Aquamarine	Blue	Mutable	Water

Examining the birthstones through the polarity of signs helps in understanding the energetic properties of the signs and even provides a balanced use in working with stone energies through the birth sign. To work in a more integrated way with astrology and birthstones, wear and/or meditate with the four stones that represent the opposition and squares to your natal sun position. This brings the sun sign into optimal balance between the four elements fire, earth, air, and water. To obtain a deeper appreciation of the nuances of the birthstones, wear the stone, but learn its fundamental energetic properties as well. As we are bridging subtle energies with mineral science, the following table correlates the chemical formula, crystal system, and a primary subtle energetic property of each birthstone connected to the astrological signs and houses to establish more conscious alignment.

ENERGETIC PROPERTIES OF BIRTHSTONES				
HOUSE	SIGN	BIRTHSTONE	CRYSTAL SYSTEM & CHEMISTRY	PROPERTY
1	Aries	Diamond	Cubic Carbon (C)	Empower
2	Taurus	Emerald	Hexagonal Beryllium ($Be_3Al_2SiO_6$)	Generate
3	Gemini	Agate	Trigonal Silica (SiO_2)	Inform
4	Cancer	Pearl	Amorphous Calcite ($CaCO_3$)	Nurture
5	Leo	Ruby	Hexagonal Aluminum (Al_2O_3)	Create
6	Virgo	Peridot	Orthorhombic Magnesium (Mg_2SiO_4)	Organize
7	Libra	Sapphire	Hexagonal Aluminum (Al_2O_3)	Balance

			ENERGETIC PROPERTIES OF BIRTHSTONES (continued)	
HOUSE	**SIGN**	**BIRTHSTONE**	**CRYSTAL SYSTEM & CHEMISTRY**	**PROPERTY**
8	Scorpio	Opal	Amorphous Silica ($SiO_2 \, nH_2O$)	Transform
9	Sagittarius	Topaz	Orthorhombic Aluminum ($Al_2SiO_4(F,OH_2)$)	Expand
10	Capricorn	Garnet	Isometric or Cubic Magnesium $Mg_3Al_2Si_3O_{12}$ (Pyrope)	Complete
11	Aquarius	Amethyst	Trigonal Silica (SiO_2)	Innovate
12	Pisces	Aquamarine	Hexagonal Beryllium ($Be_3Al_2SiO_6$)	Inspire

As an example, in bridging crystal science and astrological birthstones, we will consider the diamond more closely. It is the first gemstone listed in the table and represents the initiating, sulfuric energy of the Aries fire sign. It is the first sign of the zodiac and marks the arrival of spring on the equinox in March. Through mass marketing, diamonds are now widely sold as marital engagement rings, but historically they have been associated with power. They are ideal for amplifying intention, but we first need clarity and purification in our alignment, or our intentions turn into disappointments. The clear diamond is pure carbon, which represents the structure of life itself. Rated 10 on the Mohs scale, diamond defines the standard for mineral hardness.

The diamond's crystal system is cubic, so it is strongly associated with foundation, but its crystal habit is octahedral (figures 7.4 [page 159] and 8.1). Crystal habit represents the external shape of crystals, while the crystal system is the lattice of crystal structure at the atomic level, a level that is not visible to us. We visibly interact and observe the crystal through its crystal habit. Crystals are highly complex, representing a composite of elements, atomic structures, and external shapes. A single crystal, in and of itself, is a complex matrix. Working with crystal grids, we bring shape and form to our intentions using the crystals as powerful nodes in the crystal grid matrix. Using the shapes inherent in the diamond crystal aligns with the energies of the diamond and helps to focus intention. In geometry, these shapes have different perspectives. Using spherical tiling and stereographic projection, the octahedron appears as three concentric circles, not unlike the triple-jewel chintamani symbol we encounter in art, philosophy, and alchemy (figure 8.2 on the following page). Through the diamond, we encounter the seeding of life through carbon, the visible octahedron, a platonic air element that focuses our thinking and intentions, but the cubic structure of the earth element grounds that intention and gives it form and substance.

In Buddhism, the highest expression of spirituality is referred to as the diamond mind and the rainbow body, both of which are expressed in the diamond. In meditating with the complex and multifaceted forms of the diamond, both its interior and exterior, we encounter the true radiance and brilliance of nature through crystals. Use these forms as crystal grids either meditatively or in creating external grids to amplify and direct attention when working with diamonds. We presented eight major crystal system

Figure 8.1. The raw diamond crystal habit shape is octahedral.

Figure 8.2. Stereographic projection of an octahedron overlaying image of a faceted diamond.
Digital composite by Kaleigh Brown

structures in figure 7.4 (page 159) as an aid to develop mental or tangible grids for focusing and embedding intention.

In astrology, squares occur when planets are positioned at 90-degree angles to one another. Each sign is organized by both modality (cardinal, fixed, mutable) and element (fire, earth, air, water), creating a three-by-four grid. All cardinal elements square one another; all fixed elements square one another; and all mutable elements square one another. Astrological squares represent work we need to accomplish, appearing as both interior and exterior obstacles in our life. They are challenges we need to face and solve in order to evolve. When working with stones energetically for healing, balance, and empowerment, it may be beneficial to work with stones that represent opposition or squares to the natal solar position whose energy we seek to transform (figures 8.3, 8.4, 8.5). For example, if a Cancer water sign needs to integrate other elements alchemically, in addition to the nurturing pearl, a person with a Cancer sun could work energetically with the garnet for grounded earth energy, the fiery diamond for personal empowerment, and the blue sapphire for mental balance and discrimination (figure 8.3). Each sign has two opposing pole stones, but four element stones to balance the whole mode.

Figure 8.3. The cardinal signs and birthstones represent initiating, sulfuric energy. Pearl is nurturing compared to garnet's grounding and strength. Sapphire offers wisdom to the power of diamond.

Digital composite by Kaleigh Brown

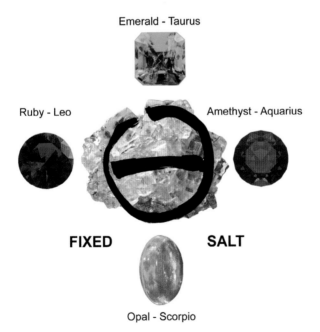

Figure 8.4. The fixed signs and birthstones are solid and are represented by the alchemical element salt. Opal offers watery transformation to emerald's abundance. Ruby is fiery compared to the cool violet of amethyst.

Digital composite by Kaleigh Brown

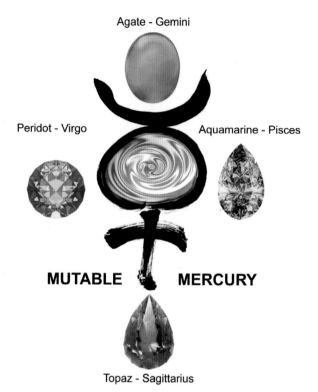

Figure 8.5. The mutable signs and birthstones are flexible through alchemical mercury. Peridot offers tangible creative power to aquamarine's inspiration and vision. Topaz intensifies focus and purpose to agate and quartz's distribution of information and knowledge.

Digital composite by Kaleigh Brown

Trines (one third of a circle) in astrology refer to planetary positions connected at 120-degree angles. They are considered complementary and can refer to gifts and talents that we develop and use. There are four triplicities, each containing all three of the same elements, creating groups of fire, earth, air, and water (figures 8.6, 8.7, 8.8, and 8.9). Each triplicity has stones that work together harmoniously as they embody the element. For example, an Aquarius is naturally innovative and offers foresight and spiritual vision, which is complemented by the violet-colored amethyst representing energies of the mental and spiritual crown chakra. To fully empower the visionary ability of Aquarius, other subtle qualities are also needed. The Aquarius

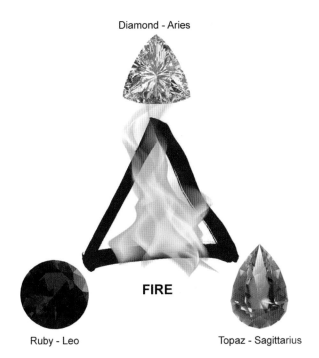

Figure 8.6. Triple gems of fire: diamond is empowering, ruby is energizing, and topaz intensifies focus.

Digital composite by Kaleigh Brown

Figure 8.7. Triple gems of earth: garnet is grounding, emerald generates abundance, and peridot is creative and organizing.

Digital composite by Kaleigh Brown

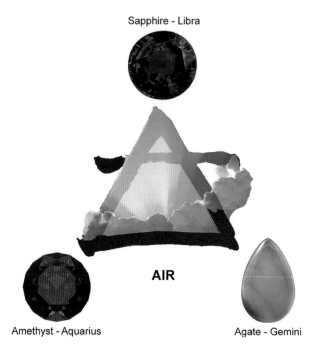

Figure 8.8. Triple gems of air: blue sapphire brings wisdom and balance, amethyst provides spiritual vision, and agate and quartz crystal accesses information and knowledge.

Digital composite by Kaleigh Brown

needs to use agate or quartz to synthesize and network information from Gemini, and the blue sapphire to incorporate wisdom, discrimination, and mental balance from Libra. Working with the Gemini and Libra air stones also helps the Aquarius to make stronger, more meaningful connections with people. Working with multiple birthstone crystals instead of just one birthstone offers an integrative method in learning to achieve holistic balance.

The point of astrology is not to focus on one sign, but to integrate all the modalities, elements, and zodiac signs to achieve wholeness. It is beneficial to acquire all twelve birthstones and work with them energetically for healing, balance, and empowerment. The birthstones offer a tangible and strategic way to align the correct energies with the focus of the intention. There are myriad ways in which the twelve birthstones could be applied to empower intention. For example, if a chart is weak in earth energy, which could manifest as blocks in abundance, (1) wear one or more of the earth stones; (2) build an earth grid

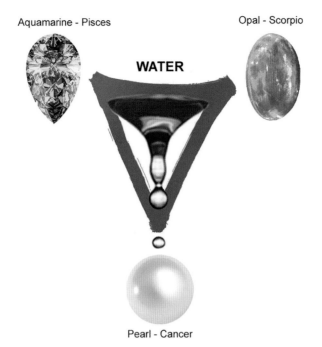

Figure 8.9. Triple gems of water: pearl is nurturing, opal is emotionally transforming, and aquamarine is creative and inspiring.
Digital composite by Kaleigh Brown

using the three earth stones emerald, peridot, and garnet; and/or (3) meditate with one or more earth stones while focusing on the subtle properties of the sign and the stone (generating, organizing, and completing). The twelve birthstones provide a tangible way to build personal grids useful for aligning with energies of lunar cycles, solstices, equinoxes, and other astrological phenomena. There is a link between the birthstone, its color, and the astrological sign's season. Wearing gemstones during the season in which the sign appears is beneficial, as it harmonizes the wearer with the season. The zodiac is like a medicine wheel that is a guide for aligning with the signs, the planets, and the seasons at the right time (figure 8.10 on the following page).

The Navaratna

Historically, the association between gemstones and astrology dates from antiquity, and arguably the earliest recorded associations originate from India.

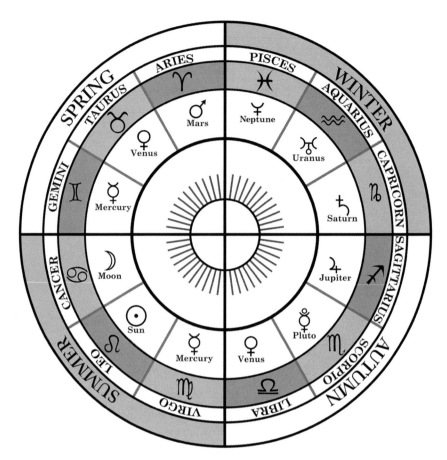

Figure 8.10. The zodiac presented as a medicine wheel
showing the signs divided by the four seasons.

Indian or Vedic astrology is intimately associated with the use of gemstones
to such an extent that astrological readings in India typically incorporate a
gemstone prescription. Unlike Western astrology, Vedic astrology connects
gemstones with the planets rather than the zodiac signs. Vedic astrology does
not recognize planets in the solar system beyond Saturn but does include
gemstones for the north and south nodes of the moon (Rahu and Ketu),
which are considered shadow planets. Collectively, these stones are referred
to as the Navaratna, Sanskrit for "nine gems" (see table). Astrology, known
as Jyotish, and its connection to gemological science generally date to the
sixth century CE, although the Navaratna developed gradually over a longer period. The interconnectedness between the chakras, planets, gemstones,

colors, herbal medicine, and mantras make this a complex system of healing, balance, and enlightenment useful for alchemically transformative practices. The Navaratna is recognized in most Asian countries and specifically in the Indian religions of Hinduism, Buddhism, and Jainism. In Thailand, the Navaratna is important to the Thai Royal Family, who award the Ancient and Auspicious Order of the Nine Gems.

THE NAVARATNA: VEDIC ASTROLOGY GEMSTONES					
NUMBER*	**PLANET**	**SIGN RULERSHIP**	**GEMSTONE**	**CRYSTAL SYSTEM & CHEMISTRY**	**QUALITY**
1	Sun	Leo	Ruby	Hexagonal Aluminum (Al_2O_3)	Authoritative
2	Moon	Cancer	Pearl	Amorphous Calcite ($CaCO_3$)	Attractive
5	Mercury	Gemini	Emerald	Hexagonal Beryllium ($Be_3Al_2SiO_6$)	Intelligent
6	Venus	Taurus, Libra	Diamond	Cubic Carbon (C)	Creative
9	Mars	Aries, Scorpio	Coral	Amorphous Calcite ($CaCO_3$)	Courageous
3	Jupiter	Sagittarius, Pisces	Yellow Sapphire	Hexagonal Aluminum (Al_2O_3)	Spiritual
8	Saturn	Capricorn, Aquarius	Blue Sapphire	Hexagonal Aluminum (Al_2O_3)	Wise
4	Rahu	North Node	Hessonite Garnet	Isometric Magnesium ($Mg_3Al_2Si_3O_{12}$)	Rebellious
7	Ketu	South Node	Cat's Eye Chrysoberyl	Orthorhombic Beryllium ($BeAl_2O_4$)	Mystical

*The numbers refer to placement in the Navaratna grid as shown in figure 8.12, page 187.

Rather than wearing individual stones representing a specific planet, it is common to wear the Navaratna, all nine gems set in gold in a special grid with the ruby representing the central sun in the center and the other planetary stones circling the center (figure 8.11). The circular configuration of the stones is laid out like a compass with directions. In this sense, the stone grid is serving as a directional unit in symbolic space. The grid shows Jupiter (yellow sapphire) representing north and Mars (coral) representing south. The Navaratna can also be set as a rectangular grid of nine stones (figure 8.12). There is a specific arrangement of planetary stones both in the circular and in the three-by-three square grid. The top half of the Navaratna grid is comprised of benefic-positive planets, while the bottom half are malefic-negative planets. The three middle stones divide the positive and negative planets via the element of fire, which in alchemy is the element used to carry out transformation. When the Navaratna is set as a numerological three-by-three grid, numeric patterns are evident in the system (for example, the sum of each vertical column is 15).

Planetary numerology and qualities in the Vedic system are discussed more fully by Harish Johari.[4] The Jyotish gemstones are worn with the intention of transforming or amplifying a planetary energy in a native's astrological chart. There are complex rituals associated with the gemstone's purchase, purification, and setting that activate and fuse the energy of the stone with the wearer. The stones correspond to colors, chakras, and mantras in the complex Jyotish system and "when wearing gems in rings . . . if the gems are positioned according to their corresponding planets, alliances with those planets form."[5] Vedic astrologers perceive gems as embodying the essences of planets, which can balance a variety of spiritual, emotional, and physical conditions. Johari says that "astrologers and gem therapists use gems to compensate for the loss of energy caused by the weak planets (i.e., debilitated, exiled, badly aspected), to provide missing chemicals and reestablish electrochemical balance, or to provide more strength to the exalted favorable planets."[6] The light radiating from the seven classical planets and two nodes affects Earth in subtle ways and, according to Jyotish, this light can be enhanced and directed through gemstones that align with the channeled light from the respective planet. One reason why Jyotish does not recognize planets beyond Saturn is simply that the light from the outer planets, Uranus, Neptune, and Pluto, is not visible to the naked eye.

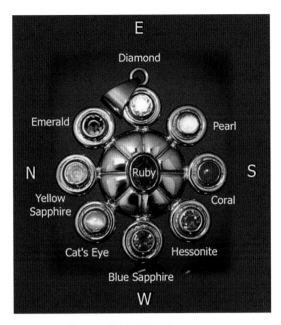

Figure 8.11. The Navaratna.

5	6	2
Emerald	Diamond	Pearl
3	1	9
Yellow Sapphire	Ruby	Coral
7	8	4
Cat's Eye	Blue Sapphire	Hessonite Garnet

Figure 8.12. Square three-by-three grid of Navaratna gems.

Using gemstones and crystals to heal, balance, or empower subtle energies is a combination of working with chemistry and the physics of energy and light. As an example, there is a parallel between the Jyotish association of Saturn with the blue sapphire gem and recent NASA discoveries.

Blue sapphire is a corundum crystal colored by trace elements of iron and titanium. Sapphire crystals form as a hexagon in nature, both internally and externally (figure 8.13). Is it a coincidence that the planet Saturn has a hexagon perfectly formed at its north pole? Saturn's hexagon represents a powerful vortex jet stream of energy whose function is not fully understood by astronomers (figure 8.14). Saturn is a gas giant predominantly comprised of liquid metallic hydrogen, a state of matter that does not exist on Earth, but which has been likened to liquid mercury, meaning that it is a highly conductive metal. There are energies on Saturn that are alien here on Earth, which could be one of the reasons why Jyotish likens Saturn to uneasy and sometimes difficult to understand energies considered malefic or harmful. Saturn is considered the Lord of Time and is associated with karma. The blue sapphire is designed to teach patience, dedication, learning through difficult experience, and wisdom through the activation of the third eye. It is by working through Saturn's difficult energies that it is possible to learn how to break free from the limitations caused by the Wheel of Time. The energy of the hexagon, with its six sides, symbolizes structure and order. Saturn, the hexagon, and the blue sapphire of the third eye have connections to the Wheel of Time and are a key to understanding the chintamani matrix.

Figure 8.13. Internal and external hexagonal
crystal pattern in raw sapphire.

Photo by Rob Lavinsky

Figure 8.14. Hexagon jet stream at the top of Saturn's north pole.
Image taken on September 9, 2016, by the Cassini-Huygens spacecraft
using a wide-angle camera at approximately 750,000 miles from Saturn.
Image courtesy of NASA/JPL-Caltech/Space Science Institute

Another configuration that is more important in Vedic astrology than modern Western astrology is the nodal dragon, which is comprised of both north and south nodes. The degree in which the north node is placed in the natal chart is a highly significant. In the Navaratna grid, there are two shadow planets, Rahu and Ketu, which are positions the moon makes crossing the ecliptic and are connected to eclipses. The nodes have a pronounced effect on our emotions and important lessons to teach us about karma. Rahu, the north node, represents the head of the dragon and provides ambition and drive to overcome obstacles in our life while Ketu, the south node, is the tail of the dragon and represents our past. As the symbolism involves a dragon or a snake, the nodes also represent kundalini energy along the spine with Ketu at the base of the spine and Rahu at the top. Gemologically, Rahu is represented by the hessonite garnet, which is a strong life force gemstone containing a complex composite of minerals. Ketu is represented by a cat's eye chrysoberyl (or similar cat's eye stone). A mysterious and unusual stone, it literally resembles a cat's eye. Symbolically, cat's eye stone helps us to see what is hidden or veiled behind us and in the unconscious. Overall, the cardinal directions built into the Navaratna talisman in combination with the nodal dragon make the Vedic system strongly suited for amplifying intention while navigating life direction.

The Breastplate of Judgment

The Ark of the Covenant was the sacred golden chest carried by the Israelites in the Old Testament that contained the Ten Commandments. While the ark is a well-known and much sought after artifact, it is complemented by a lesser-known though equally powerful artifact, the Breastplate of Judgment. The breastplate, also known as the Hoshen, was a square golden plate set with twelve gemstones; each gemstone was engraved with one of the names of the twelve Tribes of Israel. It was worn by the High Priest when he was administering before the Ark of the Covenant during Yom Kippur, the annual Day of Atonement. Only the High Priest could enter the holy place in the temple where the Ark of the Covenant was placed. There were golden figures of two cherubim above the ark with the mercy seat placed between the cherubim. Per Exodus 25:22, the Lord met with and communed with the High Priest from the mercy seat over the ark. The High Priest was carefully instructed as to his apparel and when and under what conditions he could appear in front of the ark. The interaction between the High Priest and the energy emanating from the mercy seat was so intense and dangerous that a rope was tied to the High Priest's feet so that he could be pulled out of the holy place in case he died while in the Ark's presence.

The conditions surrounding this interaction involved a spiritual technology incorporating the gold metal of the ark, the golden breastplate with its twelve gemstones, a golden mitre on the High Priest's forehead, two onyx stones on his shoulders, and golden bells on the priestly garment. Although not specifically mentioned in the Torah, it has been inferred that the High Priest could divine the will of the Lord through the gemstones on the breastplate. Josephus, a Jewish historian in the first century CE, remarked the breastplate was also referred to as "the oracle" by the Greeks. He described the breastplate stones as "extraordinary in largeness and beauty; and they were an ornament not to be purchased by men, because of their immense value."[7]

There are detailed specifications for the High Priest's vestments outlined in Exodus that include the tribe name and placement for each of the twelve gemstones in the breastplate. Due to multiple translations, there is a lack of consensus about the gemstones and colors in the breastplate. We list the names of the gemstones from the King James Version of the Bible below and include comparative translations from the Interlinear Bible (a tool that helps identify Greek and Hebrew words with their English translation). There are several alternate versions of the breastplate gem grid that are summarized in a scholarly study by Harrell, et al., which offers a lexical, geological, and archaeological analysis of the breastplate gemstones. In their version, the probable identification of the stones are: (1) carnelian; (2) hematite; (3) serpentinite; (4) turquoise; (5) lapis lazuli; (6) milky quartz; (7) amazonite; (8) banded agate; (9) red jasper; (10) amber; (11) amethyst; (12) multicolored, patterned agate.[8]

THE BREASTPLATE OF JUDGMENT: EXODUS 28:17–20 (AV)

1. Sardius	2. Topaz	3. Carbuncle
4. Emerald	5. Sapphire	6. Diamond
7. Ligure, *Opal*	8. Agate	9. Amethyst
10. Beryl, *Chrysolyte*	11. Onyx	12. Jasper, *Beryl*

The italicized gemstones refer to alternate stones named in the *Interlinear Bible*,[9] a direct translation of the Hebrew Masoretic text (MT) compared to the AV version. The precise stone and color are much debated.

Per instructions in Exodus, the gemstones were set in a three-by-four gold plate grid. The gold plate grid was attached to the High Priest's ephod with golden chains and rings. Exodus 28:29–30 (AV) states:

> And Aaron shall bear the names of the children of Israel in the breastplate of judgment upon his heart, when he goeth in unto the holy place, for a memorial before the Lord continually. And thou shalt put in the breastplate of judgment the Urim and the Thummim; and they shall be upon Aaron's heart, when he goeth in before the Lord: and Aaron shall bear the judgment of the children of Israel upon his heart before the Lord continually.

The Exodus text explains that the High Priest is to set a specific intention in his heart while wearing the breastplate, which could be further focused or amplified through the gemstones in the golden plate. The gemstones were engraved with the names of the Tribes of Israel, so the stones were acting as representatives or containers of energy for the tribes. This connection is further facilitated by the mysterious Urim and Thummim, which are placed in the breastplate. Little is known of the Urim and Thummim, and the Torah does not specifically state what they are, but rabbinical literature has theorized that the Urim and Thummim could refer to light rays shining out of the gemstones or the letters engraved on the gemstones in order to divine the will of the Lord. The possible meaning of the words "Urim" and "Thummim" could translate into "lights and perfections." It has been theorized that the stones in the breastplate and the onyx stones on the shoulders of the High Priest would glow or radiate and that the Urim and the Thummim were special stones handed to Moses by the Lord at the same time the law was given on Mt. Sinai.[10] Graham Hancock discusses pairs of sacred stones knowns as *betyls* that were carried by pre-Islamic tribes.[11] They were thought to be meteoric in nature and had special divine powers. The *betyls* were associated with both the Kaaba and the Ten Commandments written on stone tablets. As previously discussed in chapter 6, *betyls* have also been associated with goddess worship. In Europe, these sacred stones were referred to as *lapis betilis*.* Whatever they

---

*According to Graham Hancock, *lapis betilis* may be the original or an alternate version of *lapsit exillis*, referred to by Wolfram von Eschenbach (Hancock, *Sign and the Seal*, 68–69). See chapter 5 of this text for discussion on the etymological origins of *lapsit exillis*.

were, the mysterious Urim and the Thummim were placed inside a pocket built into the breastplate over the chest of the High Priest.

This form of spiritual technology involving the intention of the High Priest, the special engraved stones over the chest of the priest, and the conductive gold metal plate inlaid with twelve engraved gemstones may have been vital in amplifying the spiritual capacity of the priest to commune with the presence of the Lord over the mercy seat of the ark. There is a theory that the Ark of the Covenant was powered by a fire stone. In their research about the ark, Frank Joseph and Laura Beaudoin theorize that Moses stole a powerful chintamani or Atlantis fire stone from the interior of the Great Pyramid and used it as a power source in the Ark of the Covenant.[12] While this theft is not mentioned in the Torah, it is recorded in Exodus that the Israelites took jewels of gold, silver, and other spoils from the Egyptians.

Just like the Ark of the Covenant, the Breastplate of Judgment disappears from the historical record, but with far less fanfare. Curiously, the breastplate resurfaces in visual and prayer form on Patrick, the patron saint of Ireland (387–465 CE). In Ireland, we have found three stained glass windows of St. Patrick wearing what is uncontrovertibly the Hebrew breastplate described in the Books of Moses. The stained glass images are located in important cathedrals in Dublin, Kildare, and Armagh (figure 8.15 on the following page). Although not explicitly recorded in historic annals, there is a tradition in Celtic Christianity that associates St. Patrick with Judaic customs. Marcus Losack provides a scholarly account of St. Patrick's possible Jewish and royal heritage, through the Roman family name Calpurnius. He mentions the stained glass image of St. Patrick wearing the Hebrew breastplate and royal robes in St. Brigid's Cathedral, which identifies him with the Temple of Solomon.[13] In the versions of St. Patrick wearing the breastplate, there is an additional item around his chest that includes a large circular medallion held by a chain that partially lays over the breastplate. This item is not part of the original vestments described in the Torah. In the Kildare stained glass, St. Patrick is portrayed with his right hand poised in a mudra position, while in the Dublin stained glass, there is a smaller pane depicting St. Patrick eradicating the snakes from Ireland while wearing the breastplate. The stained glass image in Armagh pictures St. Patrick as a king, supporting Losack's theory that Patrick was of royal lineage. A famous Irish Christian prayer or *lorica*

Figure 8.15. St. Patrick wearing the Hebrew Breastplate of Judgment.
Detail of stained glass in St. Patrick's Cathedral Armagh, Northern Ireland.
Photo courtesy of the Very Reverend Gregory Dunstan, Dean of Armagh

is titled "Saint Patrick's Breastplate" and is purported to have been written during St. Patrick's lifetime. The prayer is an invocation of protection calling Christ in the four directions and binding the power of all the elements to the self, which seems to correspond with energies in the breastplate stone grid.

The connection between Celtic and Judaic history is not only found with St. Patrick, but also with Jeremiah, the prophet from the Old Testament, who is believed to have traveled with two princesses from the royal house of Judah and the Stone of Destiny to Ireland (this is more fully explored in chapter 6). Other Celtic myths portray Jeremiah and St. Patrick as the same person, but the historical timeline does not support this theory, as Jeremiah and Patrick are separated by approximately a thousand years. There are other explanations, however, that could connect St. Patrick to the breastplate. According to the apocryphal book of Second Maccabees, Jeremiah hid the Ark of the Covenant (and other temple items) in a cave on

Mount Nebo before the Babylonian invasion of Judah.[14] As a Levite temple priest, Jeremiah would have access not only to the sacred ark but also the breastplate. Connecting this story to St. Patrick, perhaps Jeremiah took the breastplate to Ireland and started a priesthood lineage in Ireland where St. Patrick could have inherited the breastplate, or its construction and spiritual use, through an oral transmission in the priesthood. Another possible connection is that Josephus, who offers a tangible account of how the breastplate looked, as recorded in his *Works of Josephus,* may have had access to the second temple breastplate since he was the son of a Jewish priest. There may be a familial connection between Patrick and Josephus through the royal Roman family name Calpurnius. Romano Piso offers supporting research that Josephus was a part of the Calpurnius family.[15] Perhaps Patrick acquired the breastplate through family inheritance. This is all speculation, but at least offers a reasonable explanation for how St. Patrick acquired access to either the first or second temple breastplate, or knowledge of its spiritual technology. Regardless, like the Ark of the Covenant, the Breastplate of Judgment's whereabouts is a mystery.

From tangible temple artifacts, such as the breastplate, we step toward the less tangible to consider a series of mystical jewels in a spiritual network or matrix. In Jewish mysticism, the Tree of Life refers to a network of ten nodes or spheres known as *sefirot*. The sefirot are interconnected along pathways and are emanations through which the Lord creates. The word *sefirot* means "emanation," but could also mean "enumeration" or "jewel." Each sefirot embodies a different quality, but all work together in balanced unison. Like the Navaratna, when worn as jewelry, the Tree of Life is frequently crafted in metal and used as a talisman with each of the sefirot set as a gemstone. Small breastplate talismans called Hoshen are also crafted into jewelry with gemstones representing the twelve Tribes of Israel.

There is an obvious connection between the twelve stones of the breastplate from the Old Testament and the twelve stones embedded in the walls of New Jerusalem in the New Testament book of Revelation. Revelation is a series of visions written by St. John on the island of Patmos while communing with the archangel Gabriel. St. John describes the measurements of New Jerusalem: foursquare (like a cube), 12,000 furlongs, and 144 cubits. Numerologically, the New Jerusalem measurements involve numbers we have been encountering with gem grids, twelve and nine, but also a three-by-four grid, as there are three gates in each of the four walls (figure 8.16). According to Revelation, the wall was made of jasper, the city was pure gold, but like transparent glass. St. John writes about the four walls having twelve foundations garnished with precious stones. The foundations are garnished in sequence: (1) jasper, (2) sapphire, (3) chalcedony, (4) emerald, (5) sardonyx, (6) sardius, (7) chrysolite, (8) beryl, (9) topaz, (10) chrysoprasus, (11) jacinth, and (12) amethyst. The twelve gates were made out of pearls.[16] Earlier in Revelation, St. John describes the heavenly throne: "And he that sat was to look upon like a jasper and a sardine stone: and there was a rainbow round about the throne, in sight like unto an emerald . . . and before the throne there was a sea of glass like unto crystal."[17] The twelve foundation stones are similar to the twelve stones on the breastplate, but due to translation difficulties, it is not possible to make an exact comparison. The important point is that twelve precious stones, gold, and a transparent glass-like substance are mentioned in detail to describe heaven and the throne, and they are mentioned within the context of a gridded structure comprised of sacred numbers of alignment.

Not only is New Jerusalem filled with crystals and precious stones, but its shape and structure is crystalline. In research on the patterns found in medieval artwork of New Jerusalem, Titus Burckhardt says that "for the medieval spectator it would have been clear that the city was in fact not only a square but a cube . . . the heavenly Jerusalem is really a crystal, not only because of its transparent, incorruptible and luminous substance but also because of its crystalline form."[18] In the illustration of the New Jerusalem (figure 8.16), the twelve stones are portrayed as spheres in the doorways with one sphere containing a special dot. Most of the figures in the doorways wear clothing printed with the special three-dot chintamani motif that we discussed in chapter 5. The checkerboard patterns present on this and similar artworks of New Jerusalem of this time period suggest that the diagram is a grid with embedded numeric formulae. In another variation of these medieval perspectives of New Jerusalem, the foundation stones appear as orbs over the heads of the figures in the doorways (figure 8.17), suggesting that the twelve crystals are more than mere fixtures on walls—they are interpreted as representing the spiritual crystalline transformation of the twelve Tribes of Israel and the names of the twelve apostles written on the twelve gates.

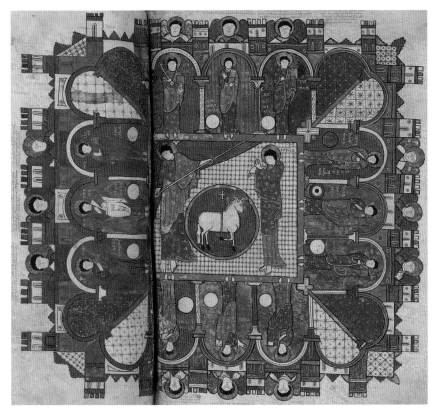

Figure 8.16. New Jerusalem grid. Note the spheres representing
gemstones in the doorways and the three-dot chintamani motifs
on the clothing. Illustrated by Stephanus Garsia in *The Saint-Sever Beatus*,
MS lat. 8878, 11th century, Bibliothèque Nationale, Paris.

Figure 8.17. Angels in the doorways of New Jerusalem.
Note the stone orbs over their heads. Detail from *La Jérusalem nouvelle.
Apoc. XXI.*, 1047, Madrid, Biblioteca Nacional.

Stone Circles and Alignments

Moving from magnificent jewels set in precious metals, we turn to humble, though no less powerful, rocks set in earthen grids. The stones found throughout the world in stone circles, alignments, cairns, and other formations also project energetic properties attributed to their placement in grids, as they would not otherwise possess these energetic properties as a single stone in the Earth's environment. Stonehenge and a few other famous stone circles have been extensively investigated. Here we consider famous sites along with a few lesser-known sites in connection with the energy and power of intention embedded in stone grids, small or large. We have personally visited and conducted energy research at several sites in the British Isles and other locations. Traveling through the British Isles, Ireland, and France, we visited well-known sites such as Stonehenge, Avebury, Callanish, and Carnac, but we also made a point to visit other lesser-known sites such as the Drombeg stone circle in Ireland, the Clava Ring in Scotland, and the Merry Maidens in Cornwall.

While it is established that Stonehenge is aligned with the solstices, we found that most of the sites we visited are also aligned with celestial phenomena such as equinoxes, moon and star rises and sets, and other astronomical events. The presence of these stones' alignments as calendrical markers of cyclical celestial events means that the stone circles are true wheels of time. Using copper dowsing rods, we investigated the energy at each ancient stone site we visited in Britain and Ireland. At every site, the dowsing rods showed a vortex energy was present. While this is not entirely surprising, the consistent and specific patterns of energy in and around the circles at the sites was surprising. It is entirely possible that people from ancient civilizations, who were almost certainly more in tune with earth energy than most people today, could feel or in some way detect the presence of subtle fields of energy in the landscape. This might have led them to build stone arrangements to further amplify the area. Since so many stone circles lay across farmland, it would seem these circles were especially agricultural in nature, but the intense focus on sky and light suggests a purpose beyond a mere calendar to mark the seasons. When using the dowsing rods, every stone circle exhibited a positive vortex of energy at the center (dowsing rods would spin either clockwise, counterclockwise, or both). The energy within the circle became neutral between the center and circumference stones, the energy became negative between perimeter stones (the dowsing rods would cross), and the energy became again neutral outside the stone circle. It seemed that the consistency of the energetic behavior of stone circles across the British Isles was a recognized, replicated blueprint.

There is an unusual stone circle construction in Drombeg, Ireland, that is atypical of other stones circles we visited because its energy configuration was far more complex. The circle was aligned with the solstice, with a triangular alignment across the circle between two portal stones and an axial stone (figure 8.18). The energy along this axis behaved differently than in other parts of the circle and this axis was not commonly found among stone circles in the British Isles. Between the two portal stones, the dowsing rods spun, but only between those two rocks and the center of the circle. How the builders knew to design energy flow in a special way across the circle is intriguing. Was

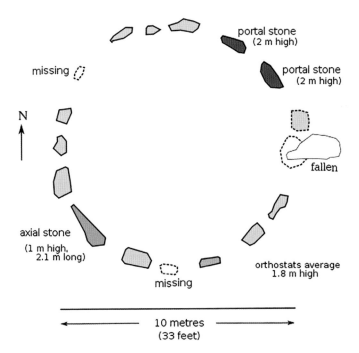

Figure 8.18. Drombeg stone circle in County Cork, Ireland, is a good example of an axial stone circle. The axis passes between the portal stones at the northeast and over the axial stone at the southwest. Based on a diagram from Seán Ó Nualláin, *A Survey of Stone Circles in Cork and Kerry*, 1984.

there a ley line running across the circle that the stones anchored? Perhaps the builders buried quartz crystal between the portal stones to create a channel of energy? Quartz crystal has been found at Celtic megalithic sites, such as Newgrange, and at stone circle sites. The Celts called quartz "sun stone" and believed it had powerful properties. At one time, the walls of the large Newgrange stone edifice were entirely covered in quartz stone.

While standing in front of two stones in an intuitive state at Avebury, one of the largest stone circle sites in the British Isles, Hara noticed a pattern of energy circulating between the standing stones. The energy was moving quickly and interlacing, looking remarkably like Celtic weave patterns (figure 8.19). Circular patterns are often carved into stones at energy sites such as the large stones in Newgrange (figure 8.20, page 202). After intuiting the energy between the stones at Avebury and observing the Celtic patterns carved onto ancient stones, we realized that the famous Celtic knot represents natural earth energy patterns that are harnessed and intensified in stone circles and other stone alignments. With the natural earth energy harnessed, the stone circle becomes a powerful vortex for prayer and intention.

Energy is found not only at stone circles, as we also experienced unusual energies with single megalithic stones as well. We visited several Pictish stones in the British Isles, some several feet tall and many with carvings of Pictish symbols. We also visited Carnac in Brittany, France, a unique site in that it was composed of massive alignments across the landscape. Hara had a peculiar experience with one large stone. We arrived at the site around dusk and walked along a series of aligned stones. Coming upon a stone in the pathway, Hara placed her hand on the large rock and instantaneously she felt jolted by a strong, sentient presence in the rock. Hara quickly removed her hand and stood back stunned and intimidated by the energy she sensed. As the evening shadows grew darker, Hara looked across the aligned stones and sensed that they could float during certain times of the year. At a megalithic site near Kilmartin, Scotland, we had the eerie feeling that we were being watched by something in the woods just outside the site. In the same area, we experienced the disappearance of a rock dolmen.* We knew we were at the

---

*A dolmen is a stone chamber consisting of two or more vertical megaliths covered by a large flat horizontal stone.

Figure 8.19. Artist's rendering of Celtic weave pattern between standing stones.
Digital composite by Kaleigh Brown

correct site and we could sense the dolmen stones, but they were not visible.

At one of the stone circles in Callanish on the Isle of Lewis along the western coast of Scotland, we noticed that as the weather changed, the energy and the mood of the stones fluctuated from benign to menacing with dark faces emerging from the ancient rocks. At Callanish I, the largest site on the island, Hara stood against one of the megalith stones in the central

Figure 8.20. Celtic patterns engraved on a monolithic entrance stone in Newgrange, Ireland. Quartz crystal embedded above entryway.

Photo by H. Hara

circle and felt like the stones had absorbed energies that were not their own. She sensed that they were quantum holders or containers of energy from stars and planets overhead. Callanish is an unusual site as it is composed of a stone circle but has other alignments connected to the circle (figure 8.21). Initially, we were confused by the presence of a large Celtic Cross across the landscape, especially since the site is said to have been built around 3000 BCE, making it about two thousand years older than Stonehenge. Later, we learned that Callanish is aligned with the star Deneb and other nearby stars,[19] which means that the entire site is probably a re-creation of the constellation Cygnus the Swan, as the constellation and the stone formation closely resemble one another in alignment (figure 8.22).

Figure 8.21. Callanish I stones aligned in the shape of a cross.
Photo by Stephen Branley

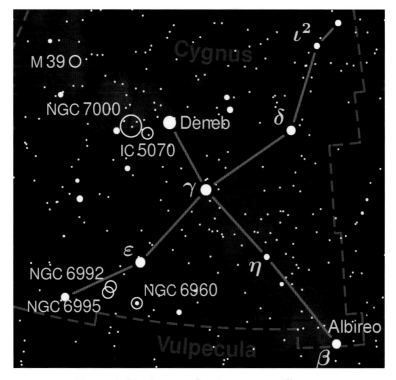

Figure 8.22. Cygnus the Swan constellation.

Building a Crystal Matrix

The author Hara has personally worked with stone circles and labyrinths and created a stone medicine wheel in her backyard. Just like the stone circles in the British Isles, dowsing rods also spin in the center of the stone circle. She often prays and meditates in the medicine wheel, and she has placed quartz and other crystals in the center to amplify the energies of the area. Whether working with gemstones, simple circles, grids of tumbled or natural rocks, or larger natural stone circles, medicine wheels, or labyrinths, stone matrices are natural amplifiers of energy and intention. But gem and stone matrices do more than energize; they provide direction in time and space.

In the ever moving and changing heavens that embody the twelve signs of the zodiac, there is dynamic, fluid movement. There is no such thing as a single power crystal that is your personal birthstone. Instead, as Earth moves through the heavens, the scenery and the energy shifts and different crystals are needed for arising energies and changing seasons. There is a sense of directionality in space with all the crystal matrices we have examined. The Navaratna is aligned with space in the eight directions like a medicine wheel. Embedded within the system are the lunar nodes, and its two gemstones, which are aligned with time, providing direction with respect to the past and the future. The breastplate, with its twelve stones, represents a blueprint of the future New Jerusalem that the High Priest carries over his chest. In this sense, the breastplate, worn over the heart, turns into a guidepost or a navigation unit leading us to our core, authentic spiritual home present in space at the center, and in the future. The stone circles and alignments represent the change of seasons aligning with the stars above. At the center of these crystal matrices is the Tree of Life, heaven, and the New Jerusalem, the Nordic tree Yggdrasil and Asgard, and Mount Meru and Shambhala. This center in time and space is where our true home and our authentic selves exist. Practicing with gems in matrix creates both the focus and the energy field to bring subtler order worlds forward as the realization of spirit into matter.

9

Chintamani Alchemy

Eastern and Western Traditions of
Cultivating the Self into a Higher Octave Gem

Tis true without lying, certain & most true. That which is below is like that which is above & that which is above is like that which is below to do the miracles of one only thing. And as all things have been & arose from one by the mediation of one: so all things have their birth from its one thing by adaptation. The Sun is its father, the moon its mother, the wind hath carried it in its belly, the earth is its nourse. The father of all perfection in the whole world is here. Its force or power is entire if it be converted into earth.

TABULA SMARAGDINA, TRANSLATED BY SIR ISAAC NEWTON

THE PHILOSOPHER'S STONE IS A NAME FREQUENTLY synonymous with the Holy Grail. The name itself conjures up ancient alchemists breaking down the elements to create gold, blending arcane notions of chemistry and mysticism in their craft. Like the chintamani and the Holy Grail, the Philosopher's Stone is equally mythical, dangerous, and difficult to attain. Like the chintamani, the Philosopher's Stone is also difficult to define. In this chapter, we examine the various definitions and concepts of the Philosopher's Stone to seek out a possible consensus regarding this metaphysical enigma and its potential in spiritual evolution. We review Western and

Eastern alchemical processes to find their connection to the creation of the Philosopher's Stone and the chintamani.

The Philosopher's Stone

Although the Philosopher's Stone is associated with the alchemical processes of transforming lead into gold, its very name suggests that the operation is more metaphysical than tangibly physical. Philosophers are intellectuals, theorists, and deep thinkers, so the stone could be referred to as the "thinker's stone" or the "thinking stone," which has similar connotations to the chintamani "thought" stone or "mind" gem. Indeed, numerous philosophers, alchemists, scientists, and psychoanalysts have thought about this stone, including Hermes Trismegistus, Nicolas Flamel, Paracelsus, Basil Valentine, Dr. John Dee, Sir Isaac Newton, Carl Jung, and many others who are famous, obscure, or hidden. The goal for the philosopher-scientist is to transform base matter into superior matter, which is at least a partially projective process. Some alchemists and psychologists approach the Philosopher's Stone by attempting to change themselves as a means of changing an object or an energy in their environment. The Philosopher's Stone and alchemy are intimately linked as the true "gold" of alchemical operations in the creation of the Philosopher's Stone. The intent of alchemy is to transform base matter and to improve upon it. This intent can be applied both to the alchemist and the matter being worked upon, so it refers to both subtle interior matter and exterior physical matter. It is encapsulated in perhaps the most famous axiom of the *Emerald Tablet,* written by Hermes Trismegistus: *"that which is below is like that which is above."* In alchemical operations, it could also be said that which is within is like that which is without.

The name originates from the Latin *lapis philosophorum* and translates to "stone of the philosophers." The Philosopher's Stone has been called other names and/or associated with other mystical stone objects such as the chintamani, the Holy Grail (reviewed in chapter 5), and the "white stone with a new name" from the Book of Revelation.* The white stone suggests the purifying

---

*"To him that overcometh will I give to eat of the hidden manna, and will give him a white stone, and in the stone a new name written, which no man knoweth saving he that receiveth it." Revelation 2:17 (AV).

of essence, but the new name refers to the re-creation of self. Alchemists have described the created *lapis* as a glassy red translucent stone.* The *lapis* has also been referred to as the elixir of life, suggesting that it is made of an essence that has healing and regenerative properties including immortality, not unlike the description of *amrita* from the ancient Vedic texts. *Amrita,* like the chintamani, originated from the primordial milk ocean. It has been referred to as the "one thing" and the *prima materia,* suggesting that the substance of the *lapis* is primordial and is a quintessence† that exists as the subtlest and most refined matter. As the "first matter," it also refers to the energy of primordial chaos and formlessness. The Philosopher's Stone has been called so many names and is referred to as bearing so many qualities that it may lie outside typical comprehension because it continuously shifts to serve the environment or the condition in which it is invoked. The *lapis* coexists in both the material and spiritual worlds, so to understand or create the stone, it is necessary for the alchemist to shift away from an exclusively materialistic perspective of the world. The *lapis* is made of an essence that lies outside the boundaries of the five basic senses.

The Emerald Tablet

It would be difficult to discuss the *lapis* or alchemy without reference to the *Emerald Tablet,* which is, in a sense, a short treatise on the essential operations of alchemy and the creation of the *lapis.* Hermes Trismegistus is intimately linked with the tablet as both its writer and master of hidden operations who discloses its secrets to the initiated. Hermes has been recognized as the Greek god of the same name merged with the Egyptian god of writing and magic, Thoth. It is difficult to separate myth from historical fact to identify Hermes Trismegistus, whose name means "thrice-greatest Hermes." Hermes appears as a magician, an alchemist, a prophet, and a god, and is historically connected with both Enoch the patriarch and Melchizedek the priest.

Like the *lapis* and chintamani, the *Emerald Tablet's* origins are so ancient its history emerges more from myth than fact. Throughout its many legends,

---

*From this point forward, we will use *lapis* interchangeably with Philosopher's Stone.
†Quintessence refers to essence of the fifth element, ether.

the tablet is typically found in a cave or tomb, but the identity of the person who finds it changes. For example, Alexander the Great, Balinas the Wise, and Appolonius of Tyana are a few who have been mentioned as persons who have discovered the *Emerald Tablet*. Alexander the Great took possession of the tablet when he conquered Egypt in 332 BCE and placed the *Emerald Tablet* on display in Heliopolis. The tablet was engraved in Phoenician, but scholars translated it into Greek and we rely on these translations today, as the original Phoenician tablet is missing. Dennis William Hauck cites an intriguing description of the tablet from an alchemical text based on the account of a traveler to Heliopolis: "It is a precious stone, like an emerald, whereon these characters are represented in bas-relief, not engraved. It is esteemed above 2,000 years old. The matter of this emerald had once been in a fluid state like melted glass, and had been cast in a mold, and to this flux the artist had given the hardness of the natural and genuine emerald, by his art."[1] We briefly introduced the *Emerald Tablet* in chapter 6 through a discussion of engraved stones and described other ancient engraved tablets with divine writing. In a way, the Ten Commandments are like the *Emerald Tablet* in that both are a series of commands written by a higher power, engraved on stone. We could view the *Emerald Tablet* as a series of supreme and essential commands for alchemical operations or creation of the *lapis* in the same way.

The *Emerald Tablet* derives its name from the Latin *Tabula Smaragdina*. The etymology of the word *smaragdina* is as mysterious as the tablet itself. The word originates from the Greek *smaragdos,*[2] but it may have a Semitic origin and connection to the Akkadian words *barraqtu,* which translates to "gemstone," and *baraqu,* which means "scintillation."[3] It may also be related to the Sanskrit word *marakata,* meaning "emerald," and its feminine form, *smaragdine.*[4] In Buddhism, *marakata* "refers to a type of jewel (*ratna*), into which the universe was transformed by the Buddha's miraculous power . . . this pearl is extracted from the beak of the golden-winged Garuda bird; it is green in color and it counteracts poisons."[5] Examining the etymology of the *Emerald Tablet* suggests that there may be a deeper meaning as to why the tablet of Hermes is engraved on an emerald or green stone. It could also be described as a green "scintillating" stone that is feminine in its energy and is connected to transformative powers. The color green and emeralds are associated with the planet Mercury, named for the Roman analog of Hermes, and the heart chakra. Mercury itself has multiple meanings, and the word "mercurial" is derived from it. The name of the *Emerald Tablet* at least suggests that its message points to the transformative center or "heart" of things.

The Magnum Opus

Alchemy has existed since antiquity and its origins date so far back that it blends into ancient myths from Sumeria and Egypt. Alchemy is considered the world's first empirical science and the mother of modern science, but its operations and philosophies were tied to subtle processes that are metaphysical in nature. In antiquity, alchemy was practiced across several cultures and, true to its name, its theories blended. Even the word "alchemy" is difficult to place etymologically, as it could come from the Greek word *chema* meaning "fluid" or "to pour,"[6] or it could be derived from the Egyptian word *kmt,* which means "black earth," "black pigment," or "black glass."[7]

Although originating in Sumer, many consider the Egyptians to be the first master alchemists. Theories in alchemy abound from Egypt, Greece, Arabia, India, Europe, and other sources. Alchemical traditions tend to incorporate religious and spiritual philosophies, so it is common to find alchemical systems blending with Eastern traditions. Consequently, there are a myriad of interpretive techniques and methods for the creation of the Philosopher's Stone. A modern scholar of alchemy, Dennis William Hauck, has comprehensively studied alchemical theories and transcribed them so that they can be applied practically to personal transformation.[8] For shamanic practices that relate to the alchemical system, James Endredy describes tangible activities for deeper levels of transformation.[9] We do not go into comprehensive detail about Hermetical models of transformation because we are approaching the Hermetical model and its relationship to the Philosopher's Stone in order to reveal its connection with the chintamani.

The alchemical stages are discussed in arcane texts in symbolic language and are difficult to decipher, which is one of the reasons so many interpretations exist and perhaps why they do not receive nearly as much attention today as Eastern alchemy models receive. Much like interpreting dreams, the success of the alchemy of transformation is dependent on the alchemist.

Thus, to practice the alchemical process in too linear a fashion would lead to disappointing results. The practice of alchemy requires a combined right- and left-brained approach toward the transformation of energy and/or matter. The results of alchemical experiments are as much influenced by the intention and energy of the alchemist as they are on the matter that is being transformed through specific operations. While defining the steps through chemistry terms initially seems to focus on tangible matter, we recognize that there is controversy around the tangible existence of both the Philosopher's Stone and the chintamani. Based on our experience and research, we posit that the stone exists on multiple levels including the mind, the spirit, and in matter, but the alchemical process begins in the present, in tangible matter. From there, we reach upward, to connect to spirit. As succinctly stated in the supreme text for the Philosopher's Stone, *The Emerald Tablet*: "As Above, So Below." This quintessential formula is both a starting and ending point. In alchemy, and other spiritual philosophies, the practitioner creates a sacred stone of remembrance. Studying the alchemical process of transformation makes the process conscious so that the alchemist becomes a co-creator with higher or subtler spiritual forces to create an immortal stone.

In Hermetical alchemy, there are three essential principles or properties that Paracelsus (1494–1541) called the *tria prima*: sulfur, salt, and mercury. He relied upon these three basic properties in his work associated with spagyrics that used alchemical medicine to create the elixir of life (see table). The three properties correspond to the modalities in astrology, which are cardinal, fixed, and mutable, respectively. There are four stages connected to the four elements, the cornerstones of matter: fire, earth, air, and water. A fifth element, ether, is sometimes incorporated in alchemical systems. These four elements are also the foundation of the astrological signs. The twelve signs are divided into four groups of three, representing each of the four elements, and also into three groups of four, representing the modalities. The blending, unification, and balancing of the elements and their properties are critical in alchemical processes. There are seven classical operations in alchemical theory. While many more stages and operations have been discussed and theorized, including three-, four-, seven-, twelve-, and fourteen-step models, for the purposes of our discussion, we will focus on the simpler, more foundational three principles, four elemental stages, and seven-step operations.

THE THREE PRINCIPLES						
PRINCIPAL	**SYMBOL**	**NAME**	**MODE**	**ELEMENT**	**GENDER**	**PROPERTIES**
Sulfur	♁	*Anima*-Soul	Cardinal	Fire	Male	Inflammability
Salt	⊖	*Corpus*-Body	Fixed	Earth	Neutral	Fixity; incombustibility
Mercury	☿	*Spiritus*-Spirit	Mutable	Water	Female	Fusion; volatility

The four alchemical stages with the elements are listed in the table below. The elements are also referred to as stages in the great work of creating the *lapis* and are represented as symbols in alchemy. The elements or stages of the work represent a core process that are integrated to create the *lapis,* which is known as squaring the circle illustrated in figure 9.1 on the following page. The geometric image represents the harmonious integration of the four elements and is considered a symbol of the Philosopher's Stone (figure 9.2).

THE FOUR ALCHEMICAL STAGES WITH THE ELEMENTS					
STAGE	**NAME**	**COLOR**	**ELEMENT**	**SYMBOL**	**STAGE OF THE WORK**
I.	*nigredo*	Black	Earth	Black raven	Putrefaction; decomposition
2.	*albedo*	White	Water	White dove	Division; purification
3.	*citrinitas*	Yellow	Fire	Yellow flower	Transmutation; awakening
4.	*rubedo*	Red	Air	Red phoenix	Integration; synthesis

The Azoth mandala (figure 9.3, page 213) is a graphic primer for understanding the Hermetical system to create the Philosopher's Stone. The term "Azoth" was another word for mercury but could also represent a universal solvent. Published in 1678, the mandala has been attributed to Basil Valentine. Meditating on the points and the symbols in the mandala is itself an initiation into the great work. Inside the Azoth mandala, the central bearded figure is surrounded by the four elements and the properties residing within a triangle written in Latin: *anima, spiritus, corpus* (soul, spirit,

Figure 9.1. Creating the Philosopher's Stone and squaring
the circle. Michael Maier, *Atalanta Fugiens*, 1617.

Figure 9.2. Diagram of
the Philosopher's Stone
representing the integration
of the four elements through
squaring of the circle.

body). The three properties are also encoded with alchemical symbols in
three of the rays: sulfur, mercury, and salt. There is a seven-pointed star representing the operational steps of the work with the planets embedded in the
star rays to represent the energy associated with each process. The operations
include calcination, dissolution, separation, conjunction, fermentation, distil-
lation, and coagulation (see table). Images within circles conceptually show
the process, but they are subjective images that work with the unconscious
part of the brain to represent the creative process. This is a Renaissance map
showing the creative process involved in alchemy, but it could also represent
the creative process over one's lifetime. Rather than exclusively considering

alchemical operations as transforming lead into gold, these steps may refer to both micro and macro processes.

Figure 9.3. Azoth mandala, showing the seven operations of alchemy, by Basil Valentine, 1678.

THE SEVEN ALCHEMICAL OPERATIONS				
OPERATION	**PLANET**	**COLOR**	**METAL**	**QUALITIES FROM CHEMISTRY**
1. Calcination	Saturn	Black	Lead	Purification through heating
2. Dissolution	Jupiter	Purple	Tin	Dissolving solid into liquid
3. Separation	Mars	Red	Iron	Conversion of mixture into separate constituents
4. Conjunction	Sun	Yellow	Gold	Joining of two compounds
5. Fermentation	Venus	Green	Copper	Metabolic process releasing energy
6. Distillation	Mercury	Orange	Mercury	Extraction to separate components of mixture
7. Coagulation	Moon	White	Silver	Liquid changing to solid or semisolid (gel) state (or possibly ionic plasma)

Reviewing an alchemical image by Stephan Michelspacher (1654) in figure 9.4, the operations are symbolized through steps on a stairway leading into a temple, which may refer to gradual steps of transformation over a lifetime. While the image is linear and easier to understand, the circular Azoth mandala may infer that the operations are interrelated and do not have a specific ending or beginning. The stages and operations may not occur in a strict linear sequence but are, instead, interdependent. The operations help expand upon the initial four stages. The stages could be steps, while the seven operations are processes within those stages.

Figure 9.4. The seven alchemical stages.
Stephan Michelspacher, *Konjunktion in der Kabbala*, 1654.

There are hidden codes and symbols embedded in the Azoth mandala. Inside the ring of the mandala, there is a Latin phrase: *Visita Interiora Terra Rectificando Inuenes Occultum Lapidem.* The phrase has commonly been translated as: "visit interior earth correcting find secret stone." A more thorough examination into the translation of the phrase yields intriguing differences. As the phrase was first published in 1678, it is presumed that the language is Renaissance Latin. However, *Rectificando* is not a Latin word but derives from several romance languages and translates to "rectifying" or "correcting." The word *Visita* is an imperative command. We offer several other possible translations of the phrase, as we concluded that the writer was intentionally ambiguous.

1. *Rectifying deeper earth, you will find the secret stone. See!*
2. *Bringing deeper earth into existence, you will invent the secret precious stone. Go!*
3. *Moving linearly in earth's depths, you will reach the secret stone. Go often!*
4. *Plumbing earth's depths, you will get the hidden precious stone. Visit!*
5. *Refining earth's depths, you will invent the hidden jewel! Go often!*

Each of the above translations offers a different shade of meaning. Possible alternative actions include inventing, seeking, finding, and obtaining. Working with the earth also takes on different meanings: rectifying, refining, or moving into the earth. There is also a simple cipher hidden in the words. Taking the first, capitalized letter from each Latin word, VITRIOL is the resulting code word. Historically, Basil Valentine was considered an inventor of modern sulfuric acid via vitriol. An extremely corrosive chemical, vitriol can oxidize any metal except gold, which would have been of great interest to the alchemists. The word "vitriol" is also of etymological interest, meaning "glass," since vitriol can harden into a substance that resembles glass. The alchemists considered glass to be a precious and remarkable substance, as it could be transformed from sand into a material that resembled rock crystal and gemstones.[10]

There are other hidden messages within the mandala. Hauck suggests that there is an eighth operation embedded in the Azoth mandala.[11] A cube drawn at the bottom of the triangle is labeled "corpus," and the Saturn ray points to the cube at the bottom center of the mandala, which represents the first stage of matter (salt) but also refers to a hidden eighth stage of completion that results in the transformation of matter into the *lapis*. As the first ray, Saturn, is pointing to the cube, which is the stone, Saturn may represent both the first ray and an eighth ray in the circle. Interestingly, the alchemists considered Saturn to be a key in the work regarding the stone, and they frequently represented the ringed planet as a black cube. Hauck theorizes that the five stars surrounding the *lapis* cube represent the four elements plus ether. The Azoth mandala abounds in less obvious secret codes. The author's name, Basil Valentine, seems to be a pseudonym, since there are no historical records showing a Basilius Valentinus. Interestingly, the name Valentinus means "powerful king," which may be a hidden code for the alchemical operation involving the solar king in the mandala. Most alchemical texts should not be taken literally, because while the operations may involve tangible mixtures and solutions, they combine both tangible matter and the more subtle "spirit" or "ether" of matter. Alchemical texts communicate on many levels and require patience and careful study to tease out the hidden meanings of the text and images.

Carl Jung wrote extensively about his explorations and interpretations of the subtle, hidden meanings of alchemical texts, popularizing them as representing the psyche and processes of interior psychological transformation. The *Red Book,* Jung's private illuminated manuscript first published posthumously in 2009, reveals his personal alchemical drawings and mandalas, suggesting that his pursuit of the stone was personal, not merely academic.[12] The *Red Book* is filled with images resembling a sacred stone. He studied alchemical manuscripts exhaustively, if not obsessively, and brought forward not only an extensive psychological explanation for alchemical operations but an even more mystical explanation as a basis for the creation of the *lapis.* He alludes to alchemists perhaps seeking out something more than transforming base matter into gold or even personal transformation; he theorizes that the alchemists were searching for the quintessence or spirit in matter, something that modern man no longer understands. He explains that this lost knowledge of quintessence is the reason why the alchemical texts elude us.

In Jung's research, he discusses that in the production or creation of the stone, the intent or true imagination of the alchemist is as vital as the tools or chemicals used. He discusses how the alchemical scientist influences and affects the experiment, proposing what was later verified in modern observer effect experiments discussed in chapter 7. He lists certain psychological qualities of the alchemist that are important in the creation of the *lapis,* which he gleaned from alchemical texts. Qualities such as concentration, true imagination, and focus of feelings, senses, reason, and thoughts are important in initiating the great work. Jung counsels that "the stone will be found when the search lies heavy on the searcher."[13] It was ill-advised for an alchemist to embark on the great work without the proper mental discipline, as it would affect the outcome of the experimental creation of the stone. These protocols suggest that what is most important in either the creation, quest for, or discovery of the Philosopher's Stone is purified *intent.*

Jung warns that the *lapis* is found in the serious and discriminating study of the ancient philosophers and not in the practice of magical filth, a warning not to be taken lightly as alchemical practices both old and new abound with questionable practices and formulae.[14] Jung's works contain some other clues that help us in a deeper understanding of the *lapis.* While Jung's extensive study of the *lapis* is used to support his groundbreaking theories in psychology, his commentary approaches the mystery and mysticism of the sacred stone that eludes explanation. He discusses the stone as more ancient than alchemy and states that the stone is both internal and external, but that "there is no real consensus of opinion in regard to its actual form."[15] In trying to describe the mystery of the stone, Jung states that it comes "from those border regions of the psyche that open out into the mystery of cosmic matter."[16] He described the *lapis* as composed of the four elements and that it is not exclusively matter or spirit but composed of body, soul, and spirit.

The Lapis and Alchemical Integration

Carl Jung characterized the stone as a tool to bring together opposing energies in the mystical marriage of the *animus* and *anima* (male and female). The stone serves as a mediator, but it is within the female *anima* energy that the secret of the *lapis* is to be found. This is a theme that is pervasive in alchemical texts throughout the ages and seems to be best represented in the ancient symbol of the caduceus. The caduceus, as ancient as the *lapis,* is associated with the staff of Ningishzida, an ancient Sumerian god whose name means "lord of the tree." Early images of the caduceus date to around 4000 BCE. Technically, the caduceus as we know it today is the staff of both the god Mercury and the staff of Hermes Trismegistus, the alchemical master of the *Emerald Tablet*. Mithras, an ancient Roman god of the mysteries, is also connected to the caduceus. There are many images in antiquity and in alchemical texts showing Mercury and Hermes holding the caduceus. The caduceus is a staff with two snakes entwined in a perfect symmetry around the staff. The staff sometimes also bears wings at the top, which are considered the wings of Mercury (figure 9.5). It is frequently represented with an orb at the top. That the orb represents the Philosopher's Stone is supported by Hermetic alchemical texts.

In the *Hermetical Triumph,* a German alchemical text from the seventeenth century, there is an engraving (figure 9.6) explicating the operations at play within the caduceus symbol. At the bottom of the vertical center of the image are two operations of fire purifying the base, both within the vessel and under the vessel, deep in the earth. From a middle crown springs forth the sun and the moon, a staff and two intertwining snakes whose serpent or dragon heads meet at an orb placed between the king and queen crowns. The organic matter represented by the snakes is conjoined and inte-

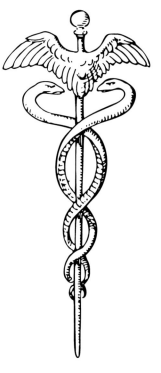

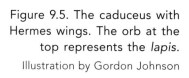

Figure 9.5. The caduceus with Hermes wings. The orb at the top represents the *lapis.*
Illustration by Gordon Johnson

Figure 9.6. *The Hermetical Triumph*, Leipzig, Germany, 1604.

grated below at the base while conjoining and meeting at the orb. Subtle influences from the sun and the moon are involved in the operation with the feminine energy radiating from moonlight on the left and the masculine solar energy shining on the right. The mysterious orb or dragon pearl is wedged between the crowning energies of the masculine and feminine. This conjunction results in the unification of the perfect cross, representing the four elements. From this unification springs forth a triangle that is said to represent the *lapis,* the crowning achievement. Inside the triangle is the phoenix. The cross and the triangle above it also represents the element sulfur. A splendid crown, larger and more ornate than the separate male and female crowns, adorns the top of the staff: a crown with three layers instead of one, with an orb with a cross above it at the top. Above the crown is the constellation Taurus flanked by its nearby signs Aries and Gemini. The three signs represent the principles sulfur, salt, and mercury.

A band intersects the signs with stars, indicating that the symbols represent the zodiac. The symbolic image moves upward, including the triangle that is pointing toward the crown and heaven.

A Latin phrase in the caption below the illustration says: *"De cavernis Metallorum occultus est, qui Lapis est venerabilis HERMES."* Like most alchemical texts, the Latin phrase has multiple interpretations. It could mean: "Down the depths of metals, it is hidden. Which venerable jewel exists?" Another possible meaning is: "From the celestial sphere of reflections, it is hidden. How does the venerable stone exist?" The phrase is posed as a contemplative question from Hermes. Hauck maintains that the seven steps and their corresponding metals are represented in this alchemical ladder ("The Seven Alchemical Operations" table, page 213).[17] The three central channels of the human energy field are represented in the caduceus with its intertwining male and female energy along the central column. The crowns on the caduceus unite heaven and earth. The Philosopher's Stone is represented by the round orb between the two crowns, but the creation of the stone allows for a bridge with the celestial plane, connecting heaven and earth, resulting in the rising of the new self, symbolized by the phoenix. The final process results in a victorious crown, a symbol of enlightenment.

A potent alchemical image from the *Ripley Scroll,* named after famed alchemist George Ripley (1415–1490), is filled with the symbolism of the triple gem chintamani (figure 9.7). The triplicity begins at the bottom of the image inside an orb with flames arising from the three orbs. The dragon is biting down on the integrated, three-phase chintamani. The top of the image shows the triple chintamani: the red stone, the black stone, and the white stone bonded together in a ring like atoms. The triple chintamani rests inside the integrated image of the sun and the moon, a mystical marriage of masculine and feminine energy.

Eastern Alchemy

As in the West, there are alternative Eastern paths that depend upon the alchemist's purpose. The first is turning base metals into gold, which is also about the ability to transform the material universe at will. Another popular purpose is the pursuit of immortality of the physical body. Medicines

Figure 9.7. Detail from the *Ripley Scroll* showing
the alchemically created triple gem.

Ripley Scroll, Golden winged bird, Wellcome Images

and cures are perhaps the most popular alchemical discipline. The pursuit of *siddhis,* or supernormal powers, is another set of disciplines to confer great mental, social, or physical skills. Finally, there are paths that aim at complete spiritual realization. These different alchemical disciplines, which are more usually described in Asia as systems of yoga or qigong, have outer, inner, and secret practice phases. Minerals, crystals, and gems are used in each of these transformative paths that serve an overall intention as part of the outer, inner, and secret yogas. Lesser and greater chintamanis appear in the course of each of these alchemical yogas.

A Western four-step alchemical model is also found in the East; both are organized around the progression of the elements. In chapter 7, we discussed the five elements in relation to Platonic solids, the shape crystals take, and the correspondence and resonance of shape with energy. There is also a more direct relation of the elements to the lower chakras. The five elements range from denser to more subtle states of matter, while the chakras arranged along the spine correspond with each element's density. Each chakra actually interlocks with a different elemental density, accessing a particular level of energy and consciousness. Our outer experiences are conditioned by the element whereas our inner experiences of that element are conditioned by the interlocking chakra. As the chakras ascend, they open human experience to finer and finer levels of elements, energies, and consciousness. Another function of a chakra is as a repository of karma, whether created in a past life or earlier in this life. Each chakra engages a particular level of energy, consciousness, and experience. This is where the spiritual science of astrology enters.

At the moment of birth, humans do not spontaneously manifest a complete lifetime of events and experiences on the physical, emotional, mental, and spiritual levels. Rather, events unfold in a time sequence, sometimes seeming in chaos, sometimes in order. They unfold uniquely for each person, depending on all the initial and added individual karmas and the timing of their activations. In Vedic and classical Western astrology, six of the major chakras have been paired with the seven visible planets. This results not in a four- or five-step element alchemy, but in a seven-step planetary model that includes elemental yoga. The activation of karma is timed by the orbits of planets as they sequence through angles and cycles. In any of the alchemical yogas, timing is a crucial factor favoring success. In this book, we are presenting the alchemical path intertwined with the chintamani that is aimed at complete spiritual transformation and realization.

Daoist Yoga

Each of the Asian yogas presumes an understanding of not just the physical body but also of the subtler energy bodies. Each Asian system describes details differently and has a unique set of practices that address their understanding of subtle or spiritual anatomy. The Daoist (道) approach either to immortality or spiritual realization is based on the *jing luo* system of meridians and acupuncture points.[18] The *jing* meridians are the twelve major energy channels plus the central yin and yang channels near the spine. The *luo* meridians are minor connecting channels. The twelve *jing* meridians are really twenty-four channels, because each of the twelve has a yin/yang twin channel with one on the left and the mirror twin on the right side of the body, similar to the snakes entwined on the caduceus. Each of the twelve *jing* meridians relates to an element pair of yin/yang organs. The math might imply there are six elements, but in the Chinese system, there are five elements named differently than in the West: wood, fire, earth, metal, and water. These form a cycle that corresponds to the seasons, with wood being spring and water being winter (figure 9.8 on the following page). So to get six elements to correspond, one gets repeated. You might guess the repeated element is water, since water does make up more than 70 percent of the human body, but actually there are four fire meridians instead of the two that all the other elements have. The emphasis on fire in the Chinese systems of astrology and medicine reveals humans as beings designed for intensive transformation. Fire is also the element needed at each stage of the Western alchemical systems.

The basic goal of Asian yogas is to conserve, control, and amplify the human energy system that permeates both the body and aura. This life energy is a more subtle energy bandwidth than food chemically transformed through the ATP-CP cycles into energy that powers the body.* This subtler but very palpable energy is called qi in Chinese, *ki* in Korean and Japanese,

---

*ATP-CP refers to Adenosine Triphosphate-Creatine phosphate in the cycle of chemical conversion of nutrients into heat and energy.

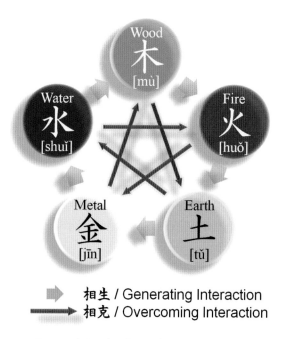

相生 / Generating Interaction
相克 / Overcoming Interaction

Figure 9.8. The five Chinese elements
Illustration by Parnassus

prana in Sanskrit, and *lung* in Tibetan. Qi (氣) flows through the *jing luo* channels within the plane of the physical body and through the subtler meridians that surround the body. Traditional Chinese Medicine (TCM) is based on assessing and balancing the flow of qi, which determines the overall level of health or disease that humans and animals experience. The first level of qi practice is to create a stronger immune system and life health force. The next level is to collect qi scattered throughout the peripheral meridians and concentrate it instead toward the center channels to reduce mental distractions and prepare for a quantum leap of consciousness. As we expend our energy and focus on a circus of negative or neutral worldly activities, we fail to amass sufficient life force qi to propel our minds to higher levels of conscious awareness, action, and possibilities. The practice that increases qi for health or cultivates higher levels of consciousness is called qigong (氣 功). In other systems, such as Tibetan tsalung and tummo, it is called the yoga of fire. There are thousands of particular qigong practices depending on the type of obstacles to overcome and the ultimate intention to accomplish.

Higher level qigong practices focus on concentrating, circulating, and fusing energies of the elements, chakras, and channels. These are different stages of Daoist practice, similar to stages in Western alchemical systems. The ultimate self-transformation goal is to unite with the primordial energy of the Dao. This final practice will not succeed unless the yogini or yogi has completed prior required transformations sufficiently. The completion of the Daoist alchemical path involves uniting three energies, qi or vital energy, *jing* or sexual generative energy, and *shen* or spirit energy.[19] Each of the energies must be collected, refined, and heated precisely by breathing, and then stored until all three energies have been transformed. The process leading to refined *jing* results in the blossoming of the Lead Flower, refined qi results in the blossoming of the Silver Flower, and refined *shen* results in the blossoming of the Golden Flower. When all three energies are refined into flowers they rise together and unite at the top of the head. The three united energies merge and return to the undifferentiated state. This fused energy descends to the abdomen to create the immortal fetus that requires an incubation period of practice. At the conclusion of the spiritual pregnancy, the immortal fetus emerges as *yuan shen* (原神), or original spirit, and rises to the top of the head (figure 9.9). From then until death, consciousness once split at birth into the human body, energy, and mind learns to inhabit and function through the reunified original spirit. Then we can return to where we were before we were born.[20]

Figure 9.9. Golden Flower Meditation. "The Immortal Fetus" in *The Secret of the Golden Flower*, 1962.

Kriya Yoga

An altogether different approach to spiritual alchemy is the path of Kriya yoga, which is based upon the *Yoga Sutras* of Patanjali, a classic text that defines the stages of yoga. The text begins:

Yogas citta vritti nirodhah
Tada dhrastuh sva-rupe avasthanam[21]

or

Yoga is stopping the flux of mental activity
So the Seer abides in self-aware nature.

Yoga is Sanskrit for "union" and gives rise to the English cognate word "yoke" in the sense of joining at least two in one direction. Patanjali's text is simple and spare and is divided into four *padas* or book chapters with a total of 202 terse verses. Patanjali lays out the *ashtanga* or eight stages of yoga. The first set of practices is *yama,* or disciplined willpower to avoid behaviors that disturb the body and mind, and to cultivate a lifestyle that limits effects of negative actions. *Niyama* is the second positive practice set of virtues of non-violence, truth, conserving life force, non-stealing, and non-possessive behaviors. The third practice set is asana, which is ultimately about continuous awareness of how body posture affects us in each instant, and how it influences long-term physical health and mental attitude. Most Westerners associate all of yoga with just this one practice from the third practice limb. The fourth practice set is pranayama, which is first about controlling how we lose and gain life force energy known as prana, which we identified as qi in Chinese. As in Daoist practice, there are several breath exercises that improve health and result in self-realization. Ultimately pranayama is about joining individual energies with cosmic energy. This practice set also includes allowing the reservoir of life energy at the base or Saturn chakra to rise through the chakras to the third eye and crown chakras without diversion. This alone constitutes a variety of practices known collectively as kundalini yoga.

THE EIGHT STAGES OF KRIYA YOGA ACCORDING TO PATANJALI

YOGA STAGE, SANSKRIT	YOGA STAGE, ENGLISH	DESCRIPTION
Yama	Behaviors to avoid	Disciplined lifestyle avoiding body/mind negativity
Niyama	Positive behaviors	Adopting positive diet, exercise, and morality
Asana	Posture	Relaxing and controlling the body through posture
Pranayama	Breath and energy	Increasing subtle energy by breathing practice
Pratyahara	Sense withdrawal	Directing the senses to their source
Dharana	Concentration	Attaining one-pointed focus of body/mind
Dhyana	Meditation	Energy flow reunifies with continuous awareness
Samadhi	No-thought trance	Abiding in the state beyond thought and karma

The final four yoga practice limbs rely on substantially mastering the prior stages (see table). As with Daoist and Western alchemies, each person has different health conditions, talents, and skills. This means that each person's path to mastery may be automatic, straightforward, or difficult at any stage of practice. The fifth practice set is *pratyahara,* which initially involves detaching the six senses from attachment to outer world objects.* The senses and their sense consciousnesses are inwardly directed to explore and reconnect with the inner world at the source. This practice removes automatic conditioning and liberates psychic energy so it can be directed easily wherever the yogini or yogi chooses. The sixth practice set is *dharana,* which is about increasing the ability to concentrate with relaxed attention and to focus comfortably for longer and longer periods of time. This leads to the seventh practice, *dhyana,* or meditative flow, which develops deep

---

*There are five sense consciousnesses plus the sixth, mind consciousness, which assembles all five sense inputs as knowledge of experience.

contemplative power. In *dhyana,* continuous conscious awareness gently yet powerfully reunifies with continuous energy flow. The eighth practice is samadhi, a deep trance state completely without thought. The self, previously limited by time and space, completely dissolves in samadhi beyond the restrictions of karma, dissolving in turn the subtle default patterns of the body, emotions, and mind at the source. When *dharana, dhyana,* and samadhi are all achieved, they transform into balanced self-awareness called *samyamna.* This ninth ability emerges as *prajna aloka,* or dynamic wisdom that is unlimited by and transcends place, space, and time.

The Three Central Channels

Another Eastern spiritual alchemy system is found in the Buddhist tradition, particularly within Tantric or Vajrayana Buddhism. The languages and cultures that have developed and transmitted this Tantric system are spread across Asia, which at one time included the area from the Middle East to Indonesia. Most of the Tantric systems that have continued to flourish are currently in India, Tibet, China, and Japan. There is also an Indian Tantra yoga based in Hindu learning, which shares practices but also has differences with the Vajrayana Buddhist Tantric yoga. When you examine all the Daoist or Buddhist spiritual alchemical systems, you will find many variations within each broad tradition. The information we present here is to gain an understanding of the common ways of transforming the born human so she or he can abide in the unborn primordial condition. A common problem found in alchemical systems is working with the three central channels that are represented in the occult West by the god Mercury holding the caduceus, a straight staff intertwined by two snakes.

In Vajrayana Buddhism, the central channel is variously called the *shushumna* or *avadhuti* channel. It is entwined by two spiral channels variously known as the yin and yang, *ren* and *du, ida* and *pingala,* or *lalana* and *rasana* channels. The three channels rise together and intersect each chakra, although only the central channel rises above the third eye chakra to the crown (figure 9.10). Networks of peripheral channels all connect especially at each chakra nexus. Qi flows through all the channels but alternates in strength of activity during the cycle of day and night. A common problem of qi flow in people who are agitated and on edge is that the flow is rough, uneven, and tends to flow outside channel boundaries. This pattern is detrimental to health. As qi flow becomes more tranquil, the flow becomes more even as it moves through the center of channels. A person who experiences this tranquil flow is more patient and peaceful. When the flow becomes too lethargic or diminished, health also declines. The common obstacle to spiritual realization is that the energies are scattered throughout all the channels, while spiritual transformation requires that life force energies be increased and concentrated to precipitate the quantum leap to higher orders of being and consciousness. Chakras too can be tranquil, agitated, or an alternating mixture of both. As the central channels pass through a stormy chakra, energy will divert from ascending easily. Each chakra impinges on all three middle channels to diminish upward flow. Each chakra requires balancing and opening to allow the upward flow of transformation to continue. Even when all the chakras are open, the two main side channels continue to impinge on the central channel, also diminishing energy flow into the central channel. Therefore, the yin and yang channels need balancing and opening to allow energies to move to the middle channel so the ultimate transformations can occur. Each alchemical system needs methods to

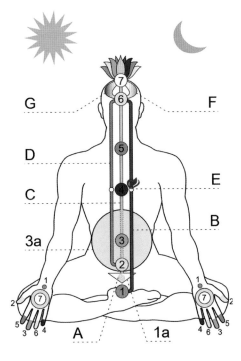

Figure 9.10. The three central channels and seven chakras.

overcome common obstacles to the human energy condition, but also needs methods that lead to transformation for sincere practitioners with a wide variety of personal conditions.

Zen and Vajrayana Approaches

Another set of alchemical systems of spiritual transformation exist in the Theravada, Mahayana, and Vajrayana schools of Buddhism. Buddhist schools begin with the understanding that the conditions of ignorance fog body, emotions, and mind so that they cannot recognize the true basis of consciousness. Certainly both Western and Eastern alchemical paths also rely deeply upon self-reflection to create motivation and momentum to complete the long process of self-transformation. In Buddhism, the fundamental exploration is to understand how our attachments to short-term desires based on our own afflictive emotions create suffering now and into the future. The intention to extinguish the flames of those counterproductive desires is quite literally what the Sanskrit term *nirvana* means. Catering to minute-by-minute desires creates the agenda of karma from lifetime to lifetime. So the first resolve of this alchemy is to extinguish the causes and results of the cycle of birth, death, and reincarnation. The next intention, which is the hallmark of the Mahayana or Bodhisattva path, is to undertake the transformative process of enlightenment in order to benefit all sentient beings. This is usually called the Bodhisattva vow, but we are referring to it here also as the chintamani vow. When the wish-fulfilling gem is activated to manifest near-term, self-satisfying gains, its potential power to end widespread suffering is cut short and remains unrealized. The vow to benefit other beings is the tonic for this calamity. Only completing the Bodhisattva transformation assures that universal and beneficial results will arise when activating the chintamani.

The Zen and the Vajrayana paths are similar Buddhist alchemical systems to each other, but they are nonetheless unique. Both rely extensively on engaging and transforming energy and the subtle bodies so that we can recognize *rigpa*, the innate presence of enlightened nature in Vajrayana, or *daigo*, supreme enlightenment in Zen. Once the underlying awakened mind becomes continually remembered, practitioners of either path deepen their connection with the great perfection of uncreated nature, and integrate the expression of their energies with that original nature. In the Tibetan Vajrayana schools, this results in manifesting the rainbow body. We will examine the Buddhist Vajrayana system of alchemy, also known as Tantrayana, or the path of Tantra yoga, in the next few paragraphs. More than any other system we have considered, teachings and imagery of the chintamani are everywhere apparent in Tantrayana, and there are many specific chintamani practices, some of which we discussed in chapter 3.

Yoga Tantra

There are 84,000 kinds of personal obstacles, 84,000 dharmas, and 84,000 doors to enlightenment. There are even 84,000 million Buddhas in as many world systems in the multiverse. This teaching is repeated throughout the sutras and the commentaries by realized teachers on how best to practice. In other words, there is not a single pattern for effective transformation. Depending on what arises during the self-realization process, a different or improvised next step is not only acceptable but may be required. Alchemy, Eastern or Western, is an empirical process. The starting point of the process disguises underlying assumptions and the root intention. As the great work progresses, the assumptions and intention reveal themselves. In Tantra yoga, the initial intention is first carefully considered and then invoked many times a day so that not only is the intention an intellectual pivot but it becomes imbued with ever deeper feelings to fuel the flames of accomplishment. The intention is always for the greater good first, and for our own good a close second.

Next the three jewels must be activated, again, on a daily basis. This means relying on (1) the Buddhas, or those who have accomplished the path to enlightenment, (2) the dharma, or the truth and teachings about successfully following the path, and finally, (3) the sangha, or those current companions and gurus who are engaging the path with deep resolution. This reliance is external and provisional in the beginning until we manifest the transformational path, at which point our reliance shifts internally to our own awakened consciousness as a true guide. What is different in Tantra yoga is that practitioners also rely on the second formulation of the three jewels—the guru, yidam, and dakini—which is parallel to relying on the Buddha, dharma, and sangha. The guru is a masterful teacher who has the proven ability to lead you to liberation. A guru is different from a mentor in that the spiritual connection is much closer, perhaps lifetime after lifetime. Mentors and gurus are both trusted guides, but the guru, with your devoted and enthusiastic practice, doesn't just impart a great skill but leads you to ultimate spiritual realization. There is a trust that develops between guru and disciple that extends beyond appearances and seems to have its source before time began. Recognizing that connection as primal creates an energy for the disciple to persevere in dark moments and to call on phenomenal love, wisdom, and power at crucial moments on the path to resolve all impasses. Ultimately, we come to recognize that the outer guru is one and the same as the inner guru.

The path of the *ishtadevata,* or yidam, is common in Hinduism, yoga, and Tantrayana, but the practice differs in goal and method in each system. Ishtadevata in Sanskrit means preferred or personal deity, whereas yidam is the Tibetan term for chosen meditational deity. The basic practice is to recognize that you, however you may appear to yourself or others, are an enlightened being endowed with all the qualities of an enlightened being. You can engage a relation to the yidam in various degrees of self-identification, but it begins with an image of the yidam, usually a Buddha or Bodhisattva. We discussed some of these images in chapter 3. The point of the meditation is to engage your imagination and direct your senses so that you experience the world in which the yidam abides. With each meditation, the experience becomes more vivid as you chant the mantra of the yidam while exploring all the particular appearances of the enlightened dimension in which you immerse yourself. As you continue to nurture the yidam vision with your attention, energy, and presence, the image changes from being a static tableau into dynamic interaction. You may notice the yidam moving or speaking in a dream, or you may notice elements of your dreams and imaginations appearing as outer symbols and messages in the course of everyday living. When the yidam begins to interact with your conscious mind, a whole new level of practice arises in which you can ask for advice, receive valid guidance, and change the outer circumstances of your life from the inside. This type of practice neutralizes whatever negative karma, habits, or life patterns cause you distress. This phase is referred to as the development or creation stage.

The main variable of this practice is the degree you come to identify with the yidam. Do you experience the yidam externally as a deity far, far away, or as close by? Do you experience yourself directly as that enlightened Buddha or Bodhisattva? Usually one is required to receive an empowerment, a sadhana method, and instructions in order to practice oneself directly as the yidam and to recite the yidam's secret mantra. There are three practices, however, in which no empowerment is strictly necessary to experience yourself as a yidam: Bodhisattvas Avalokiteshvara (Chenrezig), Green Tara, and Medicine Buddha.* Additionally, no empowerment is necessary to chant the mantras of Manjushri or Amitabha, but empowerment is required to practice oneself directly as either. Important to any of the yidam practices is that we visualize the yidam as arising from empty space and we see the yidam as composed of rainbow light (figure 9.11 on the following page). Neither the yidam, nor we, are solid. Taking the illusion of solidity as real is what is at the root of how we misperceive ourselves and the world. At the conclusion of practice, we visualize the form of the yidam dissolving into space, and then we rest our awareness in the empty essence of the yidam for the rest of the meditation. This yidam practice shifts our ego-sense from a limited construct of self to an enlightened being whose form arises and dissolves, but whose presence is continuous awareness.

The next phase of yidam practice is called the completion stage, which may often begin before the creation stage is wholly accomplished. The completion stage involves a number of yogas organized as *anu*-yoga or as the six yogas of Naropa. The first is fire yoga (*tummo*) that transforms the capacity of the energy body by working with the channels, energy flow, and movement of collected energy essence orbs called *bindus* through the body complex. This capacity building of the energy body also includes charging and opening the mostly dormant energy meridians that exist outside the body. Depending on the school of practice, these meridians are thought to be as few as 36,000 or as many as 108,000 extracorporeal channels that collectively compose the human energy field or aura. When bindus melt and can move freely through open energy channels, our path to greater skill, vision, and enlightenment accelerates. A second, clear light yoga is about maintaining and increasing luminosity in deep sleep, in other words, learning lucid

---

*The mantras for these yidams are included in appendix 2.

Figure 9.11. Guru Padmasambhava transformed into a rainbow body of light with wish-fulfilling gems appearing in front.

dreaming. This awareness is carried from sleep to waking and back in and out of sleep as a continuous conscious thread. The next is dream yoga, in which we learn to remain aware when dreams occur, to recognize we are dreaming, and to alter dream content to change our waking experiences positively. Further, while dreaming, we aim to perceive ourselves not as our body or ego, but rather as the yidam we practice during the daylight cycle. Two more of the six yogas are learning about the dying, death, and reincarnation process, and then mastering the art of dying in order to transit consciously through the life and after-death *bardos* or intermediary states. Finally, there is the yoga of the illusory body, in which we completely dissolve all remaining subtle thoughts and energies that support identity with our physical body and ego complex. In this yoga we definitively transfer the flow of continuous awareness to establish the seat of our consciousness in the non-corporeal, subtle bodies known as *kayas*.

The last of the Tantrayana three gems is the dakini, which means female sky-goer. Dakini, or *khandro* in Tibetan, colloquially can refer to all women, but in the tantric context it usually implies wisdom or enlightened dakinis.

It is female life expression that catalyzes the transformation of life energy into wisdom. In Hindu tantric yoga, the feminine energy principle called *shakti* is also recognized as essential for any alchemical transformation to occur. Dakinis are the ones who grant *siddhis* to the yogini or yogi. *Siddhis* simply are the accomplished results of long and concentrated practice and are of two types, supreme and mundane. The supreme *siddhi* or power-ability is realizing enlightenment, whereas mundane *siddhis* are super-skills such as clairvoyance, invisibility, unconventional healing, levitation, or knowledge of past and future. The tension in the exercise of supreme and mundane *siddhis* is the heart of the chintamani dilemma. Mundane *siddhis* create greater means to benefit many more sentient beings, whereas the enlightened mind endowed with wisdom, compassion, and the intent to ease suffering prevents negative effects when exercising the mundane *siddhis*. The self-transformative alchemical process is so long and tedious that practitioners may regard the arising of mundane *siddhis* as proof positive of progress in the great work. That may or may not be true. It is possible to sidetrack to seek to attain ordinary *siddhis*. It is also a sidetrack to substitute attaining the supreme *siddhi* for a few mundane *siddhis*. An important function of the dakinis is to focus developed practitioners toward applying their wisdom very practically to complete the supreme path, and to create benefit for the community of all sentient beings.

Activating the Kayas with the Chintamani

In humans, there are many latent layers. Though we see the physical body and can measure its functions and movements, it is the densest but not the sole component of human architecture. According to Vedic philosophy, Kriya yoga, and Tantrayana yoga, we are comprised of layers and bodies. Like the elements, the bodies—which Kriya yoga calls *sharira* and Tantrayana calls *kaya*—ascend in increasing levels of subtlety and vibrant essence. The denser a person's energy and awareness, the less likely they are to perceive even the presence of these subtle bodies. The denser person is also less likely to activate these *kayas* through a series of focused yogas. These *kayas* begin to function only after arising from a quantum activation of the underlying enlightened architecture. Sometimes there is a scheme of three, four, or five *kayas* posited for teaching or practice purposes. Occasionally, another term, the *vajrakaya,* or diamond body, is used to describe activating the complete set of *kayas*. The diamond body, and other *kayas,* resonate directly with the chintamani. This is true whether we think of the chintamani as a world-changing gem, a mental and energetic field of all gems, or as the activation of mind energies that will coalesce as the *vajrakaya*. This is the ultimate alchemical result.

The chintamani is the mind crystal. It reflects, refracts, and resonates through the mind's energies. The chintamani is the ground of activity and the focus of the light of intention. The chintamani is the treasure, the map, and the holder of the supreme gem. The chintamani can rise as a mountain range to bar the self-indulgent and can open outer, inner, and secret realms for the wise and compassionate. The chintamani amplifies the meaning of life and faithfully transmits the code of evolution. The chintamani is a diamond path through the cosmos to the origins of all. Why then do so few follow its spiral path beyond time and place?

10
Creating the Chintamani
Alchemical Formulae, Mystical Art, and Treasure Vases

The esthetic image in the dramatic form is life purified in and reprojected from the human imagination. The mystery of esthetic like that of material creation is accomplished. The artist, like the God of the creation, remains within or behind or beyond or above his handiwork, invisible, refined out of existence, indifferent, paring his fingernails.

JAMES JOYCE, *A PORTRAIT OF THE ARTIST AS A YOUNG MAN*

IT IS ALMOST AUTOMATIC TO ENVISION the chintamani as a great earthly gem like the Hope Diamond and to consider it as a very rare but natural object. Even the Hope Diamond does not fit that description. Great gems like the Hope are discovered not by noticing them on the ground, but by mining for them, a difficult process engineered by man. Then a raw, uncut gem block must be faceted and polished to reveal some potential qualities that a skilled artisan recognizes. The lapidarist relies on faceting technology as well as personal skill to master gem-cutting techniques. Even were we to reconsider the Hope Diamond, we have to acknowledge it is not solely a product of nature but is at least half man-made. This brings us to examine a wide variety of created chintamani-like objects such as alchemical glass, spagyrics, or the Philosopher's Stone manifested as the *lapis*.

Created chintamanis share some common qualities beyond being fashioned by the mind and hand of a creator. Like the Hope Diamond, they are some combination of natural ingredients, but are compounded with sacred and scientific technologies, both of which are empirically joined. The created chintamani connects with and amplifies thought waves, especially catalyzing and broadcasting intention. The IIED invention of Dr. William Tiller discussed in chapter 7 is a good example of this quality as well as of a created chintamani. His device also interfaces with consciousness itself, bridging interdimensional fields. Created chintamanis also collect, store, and radiate a range of energies. Created chintamani objects are programmable and can retain programmed information. Finally, they can be tuned and reprogrammed to some extent.

Essentially, there are three chintamanis. The first is the mystical chintamani with supernatural powers to grant wishes. It is the chintamani of the dragons and the wind horse appearing in myth, creative imagination, and the spiritual realms. The second are tangible stones associated with mystical powers. They are highly valuable and typically possessed by the wealthy elite, the powerful of the world, or are hidden in temples or sacred places. The third chintamani is a hybrid stone, a chintamani that bridges spirit and matter. We have presented the mythical chintamani and discussed some of the power stones of the world. But it is with the unification of spirit and matter that the most powerful chintamani is found. This process can be achieved through meditation and alignment with spirit, but there are other methods by which to create the chintamani, an alchemical method akin to the creation of the Philosopher's Stone. We investigate the process of creating tangible or quasi-tangible chintamanis uniting minerals and energy with prayer, ritual, and intention. This topic significantly widened our understanding of the nature of the chintamani, and we expect it will expand your understanding as well. We present examples of created chintamanis, of which we were unaware when we began researching. We first begin with the way others have created the energetic blueprint and architecture of the chintamani, or the Philosopher's Stone, using mathematics and geometry.

The Chintamani Code

In Tibetan Buddhism, there is a symbolic seed syllable that encapsulates the complex essence of the Kalachakra tantra and is referred to as the emblem or mantra of Kalachakra, whose mandala we discussed in chapter 4. The Kalachakra emblem is also referred to as the "Ten of Power," the "Ten Syllables of Power," or the "One With Ten Powers" (figure 10.1). Embedded within the Kalachakra tantra and mandala is the Wheel of Time, thus named for its ability to transcend the limitations of time and space. This tantra is encoded within the seed syllable and the ten parts are presented with seven syllables on the bottom part of the symbol and three on the top. The top portion is represented by a solar disc, round moon bindu, and a nada wisp, which corresponds with space. The top portion of the symbol, the nada

Figure 10.1. Kalachakra seed syllable known as the "Ten of Power."

wisp rising out of the round bindu, looks very similar to the flaming chintamani. The seven syllables pictured below represent the five elements and the animate, inanimate, and formless realms, which is a harmonic alchemical blending of energy and matter. The elements also represent Mount Meru.[1] The entire image is surrounded by flame. The Ten of Power symbol brings together the alchemical processes involving energy and matter into one complex yet supremely succinct symbol. The stylized Sanskrit syllables represent a mantra associated with the Kalachakra which, when studied and practiced, is a key to open the Kalachakra and a harmonic gateway to Shambhala.*

In chapter 9, we identified the orb at the top of the caduceus staff in Hermetic alchemy as the *lapis* or the Philosopher's Stone. Here we examine the orb at the top of Hermes' staff through the work of two alchemists who were scientific geniuses of their time: Dr. John Dee and Sir Isaac Newton. While chapter 9 explored the alchemical processes along the staff of Hermes and through the chakra system on the spine, we now turn our attention to the top of the spine or staff and focus on that orb more closely, as though looking at it with a microscope. Both Dee and Newton probed into the *lapis* closely, observing it mechanistically through math, geometry, and chemistry. We suspect that their work with the *lapis* inspired their scientific advances. We also suspect their work connects with Tibetan cosmology symbolically presented through the Kalachakra and chintamani.

Dr. John Dee (1527–1609) created a synthesized and concise symbol known as the *Hieroglyphic Monad* (figure 10.2). Dee was a mathematician, astrologer, alchemist, and advisor to Queen Elizabeth I. His influence was significant as he selected the date for Elizabeth's coronation and coined the term "British Empire" during her reign. The *Monad,* also known as the hieroglyph of the stone, represented a succinct unity of alchemical processes. The symbol was published in Dee's *Monas Hieroglyphica* in 1564, an alchemical text, difficult to understand. It has been theorized that Dee purposefully presented the text in code so that it could not be understood by the uninitiated. Considering the brutality of the time period toward those

---

*The Kalachakra seed syllable mantra is found on the internet and in *The Wheel of Time Sand Mandala* by Barry Bryant. The mantra should be practiced after receiving the Kalachakra empowerment.

promulgating novel ideas, it is understandable that alchemists avoided full transparency. The etymology of the symbol's name is of interest, as it may lead to a simpler explanation as to what Dee's treatise may have referred.

A hieroglyph is a picture of a word, while *monas* is a Greek term meaning "unit." So the symbol may refer to a representation of a unit or prime unit. Astrological and alchemical symbols are integrated into the image, and the glyphs for the sun, moon, Mercury, and others are easily discernable, but integrated in such a way to show synthesis of the alchemical processes. The processes are not achieved or operated in a linear manner but are synthesized to create cohesion that Dee contemplated as the "one thing." It is a representation of the creative unit that is the source of matter. As Dee was a leading European mathematician and astrologer whose works had an enduring legacy, the symbol could be viewed as an advanced, syncretic equation. Indeed, Holy Grail researchers Michael Baigent and Richard Leigh[2] described the *Monas* as the Hermetic equivalent of Einstein's $E=mc^2$. In the *Chymical Wedding of Christian Rosenkreutz* (1616), the Rosicrucians further popularized the *monas* symbol in early writings, associating it with a magical text or Renaissance *terma* that was delivered by a divine winged being as a precursor to the alchemical wedding.[3]

The advanced mathematical formulas encoded in the *Monas* are further elucidated by Jim Egan, who considers Dee an "atomist" and decodes the *Monas* text by explaining the twenty-four theorems postulated by Dee as

Figure 10.2. *Hieroglyphic Monad* by Dr. John Dee.

parts of a treatise on geometry.[4] In his study, Egan theorizes that the *Monas* was mathematically based, but written in the code language of alchemy. When translated into modern vernacular, Egan asserts that Dee is discussing the connection between mathematics and geometry. With respect to the "one thing," which is frequently another term for the Philosopher's Stone, Dee claimed that the "Value of the ONE THING which others purport to be Chaos, is primarily explained by the Number TEN."[5] The number ten represents all the elements added together, which is the center of the *Monas*. Egan argues that Dee knew about the atom, that he discovered the cuboctahedron (a cube and octahedron combination), and that his thinking is consistent with modern synergetics. Synergetics refers to systems in transformation and is a work by Buckminster Fuller published in the 1970s. Essentially, John Dee's version of the Philosopher's Stone is a geometric model for understanding the transformation of matter, which is the heart of the creation of the *lapis,* and which describes the shape and energy system of a transformative crystal vehicle.

From the sixteenth-century Renaissance, we jump 120 years to Sir Isaac Newton (1643–1727), who was a cornerstone and founder of the scientific revolution of the seventeenth century. Newton was also an avid alchemist, a fact that has only been receiving attention more recently. It is estimated that he wrote over one million words about alchemy alone. A substantial collection of Newton's alchemical papers was offered for auction in 1936, which brought to light a unique and surprising side to his studies that had hitherto remained in the shadow and which required a revised assessment of Newton as an Age of Enlightenment scientist.[6] In 2016, a recipe for the Philosopher's Stone written in the hand of Newton was made public. Both Dee and Newton were recognized geniuses of science and mathematics in their respective eras but studied the same alchemical texts. Curiously, both attended and became fellows at Trinity College in Cambridge, England, and both were involved in cryptography.*

Newton drew an intriguing alchemical mandala titled *Lapis Philosophicus*

---

*Trinity College has a long history with cryptography. During World War II, the spies who broke the Nazi enigma code studied at Trinity College and the English Government Code and Cipher School's station was called "Station X."

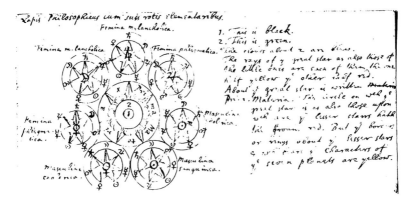

Figure 10.3. *Lapis Philosophicus cum ratis elementaribus*
by Sir Isaac Newton, c. 1690s.
The Babson College's Grace K. Babson Collection of the Works of
Sir Isaac Newton, The Huntington Library, San Marino, CA

("Philosopher's Stone with its elemental wheels") depicting a central wheel
with a star surrounded by seven smaller wheels all bearing alchemical and
astrological glyphs (figure 10.3). The seven classical planets (and their associated metals) are represented in sequence counterclockwise around the central
wheel. There are notations in Newton's handwriting for each of the seven
smaller wheels identifying their gender and humor.* To the right of the mandala wheel, Newton writes a description of the colors of the sections of the
wheels; for example, the rays are yellow and red, the center is black and green,
and the circles around the smaller wheels are yellow (figure 10.4 on the following page is a colored version of the mandala wheel). Around the circumference of the large inner wheel is written the words *Prima Materia x*. The
Latin term means "first matter" and is frequently associated with the *lapis,*
which represents not only "first matter" but also the most subtle essence
within matter, which is not solid. The presence of the *x* is intriguing and may
have a variety of meanings. First, as one of the inventors of calculus, Newton
may have been solving for *x* with respect to the *Prima Materia*. The *x* could
also mean that there is a missing element or ingredient that has not been
solved, or it could represent a secret formula that is left out intentionally so

*The humors referred to four fluids (blood, phlegm, yellow bile, black bile) and repre-
sented the balance of health in the body and behavioral characteristics.

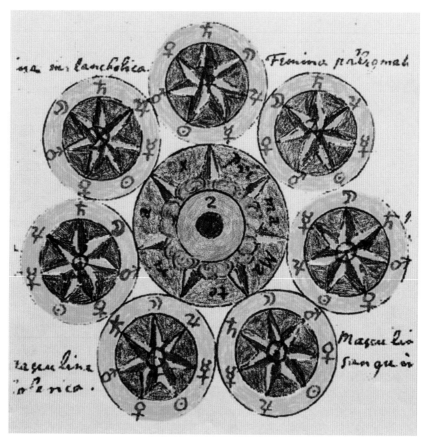

Figure 10.4. The Philosopher's Stone based on
Newton's description of the colored element wheels.
Colored version by H. Hara

that the uninitiated cannot solve the code. As a Roman numeral, X represents 10 and infers the importance of the number ten, which was found in Dee's work and the Kalachakra seed syllable. Ten is also found in the geometry of Newton's mandala. The first circle in the diagram is numbered 1, followed by the second circle numbered 2. There is a third circle that is unnumbered but contains the *x*. Around the triple concentric circles are seven elemental or planetary circles. There are ten circles in total. There is an equivalency of Newton's mandala with the Kalachakra symbol. The symbol at the top of the Kalachakra seed symbol represents three elements followed by seven syllables in the lower part of the symbol. Newton has the core components of three concentric circles at the center of his mandala image.

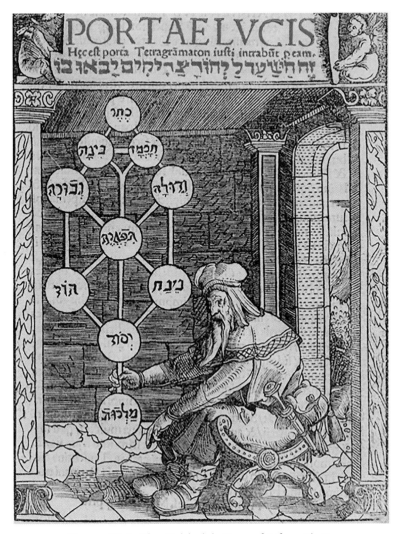

Figure 10.5. The Kabbalah Tree of Life with its
ten sefirot spheres. *Portae Lucis* by Joseph Gikatilla (1248–1325),
Augsburg, 1516, Diaspora Museum, Tel Aviv.

Correspondingly, the Tree of Life from the Kabbalah has ten circular sefirot in its matrix. As shown in figure 10.5, there are three sefirot at the top of the diagram and the remaining seven comprise the body of the image below. The three sefirot at the top are regarded as containing secret information emanating from the mind of God. The word "sefirot" has interesting etymological variations including counting, enumeration, sapphire, brilliance, and luminary.[7] The student of the Kabbalah is to concentrate on the study and purity of the self through the teachings of the lower seven sefirot. The topmost sefirot is *keter,* which translates to "crown" and is considered sublime, hidden, concealed, and beyond comprehension, as it also represents nothingness. It is through the Kabbalah sefirot that the ten utterances of creation are manifested. In the *Sefer Yetzirah,* the Kabbalistic book of creation from which the Tree of Life derived around the second century CE, the sefirot are referred to as the "Ten Sefirot of Nothingness" and the text is explicit about the number: "Ten and not nine, ten and not eleven."[8] The number and energies of the sefirot are further described as "their measure is ten which have no end . . . their end is imbedded in their beginning, and their beginning in their end, like a flame in a burning coal."[9]

Through the exponential power of 10, the Kalachakra symbol, Dee's *monas,* Newton's wheel of elements, and the Kabbalah sefirot express the core scale of the cosmos from the atomic level to the vastness of the universe. Through the power of 10 or X, the wish-fulfilling gem can be magnified exponentially either at a core atomic level or up to galactic and universal scales. The chintamani is completely expressed at the micro level but is also completely expressed at the macro level. The underlying ability of the monad to become anything and dissolve and reconstitute itself is the quality of emptiness. The essence of the "one thing" is that it is outside the model of subatomic particles, because it cannot be divided. We posit that these insights about the power of 10 express the energetic structure of the chintamani and that this chintamani is the jewel that is held by Kalachakra and Kalachakri at the center of the Kalachakra mandala, the Wheel of Time. The chintamani is also the orb at the top of the caduceus.

Chintamani Orbs and Alchemical Glass

While researching chintamanis and tektites, the authors came across an unusual chintamani "stone" on eBay. The objects are irregularly shaped spheres of two different sizes (two or four inches in diameter) and several different colors, including variations of green, blue, violet, orange, aquamarine, and black. There are rectangular-shaped stones for sale, but they are considered rare. They have a sand-blasted, pitted looking surface with many scars and imperfections. The orbs radiate a translucent glow in sunshine or candlelight that charmingly

Figure 10.6. Chintamani orb.
Photo by Kaleigh Brown

lights their interiors in deep, rich colors (figure 10.6). When lighted, each orb displays an irregular variation of colors in the same range. At the base of each orb there is a sediment coating. Merchants on eBay say that they are sacred chintamani stones and talismans. There are claims that the objects originated from Tibet and made their way to the Angkor Wat Temple and were buried nearby. Some report that they come from Buddhist caves in Thailand or were buried near Phimai Temple in Thailand after discovery by Buddhist monk Luang Por Koon. One seller shares that they are stones from the Mekong River in Thailand and may be associated with the Udon Thani Ban Chiang archaeological site (c. 2100–200 BCE), which is home to exquisite ancient pottery with intriguing patterns. Another seller stated that he was selling authentic chintamani orbs originating from India, while other sellers were selling imitations made from Chinese glass. There are claims that these stones are natural. Some orbs are reputed to be coated with funerary ash. One description speculates that the orbs originated in Tibet as a type of insignia given to Buddhist masters and gurus. The orbs are considered tools for meditative focus. The

Figure 10.7. Chintamani stones of varying colors including
three fire chintamanis (detail from a Tibetan Thangka).

objects resemble the spherical chintamani stones of varying colors that appear
in Tibetan Thangkas (figure 10.7).

We purchased a few of the chintamani spheres for research, expecting
that they would be simple glass objects, overhyped by their advertising. We
were surprised to discover that the orbs hold an unusually palpable energy.
Viewed in natural light, they are so ordinary that they are almost invisible.
They parallel our experiences with crystal skulls (discussed later in this chapter) in that they are tangible objects radiating energy but have a mysterious
and controversial history. Just like the crystal skulls, the orbs may be the
remnants of an ancient technology that has been lost in antiquity and is no
longer understood.

We questioned whether the orbs were glass-stone compositions based
on ancient alchemical recipes that shift energy fields and states of consciousness. This supposition is supported by Beretta who found, through
extensive research, that the histories of alchemy and glassmaking are deeply
entwined.[10] According to Beretta, glassmaking is an ancient art dating back
to the Mesopotamians in 2500 BCE who performed religious rituals while
making glass. It was the Egyptians though, who, around 1400 BCE under
Akhenaton,[11] turned glassmaking into a refined, albeit secretive, alchemical artform with glassmaking kilns housed in the sacred Egyptian temples.
Glassmaking and alchemy were so entwined that the alchemists considered

the creation of glass on par with the creation of matter, so much so that molten glass objects were considered a form of alchemical gold in that ordinary sand could be transformed to create so-called gems. To the ancients, glass was not considered a cheap byproduct, but rather the sacred combination of science and art that produced a magical substance referred to as "molten stone."[12] While sand and metal oxides were used to create glass, powdered quartz is reported to have been used in both Egypt and India. It is the secret rituals associated with glassmaking and the belief that glass was a transformative substance akin to the Philosopher's Stone that are most intriguing. We did find that Alexandria was a glassmaking export center due to its vast deposits of natural soda, but we were unable to connect alchemical glassmaking directly to Tibet.[13] It was also asserted by Beretta that "in India glass is made also of broken rock-crystal and that for this reason no glass can compare with that of India."[14]

Chintamani orbs are widely present in Asian art and motifs, but orbs are also present in Egyptian art. Orbs of various colors appear on top of the heads of Egyptian gods and goddesses and within hieroglyphics (figure 10.8 on the following page). Most importantly, an orb is the centerpiece of the winged disc. While the circle at the center is typically attributed to the sun, the Egyptian orbs also may have other layers of meaning. The winged disc also appears on the top of Hermes' staff, the caduceus (figure 9.5, page 218). We previously discussed the orbs above the heads of angels in medieval art (figures 8.16 and 8.17, page 197) and orbs present in Buddhist art (figures 3.4 and 3.5, pages 62–63).

It was difficult to obtain verifiable information about the Thai orbs from vendors, and there is little about these chintamani orbs in the archaeological record or other sources. We submitted two of the orbs for materials analysis and verified that the primary component of the objects is silica, which could be crushed quartz or glass. Analysis also verified trace elements as coloring agents. More detail about the materials analysis is in appendix 3. We used meditative and psychic practices as a technique to gather more information about the objects. We consulted several people who have developed skills in Reiki, shamanic practice, or intuitive abilities. Each person we consulted had strong interactions with the orbs and sensed an unusual field of energy around the objects. There were unifying themes

Figure 10.8. Horus with red orb above his head and orb at the center of winged disc at top. Egyptian Stele, Museo Egizio, Torino, Italy.

Photo by H. Hara

among those who held and meditated with them. Some stated that they felt the orbs were part of an ancient or even off-world technology. Many felt a tangible presence of energy that activated from the back of their head and rose up to the top and front of the head. Most felt the orb was both sending and receiving energy. A Reiki practitioner felt that the orbs helped her relax and that they could be useful in her healing work. After meditating with the orbs, one of the intuitives we consulted had a dream that the orbs were being returned to the ancient Buddhas who were awaking. In the dream, she cleared away leaves and debris from old Buddha statues and placed the orbs in the hands of Buddhas. The authors also meditated with the orbs to discover further qualities.

HH: *In meditation with the orb, I consistently feel an initial energetic shift, then I sense resonant waves generating around and outward from my auric field, which deeply relax me and change my state of consciousness. I sometimes feel chills at the top of my spine and the back of my head. I often see a vesica piscis formation initially before starting to drift into a deeper state of consciousness where I have experienced an ecstatic connection with higher source and, at other times, entered unending tunnels that looked like wormholes. During one meditation, after chanting Tibetan mantras, the object became warm in my hand, and in my mind's eye, I saw flames emanating from the orb. Later, after I returned to a normal state of consciousness, I realized that I had experienced the orb as the chintamani fire stone. I have found the energy so palpable and strong that I do not need to hold the orb very long. Once I am in an altered state of consciousness, I can let go of the orb and continue meditating. Over a period of time, I feel as though I have incorporated the teachings of the orb with respect to meditation because I can access that same state of consciousness without using the orb. The state is not quite as strong as when I hold the orb, but I prefer the lesser intensity unless I need to do deeper meditative work.*

One of the orbs has a doorway made of a different color than the rest of the crystal sphere. That orb led me into a different state of consciousness, or beyond a veil of illusion, awakening my third eye using a different form of seeing than my ordinary vision. During intense meditation while holding a blue-purple orb, I entered another state and walked down a long temple corridor to meet an ancient king. The temple edifice was so magnificent and large that I could not recall where it could have been on Earth, as it did not resemble any archaeological description or illustration with which I am familiar. I did not know where I had gone, but it seemed vaguely Egyptian, but also older than Egypt. After the meditation, I felt as though I actually had traveled to that ancient time.

JG: *I began with a Buddhist ritual of prayers, mantras, and meditations, as the orbs have a probable Buddhist connection. It seems that the orbs respond to Buddhist practices, but the orbs also seem to respond to other practices, including Daoist, Vedic, and several I could not identify. One orb seemed to have a long history, at least from the Tang dynasty (581–907 CE), and perhaps from an even earlier era. That orb resonated as I chanted the Avalokiteshvara mantra, but I saw the female Bodhisattva Kuan Yin, the form of Avalokiteshvara common in China, Indochina, Korea, and Japan, and not the male form of the Bodhisattva Chenrezig, common in Mongolia, Tibet, Nepal, and India.*

On a qi energetic level, the orbs can radiate a warm, comfortable field. Their qi fields become quiet when in shadow or active when glowing in light. Energy seems able to pass through them in a direction like up/down or north/south, and energy also can radiate evenly around the sphere. The orbs are able to pull qi energy into and through themselves as well. When pulsing a qi field with an orb in between, the results are unexpected. In one direction, the field collapses, but when placed at a 90-degree angle the field radiates. In the 180-degree position, the field again collapses, but again radiates in the 270-degree position. This is true if you rotate the orbs horizontally or vertically. In short, an orb can take or add energy to a person who is holding it, depending on positioning. The energy flow also intensifies when combined with crystal grids (refer to chapter 8), mantras, mudras, and rituals. The orb seems designed to function in groupings with other orbs or crystals. Grids containing volcanic and meteoric glass, jade, and the Navaratna gems produce an even more palpable result. The orbs are chintamani-like in that they facilitate intention. Although the orbs work well in astro-grid fields, that does not seem to be their original design function. The orbs seem to have an alchemical facet to their manufacture, and further have technological capability beyond just being activated by light, heat, or qi-field contact. There is a misty past from which these orbs have emerged. They are evocative and seem much more ancient and sophisticated than they first appear.

Globus Cruciger

Salvator Mundi is a recently discovered painting credited to Leonardo da Vinci that sold in November 2017 at a Christie's auction for $450.3 million.

Figure 10.9. *Salvator Mundi* attributed to Leonardo da Vinci, c. 1500.

Prince Badr, Minister of Culture for Saudi Arabia, bought *Salvator Mundi* (Latin for "Savior of the World") to be placed in the Louvre Museum in Abu Dhabi, but the painting has not yet been publicly displayed. The painting has undergone thorough conservation, including cleaning, disassembly, reassembly, leveling of the painted surface, and restorative painting. The 26 x 18 inch painting depicts Christ in Renaissance robes with his right hand raised in blessing and left hand holding a large crystal orb heart high (figure 10.9). Additionally, there are three dots painted on the orb that may represent the threefold chintamani symbol as presented in chapter 5. In fact, the presence of the three dots may be a code hidden in plain sight to communicate to the initiated that the orb is the chintamani. There are also three stones embedded in Christ's garment, which again infers the triple gem. The detailed bands on the clothing look suspiciously like complex copper circuitry, and they cross over the chest of the figure in an X formation.

Overall, more attention is placed on clothing detail then on depicting Christ, whose neck is all but invisible and whose face curiously lacks the detail so typical of da Vinci, a master at painting the human form. There is contrary evidence as to whether the painting is the direct work of da Vinci, a painter of his school, a misappropriation, or a forgery. The painted orb itself is at the center of some of the controversy, as it does not accurately portray the optics associated with glass orbs with which da Vinci would have been familiar. Despite the controversy surrounding this painting, the crystal orb maintains the same symbolism regardless of origin. There are a number of versions of this same subject by other artists depicting Christ in the same manner holding a crystal orb in his left hand. Archangels such as Michael and Uriel frequently hold orbs (figure 10.10). Because the orb is held by an incarnation of or servant of God, it implies it is the chintamani of wisdom, compassion, and universal blessing. There are also images of Jupiter, king of the Greco-Roman gods, holding a plain globe, the *orbis terrarum,* or earth orb, symbolizing dominion. Orbs are found among kings and in crown jewels. For instance, the Merovingian King Childeric was buried with a crystal orb,[15] and among the Scottish Crown Jewels in Edinburgh Castle, the top of the scepter in the royal jewels collection is a crystal orb.

By contrast, there are similar images of a sphere held sometimes by Christ or by any number of European crowned rulers. These orbs are different

Figure 10.10. *Archangel Michael with a horn trumpet and an orb,*
ninth century, Faras, Sudan, in National Museum of Warsaw, Poland.

Figure 10.11. Queen Elizabeth in coronation robes holding *globus cruciger*.
Queen Elizabeth I, c. 1600–1610, National Portrait Gallery, London.

because they are surmounted by a cross, as in the images of the coronation regalia of Queens Elizabeth I and II of England (figures 10.11 and 10.12). This symbol is known as the *globus cruciger*. A common explanation is that the cross symbolizes Christianity, with the implication that the monarch is a worldly regent wielding Christ's spiritual and temporal authority. A deeper meaning comes from the symbol for the planet Mars used both in astrology and astronomy. The Mars symbol is now a circle with an arrow at the top right (♂). An earlier symbol for Mars depicts the cross of matter directly above the circle of spirit, which is an inverted Venus symbol (♁). The *globus cruciger*, in other words, is a three-dimensional symbol of the domain of the god of war. Clearly, this is the worldly power aspect of the use of the chintamani. Another side of the symbolism is how the central figure holds the orb or *globus cruciger*. In coronation images of Elizabeths I and II, the queen holds a *globus cruciger* at the level of her Mars chakra. In *Salvator Mundi*,

Figure 10.12. The crown jewels from the Coronation of Elizabeth II. Pictured: St. Edward's Crown, Orb, Scepter with Cross, Scepter with Dove, and Ring in *Illustrated Magazine*, 1952.

Christ holds the crystal orb at the level of the higher Venus chakra. The plain orb in two dimensions is the circle or an astrological sun symbol (☉). It symbolizes mastery primarily in the realm of spirit but can project worldly dominion. Here we see the conflict between the *globus cruciger* and the clear crystal orb as a chintamani used for temporal power or universal benefit.

Crystal Skulls

A topic we did not plan to discuss originally is crystal skulls, but life events led us each to direct interactions with two famous crystal skulls. It became clear early in our search for the chintamani that the dynamic quest experience is about self-cultivation practice, revelation, actual gems and crystals, an open mind, and following the appearance of wise guidance. We are on a path, as is anyone interested in the chintamani quest, that opens in following it sincerely. The crystal skulls began showing up for us personally around a spring equinox, the first being an elder crystal skull rediscovered by archaeologist F. A. Mitchell-Hedges (MH skull) in the Mayan ruins of Lubantuum in Belize in 1924.[16] Like others, we approached the topic of crystal skulls with wonder, skepticism, information, and misinformation, but mostly with the intention to make a direct mind and energy connection. We were exploring the validity of crystal skull encounters. Besides the MH skull, we also were able to connect with the crystal skull known as "Synergy" when it also appeared close to home. We were exploring what, if any, the connection to the chintamani might be.

All crystal skulls, even imitations, are formed through some application of technology, from crude to impeccable. While investigators may dispute the minutiae of the presence or non-presence of microscopic tool marks on the skull surface, there is the fact that Synergy and the MH skull are anatomically correct in shape and human scale. Estimates are that to sculpt either of these clear crystal skulls, they would have to have been carved from a fairly clear crystal mass two to three times the size of the final skull. The angle of carving relative to the natural crystal plane is also amazing in that it would require great skill not to shatter the skull in the shaping process. Even if these crystal skulls are modern and were made in the last several centuries, the technology and skill to create the shape alone is quite advanced. Crystal skull debunkers point out that the great majority of skulls are modern and some are faked, and if most crystal skulls are modern imitations, then all crystal skulls must be modern fakes. That logic is clearly invalid. There is plenty of scientific, provenance, and anecdotal evidence to weigh, and many authors provide alternate evaluations, so we will not pursue that inquiry in any more depth here.[17]

Beyond the manufacture technology, there is inherent crystal technology present in every crystal skull. In addition, there is an energy and mind interface technology embedded in the most advanced skulls. Debatable, perhaps, but we are asserting based on our direct interactions that there are very palpable energy and consciousness fields accessible in both the Synergy and MH skulls. There are many external observations of both skulls documenting effects such as changes in light, temperature, and other phenomena that are readily available evidence. What follows are descriptions of a few of our internal experiences.

HH: *While in the same room, but not next to the skull, I sensed that my consciousness was inside the skull and I was looking out through liquid crystalline eyes. I felt I was in liquid crystal space and had access to another world or other dimensions. There was a doorway or spiral staircase going through the top of the skull, but I could look up through the top of the skull and also look down through the spine. I had the sense that looking down the spiral staircase spine, I was looking through deep time. The energy radiates down and transforms the entire human skeletal system into liquid crystal, which is useful for developing higher evolutionary states. This state could be useful for physical healing, such as in the bones, but also in higher spiritual vibratory practice, such as developing the rainbow body. I saw a crystalline rainbow crack in the quartz skull from inside. This crack represented a crack in the ego, reality, or the matrix and provided an opening to reach enlightenment. I sensed that once I connected to this liquid crystal state, I could reconnect at other times. My bones felt dynamically fluid during the connection, and I felt that I was working on inner transformation.*

The negativity associated with crystal skulls has more to do with human perception than with the skull. The skull is useful as a projective mask tool that is sophisticated and can be symbolically worn to facilitate evolution.

While in the same room with the skull, I felt powerful waves of energy and light emanating from it, and I went into a deep theta state. I sensed that the energetic waves radiating from the skull were clearing the auras and energies of everyone in the room. I experienced a stairway of light radiating from my activated third eye that had triangular, chiseled steps. I intuitively used the light bridge to communicate to other dimensions and tuned into other planets. Several small luminous white beings glided down the light bridge/stairway and entered the room. The luminous beings were from a council and were there to assist others in service of compassion. They moved to certain people in the room who were most in need of help. They formed a circle to harmonize the gathering and were participating in the session with us. While I saw the white beings interacting with others in the room energetically, I also heard people in the session asking questions about the skull, and inside my mind I could hear the answer from the skull faster than I could think. I slowly looked down and saw my bones as though I were looking at myself with x-ray vision and noticed they had transformed into a liquid crystal state and I was immersed in liquid space.

During a private session with MH, I was able to inspect the skull to look for the crack I had seen in my mind. I found a large natural fissure with a rainbow in the middle of the skull, and I knew it was a crystalline gateway. Putting my hand over the fissure, I sensed that there was a program placed in the quartz skull that aids in making breakthroughs in consciousness, ego, or matter so that other frequencies can enter. Looking into the skull was like looking into liquid outer space. During the session, with my hands over MH, I linked into energy sites around the planet including Stonehenge, Carnac, and others, and this linkage allowed for three of us in the room to send out positive energetic waves into the earth grid.

I have also had opportunities to interact with the Synergy crystal skull a few times. I noticed that the waves emanating from Synergy are more subtle than MH, but not less powerful. When the skull is placed against my third eye,

I can instantly see the island from which it came, including the blue sky and the sea. The skull itself seems to radiate a blue-sky energy. Synergy works as a beacon, and when I chant with the skull, it broadcasts a far-reaching radio signal. It can transmit across Earth and into space. During public sessions, its keeper, Sherry Whitfield, involves the group in a drumming circle with Synergy.

JG: *I encountered the MH skull twice in both public lecture and private viewing sessions and Synergy in three public practice sessions. Both guardians of the crystal skulls narrate a guided meditation as part of their presentations and are prompted to teach based on the audience as a whole. Even in a room full of people with the MH skull, I experienced a palpable energy that pulsed my third eye and crown chakras immediately. My awareness of the energy of Synergy was similar, but it radiated more subtly than the MH skull. The energy pulse seemed to create an open channel connection along which information flowed in two forms. One information set included symbols and awareness that made immediate sense, and another information set was compressed and meant to integrate over time in later pertinent insight.*

From the MH skull, I had three pivotal insights. The first was not just knowing but experiencing my own body first as clear crystal, then as a fluid crystal. That perception has been reorganizing my perspective since. Second, I became aware that the jewel net of Indra includes the entire amount of crystals in the total Earth field whether unmined and natural or shaped, polished, carved, or faceted. That jewel net connects global conscious mind. Finally, I experienced my own three central energy meridians as a spiral in flux that is removing illusive perception and increasing the mind energy complex that flows through those meridians. From the Synergy skull, I had a perception of continuous blue light emanating from the skull and also present as a light in my own chakras. The Synergy skull has a Micronesian twin that is central in ceremony to the tribe who are its collective guardians. I have the sense of the community of these twin skulls interacting across the globe and creating the jewel net of Indra, not just in crystals but in human groups as well. Last, the Synergy skull seems to add information and energy to manifest my monthly intentions, but only as they emerge, not all at once, nor in advance.

Unexpectedly, a phenomenal healer gave me a small crystal skull nicknamed Mini Max (figure 10.13). Its name and reason for being comes from the famous crystal skull Max. Apparently, Max transmitted subsets of his crystalline information to a number of smaller crystal skulls. Like other crystal skulls, Mini Max holds information that can be accessed through meditation in a deep theta state. Although Mini Max is a modern creation, he radiates palpable energy and presence—why else would I describe him

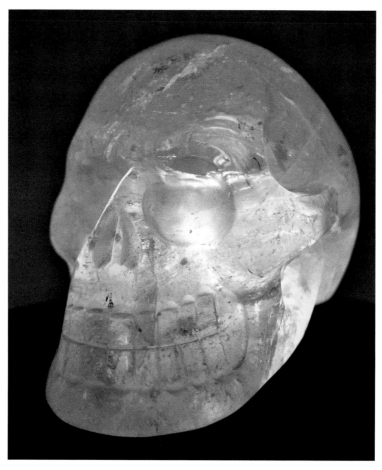

Figure 10.13. Mini Max the crystal skull.
Photo by Kaleigh Brown

with a personal pronoun? His energy field was strongest when he faced the same direction as me. Mini Max has been silent and enigmatic for the last ten years, but that has been changing as we have written this book. Energy around Mini Max has been building, suggesting he may be ready to disclose some of his secrets plainly in the near future.

The Treasure Vase

Another variety of created chintamani are treasure vases in the tradition of Tibetan Vajrayana Buddhism. Other cultures have similar practices to uphold the sacredness of Earth and its seen and unseen inhabitants. In Vajrayana practice, there are two types of treasure vases: an earth vase intended to be buried and a home, shrine, or temple vase intended to be displayed reverently. Both types of vases are created to purify and support the environment, not only close to where they are placed, but also to benefit the larger, local geography and community of sentient beings traveling that area. As Earth has been systematically mined and stripped of its treasure and abundance to fashion an artificial wealth system, placing treasure vases, and similar sacred practices, are intended to restore greater universal benefit and revive Gaia's abundant life and bounty. Treasure vases fulfill the promise of the positive chintamani path.

There are a number of lineages within Vajrayana Buddhism that incorporate treasure vases into their spiritual practices. This involves gathering sacred substances to combine in the vases, astrological timing and rituals involved in compounding vases, consecrating vases in place, and continued mantra and meditative practices in the presence of treasure vases to increase the reach of their benefit. Usually treasures vases embody the vows and compassionate activity of a particular Buddha or Bodhisattva as presented in chapter 3. At the heart, treasure vases are intended to benefit both livelihood and dharma. Treasure vases are asserted to improve a person's karma not only in this life but also in the transitionary phases (bardos) of death and rebirth. As an example, we present the treasure vase tradition of Orgyen Khandro Norlha as formulated by Dudjom Yeshe Jigdral Dorje (1904–1987).

Earth treasure vases are designed for burial, but each teaching lineage sets out particular guidelines for finding suitable places. The main criteria are to locate a spot unlikely to be disturbed by tree roots, water flow, unstable cliffs, earthquakes, or human activity. Earth vases placed on powerful energy meridians radiate all benefits of the vase over a much larger area, and therefore, such meridians make for superior locations. Earth vases are intended to re-create a deeper harmony with the Earth and all the sentient beings she carries within that eco-locale. Like many indigenous cultures, the treasure vase tradition recognizes that in addition to the beings apparent to our senses, humans share the Earth with many other sentient beings not usually apparent and often categorized as nature spirits. Treasure vases are meant to help restore right relations with our unrecognized cohabitants. Earth vases are also intended to increase the fertility of the plant and animal kingdoms, and to create a more harmonious coexistence with them. Earth vases are also intended to restore the underlying integration of the five elements in the environment and in us. There are currently a number of different organizations dedicated to creating and placing earth treasure vases around the world to catalyze greater global harmony.*

Treasure vases (figure 10.14) are designed to benefit homes, businesses, schools, or spiritual practice centers. Like earth vases, they emanate a harmonious energy field for all who dwell in an area. These vases effect all those who move in and out of the specific natural and built environment. As such, treasure vases are a strong variety of feng shui radiance. Treasure vases operate unconsciously in the background to increase a wide range of positive outcomes. Spiritual practitioners, however, can also consciously engage prayer, ritual, mantra, and meditation to increase longer-term benefits. Any practice that is generated from compassionate motivation will extend and intensify the treasure vase field. Yogic practices from the specific teaching lineage that produced a treasure vase will create a stronger harmonic field. These vases form a complex alchemy of contents, timing, and rituals.

There are hundreds of ingredients aggregated in any treasure vase gathered during a long-term process. Treasure vases mix materials from all over the world from journeys of many gurus and practitioners who personally

---

*Two examples are the Earth Treasure Vase Global Healing Project found at www .earthtreasurevase.org and Siddhartha's Intent at www.peacevaseproject.org.

Figure 10.14. Treasure Vase.

Photo by J. Govert

collect potential contents. Only superior ingredients are selected as the collector maintains an internal state of joy, peace, balance, gratitude, and compassion. The Dudjom vase is about 9.5 inches tall by 6 inches wide and weighs more than a pound. The vase can be made of gold, silver, copper, or ceramic in a shape resembling a Buddhist stupa. The stupa shape in general creates a form resonant with the stack of human chakras along the spine. Two central ingredients specific to the Orgyen Norlha treasure vase are a Sonam Lang Kor talisman and a "mother pill."*

The Sonam Lang Kor talisman is composed of an image of an elephant with a chintamani on its crown with the eight-spoked Buddhist dharma-wheel drawn by Dudjom Rinpoche and signed by him. This is wrapped within another piece of paper folded like origami into a square. A photo from a Thangka depicting the central wealth yidam, Orgyen Khandro Norlha, is placed outside. The entire talisman is then wound and bound in many circuits of threads in rainbow spectrum colors. This talisman, created and consecrated during a ritual, is placed at the inside front of the treasure vase resting on other contents.

Mother pills are a similarly complex mixture of compounds assembled during a separate ritual. They contain over 137 different substances pulverized into a powder, made into a sphere, and painted with metallic gold. The mother pill contains relics of Buddhist masters and earth from sacred buildings and cave retreats associated with realized masters and yogis. Powders of precious jewels including diamonds, sapphires, emeralds, rubies, and opals are important components. Earth and rock from all directions, sacred and highest mountain peaks, fertile fields, power spots, pilgrimage places, tranquil hollows, ocean sands, meteorite impact zones, and places that intersect other dimensions are aggregated. Pure water is collected from healing springs, oceans, rivers, sacred waterfalls, lakes, and places where the waters purify, renew, and bless the local environment. Flowers, grains, seeds, fruits, and roots are collected from prolific fields that grow high-vibration and nourishing foods. Hairs from healthy animals, wild and domesticated, are another category included in mother pills. Herbal medicines both as raw

---

*Greater detail of the Dudjom Orgyen Khandro Norlha treasure vases are described at www.treasureofabundance.com.

plants and as pills made in a variety of healing formulas are added to the mother pill. When it comes to making a particular treasure vase, only a piece of the mother pill is mixed with other vase contents.

Mantras are added in small, tightly rolled paper scrolls inscribed with thousands of lines of text. These scrolls contain mantras of the main and complimentary yidams, and are intended to confer merit, wealth, and abundance united with compassionate motivation. Yantras are symbolic images combined with written mantras intended to confer blessings, wealth, and protection. These include mandalas of the realm of *yakshas,* or nature spirits, who are one of several classes of wealth lords. Creating mantra and yantra scrolls, like producing mother pill and the core talisman, are complicated projects in themselves.

In addition, iron pyrite and magnetite minerals are added to protect the overall environment. Pyrite is specially connected to the life force of *yakshas* and harmonizes humans with them. Quartz crystals are added to the vase because they confer the very essence of wealth. Quartz is connected to the life force of nagas, the serpent or dragon beings who guard treasures and are also wealth lords. King Indrabodhi received a blue chintamani from a naga princess who lived on a golden island with great stores of precious jewels. Quartz crystals harmonize human and naga realms. Turquoise is added because it is connected to human life force and confers longevity. As the essence of intelligence, turquoise stimulates that faculty and establishes more harmonious relations across divisions of the human family.

Pearls and antique corals are added to treasure vases because they purify the environment and life force and, as a result, increase longevity of all beings. Conch and cowrie seashells are added because both confer the essence of beauty. Conch shells are connected to the life force of the devas. Cowrie shells, which have been used as a medium of wealth exchange in many cultures, are connected to the dakini realm. Placing these seashells in treasure vases is intended to harmonize the deva and dakini realms with the human realm.

The entire process of creating treasure vases is very layered and long. Tibetan astrology identifies the best days of the week and days of the lunar month in spring or summer to begin making treasure vases. Other timings include special days in the Buddhist calendar, favorable star patterns present in the skies, and positive spiritual cycles as auspicious times to start each phase of the process. Before treasure vases are made available to the public, they are consecrated during a weeklong retreat by a group of dedicated practitioners who engage in intense and extensive practice. For those who want to bury a treasure vase in the earth to create great benefit for others, there are recommended astrological timings and consecration rituals for that as well. The entire process to compound positive transformational energy into a treasure vase as a created chintamani is essentially an alchemical project.

Statues, *Murtis,* and *Rupas*

Many spiritual traditions use images of saints, sages, gurus, gods, Bodhisattvas, Buddhas, and God as positive supports for practice. Statues of religious figures are common in Asian lands. Hindus refer to these form representations of the divine as *murtis,* while Buddhists refer to these as *rupas.* Those who use statues for religious devotion developed rituals to energize a *murti* or *rupa* with the presence of the representation. The statue ceased being a symbolic reminder of a great being and transformed instead into a more direct and proximate connection to that great being. Initially, the only image of the Buddha used as a practice support were his footprints but, later, this changed. Stone sculptures of the Buddha exist only as early as the first several centuries CE. With sculpted images, rituals developed to imbue statues with a more tangible sense of the awakened mind. In Chinese Buddhism, a *kai guang* (開光), or "opening the light" ceremony, energizes a statue to create immediacy. This same ceremony in Japanese Buddhism is called *kaigen* (開眼), or "opening the spiritual eyes of a Buddha." The ceremony transforms the *rupa* to function as a direct connection to a Buddha's field of consciousness. The consecrated statue is similar to an electrical transformer that steps down the frequency of incoming energy to a more accessible and useful wave. Many Hindu and Buddhist statues are made of metal alloys that conduct electromagnetic energy. The specific alloy admixture and production process are generational secrets statue makers keep.

In Tibetan Vajrayana Buddhism, the process of energizing a statue to become an accessible presence of a Buddha or Bodhisattva resembles creating a treasure vase. Rupas in the Tibetan tradition are hollow and made with a removable bottom or with the inside open. The hollow statue interior is like an empty treasure vase that is subsequently filled with many of the same types of precious contents that fill treasure vases. Relics, semiprecious and precious jewels, scrolls of written mantras, and other items specific to the represented yidam are placed in the empty area. If the rupa is to be placed in a temple, the variety of contents involved will be more elaborate than for a home shrine room. Like the treasure vase, rupas are sealed securely and a consecration ceremony is performed to make it easier for all to access the consciousness of the represented Buddha or Bodhisattva. When the statue is one of the Buddhas or Bodhisattvas that holds a chintamani or is connected directly with the chintamani, then that light-opened rupa vibrates with closer presence and access to everything chintamani.

Chintamani Medicine

Where might a search for the chintamani lead? After compelling inner promptings, Peter Mt. Shasta, a self-described mystic adventurer, undertook a personal quest leading him to Nepal, Tibet, and India to find the wish-fulfilling gem. At Yambulagang Palace in Tibet's Yarlung valley, a girl offered to sell him what he thought might be the wish-fulfilling jewel, but someone else purchased it. Weeks later, on the eve of returning home, he was given that very crystal, but he found that it was not the chintamani.[18] What he eventually discovered as the chintamani was a particular Tibetan medicine, *rinchen ratna samphel.* After taking this medicine before dawn as instructed by a renowned master physician of *Sowa Rigpa* (Tibetan Medical tradition), he realized that the chintamani was not just an object but the very activity of compassion.[19] His quest ended with the certainty that he had obtained chintamani awareness, but the quest also presented him with an opportunity for immediate compassionate action that would require considerable generosity, effort, and discipline to accomplish.

The type of medicine Peter Mt. Shasta was prescribed is a rare category of Tibetan formula called *rinchen rilbu,* or precious pills. Sowa Rigpa blends Traditional Chinese Medicine with Ayurvedic healing of India. All three healing traditions combine herbal medicines into formulas to treat a particular person with a specific disease. Most herbal prescriptions combine three to ten different ingredients into a single formula. The *rinchen rilbu* are very different because they combine from twenty-five to over seventy ingredients into a single formula. Furthermore, the ingredients include metals, mineral and gem powders, and other ingredients beyond flowers, seeds, bark, grains, or roots of plants. They may include alchemical ingredients such as potassium nitrate, sulfur, sulfuric acid, and bitumen.[20] Like treasure vases, *rinchen rilbu* require a lot of travel, selection, processing, and consecrating ingredients to create the final product. *Rinchen rilbu* target specific disease complexes but are also directed to increase spiritual ability and realization. Mantras and practices of the Medicine Buddha are very closely connected with *rinchen rilbu* both in producing the precious pills and in taking them to dissolve disease.

Rinchen ratna samphel, the chintamani medicine, contains a secret, compounded ingredient called *tsothel*, which is considered the king essence. It contains some compounds that need to be detoxified before they can be ingested safely. *Tsothel* may include powdered pearl, turquoise, coral, *zi* (prized Tibetan opal associated with outer space), gold, silver, copper, iron, or lead. There are other non-herbal ingredients, the six superlative medicines, the three myrobalan fruits, bonnet bellflower, saffron, and other rare, expensive, and exotic herbs. Modern chintamani medicine is based on formulas with around seventy ingredients discovered by past Vajrayana masters of Tibetan medicine passed down over the centuries. Like some Daoist formulations, *rinchen ratna samphel* is the result of elaborate alchemical processes including prayers, rituals, mantras, and meditations. Like Chinese Daoist and Siddha yoga traditions of India, the pills are intended to accelerate preparation of the diamond energy body that makes higher level spiritual practices easier to accomplish.

An interconnected branch of Sowa Rigpa regards incense as medicine. In many of the rituals and yogas aimed at realizing enlightenment, various lineages include formulations of incense to accompany specific practices to connect with a meditational yidam. There is a chintamani incense formulated by Drikung Tsewang Tenpa (c. 1612–1700), who was a scholar and physician. He wrote thirteen medical texts and founded a unique medical practice lineage.[21] His formulation of chintamani incense is aimed at balancing energy disruptions (qi or *lung*). While these imbalances can cause high blood pressure, insomnia, dizziness, irritability, or joint pain among other symptoms, energy disruptions also lead to emotional and mental dissatisfaction as well. The chintamani incense, like *rinchen rilbu,* seeks to establish even energy flow through the meridians, which in turn makes happiness and spiritual progress more possible. Tsewang Tenpa formulated this incense to help others connect more easily to the chintamani as a gem or as enlightened mind.

Re-creating Self as the Chintamani

The first chintamanis that arose from the churning of the milk ocean were miraculous apparitions but were only possible as the product of an intense collaborative and technological creation of the triune God, devas, asuras, and primal animals mixed thoroughly into the elements of matter. The fourteen different ratnas brought forth weapons, beauty, celebration, abundance, power, healing, immortality, and the potential for continued chaos or infinite benefit. If we take the cosmic ocean as a symbol of the undifferentiated and uncreated level of higher consciousness, it still needs an intention vehicle to enter and navigate denser states of matter. The fourteen ratnas were very specific vehicles to reengage the creation already in progress. From primordial times, the chintamani was created to be this vehicle to manifest higher intention into the world field. The created chintamani objects that we have explored here are of the same nature. They form a wide range of responses from alchemical symbols, chintamani orbs, alchemical glass, orbs of power or light, and treasure vases, to alchemical medicines and incenses. Each of these is a unique transformation of mind into matter, and matter back into mind, all created permutations of the mind gem, the chintamani.

11

Crystal Alignment and Intention

Eleven Ways to Connect with the Wish-Fulfilling Gem

Words and paper did not seem real enough to me. To put my fantasies on solid footing, something more was needed. I had to achieve a kind of representation in stone of my innermost thoughts and of the knowledge I had acquired. Put another way, I had to make a confession of faith in stone.

CARL JUNG, *MEMORIES, DREAMS, REFLECTIONS*

IN THIS CHAPTER, WE MOVE DIRECTLY into tangible crystal practices as symbolic methods of aligning ourselves with the chintamani. Meditating with a clear quartz point, rose quartz, or amethyst may not be quite the same as the chintamani we have described thus far, but it is an important first step in grounding oneself in the present and working toward achieving a mind-gem we refer to as the tachyolithic energy state of the chintamani. If you are reading this book, you probably already own a few crystals and have practiced meditating with a crystal at some point, or perhaps you are an advanced crystal energy practitioner. This section is written for everyone, novice and expert, and these practices can be carried out individually or in unison with other practices. To gain the maximum potential out of these practices, we invite you to relax the rational left brain and play with crystal energy. When we are young, the world is a magical place where we think butterflies and dragonflies are fairies, and crystals and rocks are treasures from the fairies. Return to the innocent, playful state of the child and believe in a magical world where crystals are talking friends with magical powers. Crystal energy is very much about opening and awakening the right brain's potential for imagination, creativity, playfulness, joy, and a childlike innocence and spirit: this is where magic awakens! Like the Magician in the Tarot, you are now playing with tools to create magical intention. In this chapter, we also focus on specific practices you can use to work more meaningfully and powerfully with crystals—such as selection, meditation, sound vibration, programming, and creating sacred crystal-fused water. These practices are recommended starting points to encourage you to embrace and play with the elements. From this starting point, integrate your own intuition to advance or augment these practices.

Crystal Selection and Alignment

In spiritual practices, we often use sacred or meaningful objects to symbolize a power, God, a spiritual presence, or something we wish to attain. We place these objects on altars, but we also hold them during prayer or meditation, such as prayer beads. These tangible objects help us to focus and are used as a step toward fusing matter and spirit. Once focus has been achieved, you may no longer need to hold the object. You are using the object as a projective tool to enter a state of creative enlightenment where you can leave behind the material object and move to an advanced or deeper state of being and awareness. Prayer beads and worry stones have a tangible place in prayer and meditation. Prayer beads are used for counting mantras, but they are also held during sacred practice. There is considerable background noise originating from our thinking and nervous system. A simple practice such as counting, holding prayer beads, or rubbing a worry stone helps to calm the nervous system by literally giving our nervous state something to do that reduces interference with the higher states in meditation. Especially for those who are more nervous in temperament or are inexperienced with meditation, holding prayer beads or a crystal is a helpful tool for initiating and grounding spiritual practice.

Usually the beads or crystals we use in spiritual practice have some symbolic meaning to us, and this is part of practice alignment. During prayer, we make a request to a higher source for a deeper connection or to grant a wish. While meditation can be about listening or abiding in emptiness, there is always a reason behind the practice. Sometimes the objective is to release the ego or simply to relax the mind. Other times the objective is to align with a deva or angel. Part of clarifying intention and focusing on the power of intention is to examine each of the steps to select the tools that bring about the most beneficial result. Whether for prayer beads, crystal grids, or a single meditation crystal, when selecting crystals for a particular intention or outcome, assess the energy generated by the object and its connection to you, the practitioner. Your own energy and your reaction to the object activates the energy of the object, and your reaction and intention directs the energy of the activated object.

There are many methods to assist with selection. In chapter 3, we discussed some of the specific crystals associated with Bodhisattvas. In chapters 6, 7, and 8, we examined power stones, the properties of quartz, birth stones, and planetary stones, which can be used to align with a natal astrological chart or astrological events. You can make the ritual of alignment simple or complex. There are myriads of books and internet resources discussing the metaphysical properties of crystals. Naturally, some resources are more in-depth than others. We encourage a simpler process, allowing a personal connection in getting to know the crystal and its energy and chemistry signature. Even knowing how a mineral or crystal may be used in medicine or industry gives clues as to the crystal's energy. This aligns with science and the left hemisphere of the brain and is a practical and tangible application. Select with the right brain and learn to rely on your own intuition with a crystal rather than what others say about a crystal. Each person has a unique energy interaction with a crystal. When selecting any crystal or gemstone, check to see if you have chemistry with the stone by relying on your intuition and reaction to the crystal. The dollar amount of the crystal or another person's evaluation means less than your personal reaction. Alignment is not about investing in high quality diamonds or gold. It is about your authentic energetic interaction with a crystal.

A simple way to gain conscious understanding of attraction to a crystal is through use of the chakra color system. For example, if the attraction is toward green crystals such as emerald or jade, this corresponds to the heart chakra. If the attraction is toward red gems such as ruby or garnet, the first chakra is involved with the unconscious selection influenced by one's emotional interaction with color (see table). Finding corresponding information about the intuitive selection aids in connecting the crystal to a part of the energy body and allows blending right- and left-brain processes. The chakra system can also help with a simple selection of a crystal by consciously knowing there is a need to work with a particular chakra. For example, if alignment is needed with the solar plexus, then the chakra system provides the clue to work with yellow crystals such as yellow sapphire, citrine, or golden calcite.

CHAKRA SYSTEM AND CRYSTAL COLOR				
CHAKRA	**COLOR**	**BODY**	**CHAKRA QUALITIES**	**COMMON CRYSTALS/METALS**
1. Base	Black & Red	Base of Spine	Energy, Vitality, Life Force, Protection, Groundedness	Red Garnet, Ruby, Red Carnelian, Iron, Hematite, Obsidian, Black Tourmaline, Black Onyx, Tektite
2. Sacral	Orange	Navel	Creativity, Sexuality, Partnership, Choice, Passion	Copper, Orange Selenite, Orange Garnet, Orange Carnelian, Orange Aragonite
3. Solar Plexus	Yellow	Stomach	Digestion, Assimilation, Willpower, Confidence, Joy	Yellow Sapphire, Citrine, Yellow Topaz, Yellow Calcite, Golden Pearl, Gold
4. Heart	Green	Heart	Love, Compassion, Abundance, Generosity	Emerald, Jade, Green Aventurine, Green Tourmaline, Watermelon Tourmaline
6. Third Eye	Indigo	Forehead	Thinking, Vision, Insight, Wisdom, Discrimination	Lapis Lazuli, Blue Sapphire, Blue Kyanite, Sodalite, Iolite, Dumortierite
7. Crown	Violet & White	Top of the Head	Spiritual Connection, Higher Self, Serenity, Peace, Aspiration	Amethyst, Tanzanite, Charoite, White Sapphire, Diamond, White Topaz, Clear Quartz, Silver, Platinum

We provide four simple exercises to help with crystal selection and alignment. Naturally, you can use any technique you have already developed in addition to these recommendations. We recognize there are variations of energy and chakra systems. Rely upon those systems with which you are familiar. Think of these exercises as helping you choose the right crystal focus for your intention beyond pretty crystals attractive to the eyes. Meditate with the color and chakra symbols illustrated in figure 11.1 for deeper insight.

Figure 11.1. The chakras and a common system of color correspondences. The symbols for each chakra graphically present the complexity of the energies at each chakra. Meditate with these forms, the color, and a representative crystal.

◎ *Intuitive Alignment*

This practice is best performed with a collection of crystals spread in an array before you (figure 11.2). Have a pen and paper available so you can record your reaction.

Figure 11.2. Set of crystals correlated with colors of the chakras from base to crown, left to right.

1. Close your eyes, breathe deeply, clear your mind, and release expectations.
2. Gently bring your intention to mind, thinking and wishing for a positive outcome.
3. Slowly open your eyes and select a crystal that helps you with your intention.
4. Write down your intention, the crystal you selected, how it looks—including its color and shape—and how it feels in your hand. Record how you think the crystal can help you with your intention. It does not matter if you know anything about the crystal and its metaphysical properties. Just record your first thoughts and contemplate how the crystal can assist you.

This practice helps you to understand your intuition and is a method to bridge the left and right sides of the brain while finding creative and innovative solutions for manifesting your intention. If you do not own or have access to any crystals, you can go outside and work with nature's rocks or walk into a crystal store with the purpose of selecting crystals for your intention. Select crystals because you sense they can help you, rather than because of their beauty. It is better to select crystals in person than online, as it helps you to feel or sense the chemistry of the crystal in connection with your own chemistry.

Kinesthetic Alignment

This practice is best performed with a collection of crystals spread in an array before you. If you have a crystal collection, include earthy, grounding, and protecting crystals such as obsidian, smoky quartz, black tourmaline (figure 11.3), raw garnet, hematite, black onyx, shungite, pyrite, Tibetan black quartz, meteorite, and tektite. Have pen and paper available so you can record your selection and reaction.

1. Close your eyes, breathe deeply, clear your mind, and release expectations.
2. Vigorously rub your hands together to stimulate energy in your palms.
3. Keeping your eyes closed, use your left hand to slowly glide over the crystals. It does not matter if you touch the crystals or just sense the energy above or around the crystals. The point is you are using kinesthetic or physical sensation to sense energy and interaction with the crystal through your hand. Use your left hand as an extension of your right brain, which is more feminine or intuitive in its processes. Allow any criticism or doubt to leave your mind. If you feel like you are imagining a sensation or intuition, surrender to your imagination. Intuition and imagination are intimately linked in the brain.
4. You may feel one or more sensations from the crystals such as pulling, tingling, warmth, cold, or just an inner knowing. Select the crystal you sense will help you based on a signal from the crystal. You may feel the sensation in your palm, fingertips, or somewhere else in your body.
5. Once you select the crystal, hold it in the palm of your hand and notice any other sensations before you open your eyes. Contemplate how the crystal might help you with your intention.
6. Open your eyes and look at the crystal. Write down your reaction to the crystal—including how it felt, why you selected it, and your reaction to

Figure 11.3. Crystals like black tourmaline are protective and grounding, and they absorb electromagnetic smog from electronic devices such as cell phones and computers.

it when you opened your eyes. Did the crystal seem consistent with your initial "blind" sensation, or did the crystal surprise or disappoint you once you opened your eyes? It is important to recognize negative or disappointing feelings. It is not uncommon to pick dull or ugly crystals in this process. Sometimes the most beautiful crystals may not be the ones our body needs, or the aesthetic crystals may not be the most powerful crystals on the table.

7. Learn about the crystal you selected, especially its chemistry, so you can assess whether your body needs the mineral in the crystal. It is not uncommon for the body to signal kinesthetically about a mineral it needs. For example, if you select a calcite, your body might need calcium. If the crystal contains iron, the body could be signaling it needs iron or is not absorbing iron. Wearing crystals with certain minerals could aid in absorbing the mineral on a subtle energetic level through the auric field. Wearing crystals and gemstones is like feeding the auric field vitamins and minerals.

The kinesthetic selection process, including recording your interactions, connects the right and left sides of the brain much like the analysis of dreams, bridging the conscious and the unconscious.

◎ Chakra Alignment and Color

There are several ways in which to work with the chakras and crystal energy, even in the selection process. If you are attracted to a certain color in your everyday life, there are benefits to meditating and wearing crystals of that color. Try using the techniques described in the practices above but note the color of the crystal. The color helps to identify which chakra is associated with the crystal.

If green appears either through everyday attraction or in one of the techniques described above, then study the heart chakra and wear or place a green stone over the heart area to help stimulate subtle energies in that area of the body. Chakras correspond with different layers of the body's energetic field. The heart chakra literally refers to the heart, but also to the lungs on the physical level. There are also emotional and spiritual levels of the heart.

Evaluate which of the levels the crystal may be signaling as needing attention. It does not always mean the chakra energy is blocked or unwell; the attraction may have to do with alignment and kundalini awakening. Whatever color appears in your selection, use the chakra system to work more deeply and meaningfully with the crystal and try wearing or placing the crystal on the selected chakra even for a few minutes. The chakra system will also have associated seed syllables, mantras, and symbols that help integrate crystal and body work (see "Chakra System and Crystal Color" table and figure 11.1, pages 275–76).

◎ Astrological Alignment

Chapter 8 includes information about basic astrological correspondences with gemstones so that you may select a crystal using astrology. For example, if you are working with the earth sign Virgo, wear and meditate with green peridot to align with the creative, productive energies of Virgo. Additionally, you balance Virgo by wearing aquamarine, the stone of the opposing sign Pisces, to surrender control and expectations.

You could also create a medicine wheel astrological stone grid by choosing astrological stones for the natal cross (figures 8.3 through 8.5, pages 179–80). As an example, if you have a Sagittarius ascendant, then topaz is placed in the first house. Aquamarine (Pisces) appears in the fourth house. Agate (Gemini) holds space in the seventh house, and the tenth house is ruled by peridot (Virgo). Using astrological stones in addition to the main birthstone can be powerful and allows you to draw in and attract the energies of other signs. If you are not familiar with astrology, then start simply by using the stone aligned with your sun sign. Because there is quite a bit of misinformation concerning correct birthstones, see "Western Astrology Signs and Birthstones" table on page 174 to find the correct stone aligned with your astrological sign.

Try collecting all twelve birth stones and wear or meditate with them during the times of the year when the sun appears in those signs. Doing so aligns you more intimately with the signs and the seasons as the sun progresses through them in its annual trek through the zodiac.

Clearing Crystals and the Self

Purification is a practice found in all spiritual systems. When working with crystal energy and integrating intention, it is beneficial to use clearing rituals. Remember that clearing yourself is even more important than clearing the crystal. Not all crystals require clearing, especially the stones that are gathered outside in nature. Clearing is dependent on the practitioner and the practices for which the crystal is used. Especially when using crystals for energy healing work on others, it is important to clear crystals that are already holding energy, such as quartz-based crystals. There is research about the efficacy of moonlight to clear quartz crystal. In a study conducted at the University of Arizona Department of Geology, a set of clear quartz crystals was placed in a moonlight collecting chamber. Using the results from a Raman spectrometer, the crystals from the moonlight chamber were compared to a second set not placed in the chamber. The results showed that the crystals placed in the moonlight chamber displayed significantly less "noise" than the control set of quartz crystals.[1]

On a tangible level, crystals can be cleared and energized using simple practices involving the elements: fire, earth, air, and water. The selection of element is predicated on what is being cleansed, the intention or practice for which the crystal will be used, and the elements the practitioner and the crystal are already manifesting or with which there is a natural resonance.

Purification involving sunlight, moonlight, earth, water, indirect light, smudging, salt soaking, mineral energizing, plants, breath, candles, incense, and fire are all elemental techniques to cleanse and energize crystals. If the intention is for emotional healing, then cleansing and energizing the crystal in moonlight is in energetic alignment with that focus. Manifesting energy, vitality, confidence, willpower, and protection involves fire, so prepare the crystal by charging it in sunlight or with fire through a candle, incense, or smudging. Earth energies help to bring in prosperity, fertility, and abundance, so placing the crystal in the earth, on grass, in a tree or tree root, or in a potted plant helps to charge the crystal with growth-based energy. Placing the crystal in a salt bath, in moonlight, or a running stream brings in peace, tranquility, purification, healing, creativity, and flow. Breathwork (such as qigong and pranayama) and mental intention works with the air element to access the mind, spirit, insight, vision, and unseen realms. We will discuss working with breath in a later section. When preparing a crystal for use, it is important also to prepare yourself with similar purification and energetic practices by standing and absorbing sunlight or moonlight, taking a purifying bath, or burning incense.

The length of time to purify and energize is dependent on how much the crystal has been used and your own intuition as to its clarity. During intense crystal healing sessions, the crystal may absorb a great deal of released energy and may need several hours or even days to purify and recharge. Mild use does not require daily cleansing. Quartz requires more clearing than other types of crystal due to its ability to adapt and absorb. Many crystals function in such a way that a practitioner needs to adapt and open to the energy of the crystal. For example, an opaque and structurally ordered crystal such as red garnet already has a preprogrammed method of functioning, and this requires less cleansing because the human reacts more to the garnet. Quartz crystal usually adapts and reacts to the human energy field. Typically, translucent crystals are more adaptive and flowing and, because of that, require more clearing and energizing. Opaque crystals are grounded and dense, requiring less clearing because they absorb and are less adaptive. Use caution regarding certain clearing methods. Some crystals, such as salt, will dissolve in sunlight and/or in water. Excessive sunlight exposure can also cause color to fade in crystals such as rose quartz, citrine, and amethyst.

Figure 11.4. Crystals can be cleared using smudging, water, salt crystals, breath, sound, light, and other techniques.

We will now turn to a practice using wind or breathwork to clear a crystal and program it with pure white light. This practice energetically bonds the practitioner with the crystal. Using breathwork to clear a crystal can be done with or without any prior cleansing as discussed above. This meditation is designed for clear quartz because quartz is adaptive to programming and clearing with white light. Part of the technique involving exhalation originates from practices created by Dr. Marcel Vogel, who worked with specially cut crystals (that he invented), breathing, and intention.[2] Vogel programming techniques were designed for use with a specially cut Vogel quartz and Vogel points are best suited for use by those who are trained in healing energy practices such as Reiki (figure 7.5, page 167). Vogel used a practice involving a snorting exhalation from the nose to program the Vogel crystal. While this technique is effective, we find breathwork through the mouth is also a useful method described below. For optimum effectiveness, and if you are new to meditation and crystal energy, we recommend using a natural clear quartz crystal point in the following practice, as natural points are best-suited for daily meditation use.*

◎ Crystal Clearing Using Breath

1. Begin by holding the crystal upright in your hands so the tip is pointing toward the sky.
2. Rub the sides of the crystal to generate warmth and energy between yourself and the crystal.
3. Hold the crystal with both hands either in a prayer pose over the heart (*anjali* mudra) or in another mudra pose, while sitting in a comfortable meditative position.
4. Practice deep breathing until you feel calm. As you exhale, release all thoughts and worries to be in a receptive and clear state. Allow the breath to flow through all parts of the body, including all the chakras, to increase energy and clarity.
5. Focusing on the third eye point, visualize pure white light, as white as snow.
6. Begin to breathe the pure white, crystalline snow light into the breath, allowing it to radiate through the heart and lungs, the mind, through the arms into the fingertips, and into the crystal held in your hands, so the crystal is radiating with pure white light.
7. Visualize the white light radiating through your abdomen purifying and energizing your organs, and allow it to flow down through the legs and into the feet.

---

*This and other practices discussed in chapters 11 and 12 are available as sound recordings that can be accessed at www.chintamanimatrix.com.

8. Continue to inhale the white light. As it enters, feel the energy cool and refreshing on your breath.

9. Visualize your entire body vibrating and glowing with pure white crystal light.

10. Gradually move the crystal in your hands to your mouth.

11. Take in a deep breath filled with pure white light and exhale into the crystal with a sharp strong breath or as a sharp exhale from the nostrils.

12. Rotate the crystal to access different angles and breathe white light into other faces of the crystal.

13. Return to holding the crystal back at your heart center, then connect your heart and the crystal together energetically through the white light.

14. Sit with the crystal in the pure white field in a meditative state for as long as is comfortable.

15. When you are ready, slowly open your eyes and silently express gratitude and connection with the crystal in your hands. The crystal is now energetically cleared using breath and is also linked to your energy field. Notice how warm and comfortable the crystal feels in your hand, a sign that the crystal has been activated.

Crystal Meditation and Programming Intention

Meditating with a crystal can and should be practiced at any stage of work with crystals. Meditative attention should be present when selecting, clearing, and programming. We introduce crystal meditation as the next step after purification to make a bridge between purification and intention. Knowing what we want, what is good for us, and what is possible based on energetic pathways available to us now, as well as knowing how to be aligned with spirit, is a complex process. If you were presented with a magic genie lamp and granted a single wish, wisely choosing just one wish would require deep reflection. Programming a crystal with an intention also requires reflection as you explore multiple needs and desires. King Solomon, who wore a legendary magic ring with a wish-fulfilling jewel, was granted a wish from God during a dream. Solomon responded thoughtfully by requesting an understanding heart to judge the people.

God, pleased by the selfless request, responded that he would give to Solomon not only a "wise and understanding heart," but also riches, honor, and long life.[3] Solomon, who was a young and inexperienced king at the time of the dream, made his request in response to a personal weakness that he felt would inhibit him from fulfilling his role successfully as the leader of a nation. What Solomon requested was more valuable than any precious jewel, as it was an intangible quality that cannot be bought. If you were to win a multimillion-dollar lottery, you would be rich merely in material wealth, but still could not buy intangible qualities such as heart wisdom. Solomon's request showed that by aligning intentions with the intangible spiritual qualities, the material or worldly treasures were added automatically.

Applying the alchemical formula "as above, so below," if one is spiritually rich above, resources supporting the core spiritual mission manifest below. Use the practices in this section to "listen" to the crystal first as an aid to connect with the core intangible quality of your higher spiritual nature. Blend this intuition into programming the crystal with a spiritual intention. Although these practices can be adapted for any crystal, or even a visualized crystal, we describe these meditative practices around the use of a single, hand-held natural quartz point. There are many different types of quartz shapes and points. A few of the common types for working with energy include male and female crystal points. For purposes of simplicity, choose a crystal point that feels comfortable in your hands. Then make some discoveries about the crystal. Analyze its tip, faces, and features to learn more about the crystal and its interior fractures and inclusions. Crystals coming to a point have directed and focused energy, which is why they are called male crystals (figure 11.5). Crystals with a blunt or straight edge tip are feminine and are holders or receivers of energy (figure 11.6). So you can work with the structure of the crystal to align with your intention or use it to direct the energy field. The top of the crystal is masculine and sends energy out, and the bottom of the crystal is feminine and receptive. Most of the meditations described below involve holding the crystal so the tip is pointing toward Father Sky and the base is receiving energy from Mother Earth below.

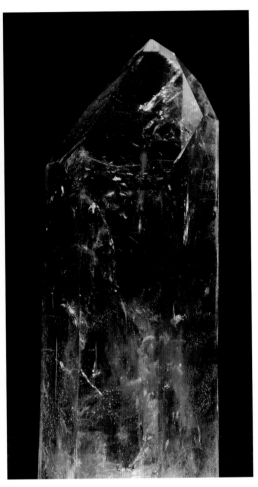

Figure 11.5. Example of a male crystal
with a sharp point.

Photo by Kaleigh Brown

Figure 11.6. Example of a female crystal
with a flat-top edge.

Photo by Kaleigh Brown

◎ Inner Crystal Silence

1. Write down your intention on a piece of paper and put it aside.

2. Begin the practice by holding and stroking the crystal in your hands until it feels comfortable or warm.

3. Once the crystal feels warm, your body's heat and energy have activated the crystal's pyroelectricity and send out harmonic waves. Observe the crystal's construction, angles, and interior inclusions. Let

your imagination explore the inclusions of the quartz crystal as though you were looking at clouds in the sky and noticing their shapes.

4. Holding the crystal comfortably in your hands, close your eyes, focus on the third eye, and relax your mind and your feelings.

5. Enter deep silence. This is a moment of freedom from your thoughts. Release attachments to what you think you want. Free yourself of your own wants, wishes, and desires.

6. Practice simple awareness. Gradually let this blank screen evolve into listening and sensing the crystal in your hands. You may experience nothing, so relax into a receptive state. You may see colors, sounds, music, or experience visions.

7. Give yourself several minutes of sitting and listening so you can more deeply experience the crystal.

8. When you finish, express gratitude to the crystal.

9. Write down what you have experienced, as this is a part of your work in discovering your core spiritual intention and how it will manifest.

Figure 11.7. Sit with a crystal and
go into the earth cave
to discover its soul.

◎ Creating Intention and Crystal Programming

1. Write down your intention on a piece of paper and put it aside. Write the intention using positive "I am" phrases.

2. Hold the crystal in your hands until it feels warm or comfortable. You have activated the pyroelectricity when the crystal feels warm and comfortable in your hands.

3. Center yourself through breathing and sensing each of your chakras and areas of your body. Release stress from your body, including your shoulders, chest, abdomen, and knees, then ground your legs and feet to the earth.

4. Once centered, continue breathing deeply and begin to visualize your intention at the third eye point. Visualize your intention as though you can see it happening in your life now—a living, moving picture. Sit with the picture.

5. Take a deep breath and slowly move the living, moving picture of your intention from your third eye point into your heart center.

6. Convert the intention at your heart center from a vision to a feeling. Feel the intention in your heart as though it is in your life now. From your heart center, give your intention all the love and nurturing it needs to take root in your life and manifest. Feel love toward your intention deeply and feel the intention in your heart and your body.

7. Take in a deep breath and expand your heart center so the intention can expand within you, and sit with the feeling of intention at the heart center until you are comfortable to move it down slowly to your solar plexus or stomach center. The solar plexus is the seat of manifestation and the seat of emotion. At this point, spend time feeling the intention instinctively in your abdomen.

8. Contemplate why this intention has not already manifested in your life. Ask yourself what blocks or fears have prevented you from manifesting the intention. In what way will this intention change your life? Be comfortable exploring your fears. If you are able, allow the fears to slowly dissipate, releasing their hold on you, and tell your instinctive self that change will be alright. If this stage of the process becomes uncomfortable and you cannot get past the blocks, it is useful to stop the process,

do some clearing practices, and restart at a later time. It is also perfectly fine to adjust, fine tune, or change your intention.

9. As you explore your intention at a deeper level, the truth about your alignment with the intention will reveal itself. When you are at peace with your intention, digest the intention and absorb it into your body. Feed your body with the intention so it becomes one with you.

10. Slowly move the intention to your throat center and let it sit there so the intention can form a voice. You can contemplate what you need to say to yourself or out loud to others to activate the intention. You can also convert the intention into a single power word encapsulating the essence of your intention and say that word out loud. That word now becomes a trigger word for you to activate the intention in yourself.

11. During this active meditation, the crystal has been energizing your heart center. Now, slowly move the crystal to your throat. Bring together all the meditative work from the third eye, heart, solar plexus, and throat into a single breath and breathe or snort it sharply into the crystal followed by the audible sound of your intention's power word.

12. Repeat this process as you change the angle of the crystal in your hands. When you have finished breathing your intention into the crystal, return the crystal to your heart center.

13. Open your heart center to receive the programmed intention and breathe deeply as you enter a calm, receptive, and magnetic state with the programmed crystal.

14. End the meditation by opening your eyes and thanking the crystal for helping you to realize your intention.

15. Record your intention and your power word, especially if the intention has changed from the point when you started the meditation. Turn the intention into a daily affirmation.

The program will stay in the crystal for a period of time. It is sufficient to program a crystal once in a monthly or lunar cycle. It is recommended to program the crystal on or around the time of each new moon. Meditate with the crystal once a day in a receptive state over the heart. On the following new moon, cleanse and clear the crystal, and renew the program or reprogram the crystal with a new intention. Meditate with the same crystal and the same intention for a full lunar cycle. This meditation can help establish a new habit within the lunar cycle. Meditate with the crystal every day to program yourself and receive and act on the intention. The crystal will radiate the program for a period of time, which will subtly affect the unconscious. You can program a crystal for your own personal intentions, for a positive intention for the world, or to help others by sending them healing, love, and support.

In traditional Tibetan medicine, known as Sowa Rigpa, Vajrayana Buddhists use programmed rocks in their healing. Tibetans select river rocks for this practice because the water has entrained the rocks to move energy. Mantras are used to program the rocks. After repeating the mantra at least 108 times, the energized breath is used to blow the energy of the mantra on the selected rock or rocks. The energized rocks are then placed on the affected area of the body.

Figure 11.8. Use programmed crystals to spread light energies into the world. Glacier quartz from Kullu, Himachal Pradesh, India. Shodo by J. Govert. Photo by Kaleigh Brown.

Crystal Grids, Intention, and Meditation

As discussed in chapter 8, crystal grids unite a combination of crystals in geometric form to amplify energy. Crystal grids can be employed by a single practitioner or by a group of people unified in intention. A crystal grid amplifies the positive field of group meditation and sends a synergistic positive signal out in harmonic resonance. Quartz has been used in radio transmitters to harmonize frequency, so it is ideally suited as a tool in a meditation circle grid focused on world peace, healing, or other harmonic intention.

Grids can be simple or become a part of a complex ritual. Some involve a few crystals with a central crystal programmed with a specific intention. The crystals in the grid are then pointed outward in a circular array to radiate the intention. As mentioned in chapter 7, the particular shape of a crystal radiates specific qualities, so grid shapes made of crystals also radiate greater energy into the macrocosm. A square grid conserves energy and represents structure, grounding, and form, while a circular grid radiates qualities such as healing and harmony. Of course, crystal grids can be augmented with flowers, candles, incense, metals, beads, affirmations, written mantras, spiritual texts, and symbols to couple with consciousness to imbue greater meaning into the grid, while the crystals perform the functions of increasing energy, resonance, and transmission of the core intention. The type and combinations of crystals forming the grid should create the most congruent array to amplify the intention of the grid. Color is a simple way to connect with the energetic properties of a crystal. For example, a grid with yellow citrine and golden pyrite will help manifest abundance, while a grid with purple amethyst and clear quartz will promote peace and serenity.

◎ Radiate Intention

On a power day such as a new moon, follow this process to build a grid.

1. Write down an intention and then select a place such as an altar, feng shui wealth corner, or spiritual spot in the home or garden that is connected with your intention.

2. Start with a few clear quartz crystal points that have been cleared as described above (four to ten crystal points is a good number for small grids).

3. Select a few more colored crystals that support your intention (e.g., purple amethyst for spiritual growth and peace; blue lapis for vision and inspiration; sky blue aquamarine for communication; pink rose quartz for relationships; green aventurine for growth and abundance; yellow citrine for wealth; orange carnelian for creativity; red garnet for energy and strength; black tourmaline for balance and protection; and clear white quartz for purification).

4. Place these crystals in a ring inside the circular quartz grid. Face the quartz crystal points outward. In the center, place your written intention or a power word or symbol representing your intention and then place a crystal on top of the words or symbol.

5. Once a day, pray, meditate, and/or chant over the grid to activate the crystals and direct their energy toward manifesting your intention.

6. Periodically incorporate other elemental energies in or around the grid, such as incense, smudging, candlelight, sacred water, singing bowl, harmonic music, fresh air, plants, sunlight, moonlight, and fresh flowers, to increase the potency of the grid. Increase the energy of the grid and refresh it on full moons. Practice thankfulness and gratitude for what is

Figure 11.9. A circular crystal grid composed of rose quartz radiates compassion and love.

manifesting in your life. Dismantle the grid and cleanse the area at the end of the lunar cycle so you can start fresh and build a new grid on the following new moon.

◎ Create a Mind Gem

To prepare a medicine wheel grid to integrate multiple crystals and create an external mind gem, follow these steps.

1. Using the methods described in the crystal selection and alignment section earlier in this chapter, select at least four crystals for a medicine wheel grid (figure 11.10). You want to have a crystal for each of the four sections of a medicine wheel to represent the north, south, east, and west polarities.

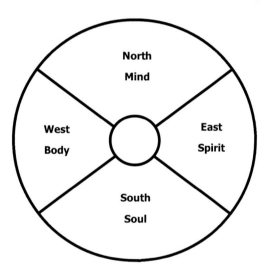

Figure 11.10. Medicine Wheel for focus, integration, and orientation in crystal meditation and building grids.

2. You can place the crystals in the sectors and, using a compass, orient your medicine wheel stone circle with magnetic north.
3. In the center, place your intention with a programmed clear quartz crystal. Hold your hands over the medicine wheel and blend the energies into the center crystal. This center crystal integrates the crystals in the grid and creates an external mind gem.

For a more powerful meditation technique, creating an internal mind gem, try this medicine wheel practice.

1. Select four different stones and seat yourself in meditation facing magnetic north. This meditation is more powerful when practiced outside in nature or in a garden.

2. Place the north stone in front of you, the south stone behind you. Place the east stone to your right and the west stone to your left.

3. Practice deep breathing and center yourself with Mother Earth energy beneath and Father Sky energy above.

4. Once centered in meditation, call on the stones one-by-one and bring their subtle, intangible energy to your heart center. Start with the north stone first and bring its energy into your heart. Call in the second stone and bring its energy to you, blending it with the north stone. Continue with each stone, bringing the stone's energy into your heart center. Once all four stones have been called into your heart, blend them together and create a new stone. This is your chintamani mind gem, which you have created using spirit alchemy.

5. Blend your intention into the mind gem in your heart and give love to the chintamani that you have created so it can radiate your intention in harmonic wavelengths outward from your energy body. This is a powerful meditation, so spend time with each stone and with your imaginative blending.

The visual mind gems created through this meditation are unique and sometimes surprising. This is a form of alchemical meditation accessing primal creative activity that helps you become a powerful manifester.

Working with Crystal Shapes and Objects

Cut and polished crystal shapes are fairly easy to obtain. They are useful on their own in meditative practice or for use in grids. The minerals are carved in a variety of shapes and the mineral will radiate a particular type of energy that is then augmented by the shape in which it is carved. Some of the more common shapes include spheres, eggs, hearts, cubes, triangles, and pyramids. These shapes correspond with the elements so they can be used strategically to enhance a particular intention or quality. The sphere is associated with water and feeling and radiates in all directions. The egg shape is spherical and can be used to start a new phase in life, a birth of a new idea, fruition, fertility, and growth. The cube represents earthen qualities and is a container of energy for intentions centered on grounding, protection, building, and foundation. Triangles are associated with fire and the energy of passion, enthusiasm, and focus. The pyramid and obelisk shapes combine both the square and the triangle and are useful to support the combination of the elements of earth and fire. If your focus is on relationships, harmony, love, compassion, and peace, the sphere and heart shapes support those intentions. Amorphous shapes can be used to represent the quality of air or ether, both of which are difficult elements to represent in a solid form. Crystal skulls are a more complex form. Working with this shape helps to amplify mental abilities and aids in connecting to the collective mind through meditation.

The sphere is a particularly powerful shape because it radiates energy in all directions and, because it is spherical, manifests the energy of "no beginning or ending." It works well to represent the shape of planets such as Earth and, because of its roundness, represents concepts such as fluidity, harmony, and equality. Clear crystal balls have been used for hundreds of years in intuitive practices such as gazing and scrying to induce visions. For these divinatory practices, it is preferable to use a very clear quartz sphere. In order to activate the pyroelectrical properties of the quartz, the gazer rubs the quartz sphere with the palms of their hands. The gazer enters a meditative or trance state, then begins to see images in the crystal ball. Once a resonant connection between the crystal ball and the gazer occurs, the crystal ball acts as a screen or mirror of the right brain images for psychic seeing. This state can be enhanced using subdued lighting such as candles or moonlight. Meditating with quartz increases intuitive states, provides clarity in visionary states, and opens access to the right brain, which allows access to dream states, clairvoyance, channeling, and astral travel. The Hindu-Buddhist goddess Manimekhala, guardian of the seas, held an orb while flying, suggesting that crystal orbs may be useful for interdimensional or astral travel (figure 11.11).

Crystal mirrors act in much the same way as crystal balls, serving as a projective screen or tool to make visible what the right brain sees. Black obsidian glass balls and mirrors are also used for scrying. Dr. John Dee, the astrologer for Queen Elizabeth I, used crystal balls and was also in possession of an Aztec black obsidian mirror that he purportedly obtained from British pirates

Figure 11.11. Manimekhala flying with her glowing crystal orb, 1850–1899, *Illustrated Book of Thai Poetry* in Bavarian State Library, Germany.

who had raided Spanish treasure ships. Obsidian glass is an amorphous crystal structure while quartz crystal is trigonal. Therefore, obsidian may result in less predictable results but may be useful for developing the intuitive faculties outside our senses. Black obsidian helps to peer into the unconscious or dream time. The Tibetans use a turquoise mirror for scrying, which comes from practices associated with the deity Dorje Yudronma, Turquoise Lady, a nature spirit princess who is an earth and dharma protector.

The following practice is simple and utilizes a crystal sphere or ball made of clear quartz, rose quartz, or amethyst, all three of which are fairly easy to obtain as spheres and are pyroelectric when held in the hand and warmed by natural body heat. When working with crystal orbs, it is best to start simply by first feeling the radiating energy emanating from your hands around a crystal sphere while becoming comfortable with meditation and intention. This practice is useful for both the novice and those who are experienced with crystals and meditation.

◎ Radiate Compassion

1. Hold the crystal sphere, stroking it until it feels warm or comfortable in your hands. Hold the orb at heart level with both hands while breathing deeply, and enter into a clear and meditative state.

Figure 11.12. Crystal balls are used to amplify psychic energy.
Photo by Kaleigh Brown

2. Meditate on the feeling of compassion in the heart, allowing the feeling to radiate from the heart center, through the arms, and into the hands flowing into the crystal ball. While the heart is radiating with compassion, feel that compassion glowing from the orb. Breathe in deeply while making this heart connection between yourself and the orb.

3. Bring the crystal ball up to the throat chakra, take in a deep breath charged with love and compassion, and breathe it into the crystal ball.

4. Repeat this breath exercise at least three times, rotating the position of the orb each time.

5. Return the sphere to heart level and connect the heart energetically with the orb, giving and receiving compassion from the orb. Sit in

meditative silence and visualize the orb as planet Earth while radiating compassion. Send out waves of compassion flowing through the self, the immediate area, the region, the country, and out into the world, until compassion embraces the entire planet Earth and continues out and beyond into space.

6. When you are finished radiating compassion, bring your attention back to a simple heart connection with the orb, open your eyes, and express gratitude back into the crystal ball for helping to radiate compassion into the world.

Preparing Gem Elixirs

"Elixir" is a term rooted in alchemy. Per Merriam-Webster, it is from the Arabic *al-iksir* but ultimately derives from a Greek word meaning "desiccative powder."[4] Desiccation involves drying a substance into a powder. Elixirs were also produced by crushing gemstones into fine powders, mixing them with liquids, and ingesting them. These processes evolved into modern-day pharmaceuticals but now exclude the spiritual component prevalent in the development of alchemical elixirs. Grinding minerals and gemstones into powders is still practiced across the world. For example, it is a Chinese practice to grind pearls into fine powders and use them for therapeutic remedies, including beautifying creams and remedies for digestive disorders, due to pearl's calcium content. Transmutation was at the heart of this process, the goal being that the substance was broken down to its core essence and, with this substance, the elixir could be created. We do not advise that you crush your minerals and gemstones into fine powders and ingest them, because many minerals are toxic. However, there are some simple alchemical processes that can be safely performed and even ingested when carried out properly.

At a simple level, a crystal programmed with an intention and then placed into a liquid helps to energize and focus the substance. Small quartz crystals or Herkimer diamonds are ideal for this type of practice. Program the small crystals using the technique described earlier in this chapter. Place the crystal in water, essential oil, spray, or cream. Be sure that when placing crystals in drinking water, only polished or tumbled quartz is used. Clean and polished clear quartz, rose quartz, amethyst, and citrine are safe for placing directly in drinking water. Do not place other crystals in drinking water as they may be chemically toxic and leach into the water. Raw pieces may have small fragments that can break off and are not safe for drinking water. Instead, use the indirect method of energizing water with crystals by placing the crystals in a sealed glass container and placing the sealed container into the water (figure 11.13). This is a safe transfer of energy, preventing toxic minerals or broken pieces from contaminating the water. The following practice is described for use with polished, tumbled quartz crystal.

◎ Create Chintamani Water

1. For this alchemical practice, gather your materials first. Select a clean glass container, water pitcher, or bowl.

2. Place a programmed quartz crystal (clean and polished) into the container. Pour purified drinking water into the container.

3. Depending on how you want to program the water, stand in either moonlight, sunlight, or starlight and pray over the water with your intention. State the intention over the water several times while using your hands to send energy into the water. You can chant *Aum* over the water or another mantra such as *Aum Mani Padme Hung!* You can also use singing bowls to add vibrational energy.

4. Place the container of water in sunlight, moonlight, or starlight for several hours (either overnight or for a full day). The time of the full moon is ideal for charging water overnight. If you want to charge the water with a particular planet (such as Venus) or star or star group (such as the Big Dipper or Orion), be sure to place the water container in a place where the planet or starlight is radiating on the water for a period of time.

5. After the water is finished energizing, use the water in the same way as you would holy water, such as sprinkling yourself and others with the water, sprinkling a space, or anointing an altar or crystal. When drinking the water, open yourself up to receive the intention of the programmed and blessed water and visualize yourself drinking the water of life. After drinking and sprinkling yourself with the water, meditate on your intention while absorbing the water into your body.

Figure 11.13. Examples of creating energized crystal water
using the indirect method.
Photo courtesy of Franziska Schulz and VitaJuwel USA

Crystals, Sound, and Mantra

Mantras are frequently mentioned in our crystal meditation practices because crystals can broadcast the mantra into sound waves, much like a radio signal broadcasts. Mantras are also useful tools for activating and focusing the mind. One translation of mantra is "mind tool," which highlights how mantra can help focus consciousness on outer or inner objects or even upon awareness itself. Mantras are word sequences with linguistic meaning but are more importantly sound sequences vibrating structures of the physical and subtle bodies. Mantras are designed to be chanted or hummed; they are meant to be felt as much as heard. Mantras are intended to operate beneath the surface of discursive thinking to rearrange deeper energy patterns into more positive expressions. They can release automatic responses that have created repeated but negative behaviors and outcomes. After deeper releases of emotions and energies, mantras can be combined with other self-transformational techniques to create and integrate a new array of more positive intentions.

The most common question about any particular mantra is: What does it mean? Many mantras originate in Sanskrit and have been used by non-Indic cultures and transliterated into spoken sounds familiar in the transplanted language. Mantra words also derive from other cultures, languages, and realms. Usually a mantra can be translated so it has linguistic meaning. For instance, the mantra of Avalokiteshvara, *Aum Mani Padme Hung!* is often rendered as: "hail gem in the lotus." This could work if you equate *Aum* to hail, but *Aum* is a very careful combination of every vowel connected in a continuous sound from the back of the throat to the front of the mouth. It has no semantic meaning, but it opens every energy channel. *Hung* similarly has no meaning, but it opens the heart chakra. Instead of speaking a mantra as an ordinary sentence, chant it as an ordered set of vibrations to clear, open, or connect energies. As mantras are repeated, the processes of clearing, opening, or connecting become strengthened and stabilized to accommodate more subtle flows of energy, information, and wisdom.

Mantras have been characterized as affirmations or prayers, and that is partly true. If we repeat thoughts often enough, they manifest in the physical world. Affirmations, however, have to first neutralize a sea of thoughts and emotions to become effective. Mantras engage surface awareness, which is the primary field where affirmations operate, but mantras can also engage unconscious, subconscious, and superconscious states of mind and work on each of these levels simultaneously.

Mantra and Crystal Resonance

When practicing mantras, they should be pronounced and chanted as closely to the manner they have been taught as possible. If mantras were given to you as a spiritual practice, you should honor the instruction that came with the mantra. Mantras you practice that came from a guru or spiritual teacher have more power because of the added momentum of the practice of your guru and all the lineage masters in that tradition. Usually mantra practice settles extremes of emotions and energies into even concentration, resulting in easier meditation practice with less mental effort. Mantra practice is about rhythm and flow and operates most effectively when the sound vibrations arise almost spontaneously. As you chant in a relaxed manner, you will notice variations occur in your cadence, speed, emphasis, focus, and even pronunciation. The mantra's resonant sound energy dynamically adjusts your state of feeling, thinking, and being moment by moment. You can also work with mantra more intentionally and experimentally.

In chanting any mantra, you can feel it vibrate in and through your body. As you chant, you can choose a focal point where you will especially notice the resonant vibration acting. For instance, if you are working to balance your heart area, whether for physical health or emotional equanimity, you can place your awareness at the heart and feel the vibration there. This is a good way to heal any distresses with which you may struggle. You can amplify the focal power of mantras through the field of your body and aura with crystals or other minerals. The technique is to physically hold a crystal at a focus spot like the crown chakra. Then feel the mantra sound vibrate both the crystal and your focus area together. You can further intensify the mantra and crystal by choosing a crystal with qualities benefiting your physical, emotional, or mental focus. For instance, you can use rose quartz, emerald, or aquamarine when working with the heart chakra. When you work with the resonant dimensions of crystals, you amplify what crystals can accomplish as well as increase the beneficial effects upon your mind, heart, and intentions.

◎ Crystal Energy Sphere

Although this practice can be done alone, it is better to work with a group of people in a circle.

1. Prepare by cleansing the space and clearing several hand-held crystal points and smaller crystal points. Other colored stones can be added into the circle grid for increased energy or to enhance a specific focus (see table on page 275 for colored crystal suggestions).

2. Create a centerpiece with a crystal singing bowl or a Tibetan singing bowl. Create a circle wheel of crystals pointed outward from the centerpiece. This can be complemented with a circle of other stones in a circular array interspersed with the large crystals. Incense and/or candles can be incorporated.

3. Place hands over the circle and pray and/or chant with the intention that the group meditation will benefit all sentient beings in the world.

4. Invite others to sit around the crystal circle and ask participants to choose a meditation crystal from around the circle. Once everyone selects a crystal, begin leading a guided breathing meditation first by clearing and connecting with the crystal and then programming the crystal using breathwork (as described in pages 281–91). Use a unified intention said out loud by the meditation leader. For example, love, peace, harmony, compassion, healing, or other similar themes are beneficial to all sentient beings on Earth. Guide others to meditate with these qualities in themselves first so their minds and bodies are radiating the beneficial intention.

5. When the crystals have been programmed with an intention, guide the group to point the crystal tips outward to the center of the circle and send waves of energy radiating with the intention to each person in the room. Then guide the group to visualize and direct intention into an imagined energy ball in the center of the room floating above the center of the circle.

6. Guide the group to intensify the energy of the intention from their heart center, through the voice in chanting *Aum* or *Aum Mani Padme Hung!* in unison, through the quartz crystal pointed from their heart outward to the center, and into the floating sphere above the center.

7. Continue guiding the meditation and collectively "lift" the energy orb into the sky and allow it to disperse as an intentional gift to the world. Use the resonance from crystal singing bowls or Tibetan bowls and chanting to raise the visualized crystal sphere into the sky.

8. Guide the group to return focus slowly to the self by turning the quartz crystal in their hands upright and reground. End the meditation by slowly opening the eyes, looking into the crystal, and centering the self in gratitude. Thank everyone in the group for taking part in sending this gift to the world.

Figure 11.14. Create orbs of light during crystal meditation.

Wearing Gemstones

An intuitive and easy way to work with crystals and gems is wearing them as jewelry on the body. It is no coincidence that royalty and the priesthood have historically adorned themselves with gems through their necklaces, rings, and crowns. King Solomon wore a legendary signet ring reputed to control demonic energies, which he directed to help build the first temple in Jerusalem. Solomon's ring was mentioned by Josephus in the first century CE, who reported that others had imitated the ring and were able to heal and cast out demons using an engraving of Solomon's seal in a ring.[5] To this day, agate rings engraved with the Seal of Solomon are worn for magic and protection. Nicholas Roerich believed the stone in King Solomon's ring was a chintamani.[6] Solomon's magic ring undoubtedly contributed to the popularity of wearing magic rings, but gemstone rings have practical applications as well. The hands are creative channels and extensions of the brain, so wearing gemstones and precious metals on the fingers aligns them with energies in the hands that are directed consciously by our thoughts and intentions. Wearing gemstones on the fingers is an empowering link to support our creative thoughts.

Figure 11.15. Hessonite garnet set in a gold ring. Hessonite is a gemstone useful for directing ambition and willpower toward enlightened action.

While gems are considered objects of wealth and power, many are not often consciously connected to the energetic vibrations of the crystals they are wearing. Gems have an unconscious effect on the wearer, but the energy that gems radiate can be directed by the wearer toward specific intentions or powers. Jyotish practices provide a model of rituals that unite wearing a gem with conscious intention. Some of the Jyotish gemology practices can be adapted to the Western approach to astrology as well. As discussed in chapter 8, birthstones are connected to the astrological signs while gemstones in the Jyotish system of astrology are associated with ruling planets. The fingers on the hands are also aligned energetically with each of the planets (see table). By wearing gemstones on the right hand, associated with solar energy, one is empowering the male or exterior energies such as leadership, vigor, success, and confidence. Wearing gemstones on the lunar left hand increases feminine internalized qualities such as intuition, relationships, healing, and creativity. For balance, Harish Johari recommends wearing solar gems (associated with sun, Mars, Saturn, Rahu, and Ketu) on the left lunar hand and lunar gems (associated with moon, Mercury, Venus, and Jupiter) on the right solar hand.[7] Each finger is aligned with a planet and corresponds with the energies of that planet. So the forefinger is the teaching finger and is aligned with the guru planet, Jupiter. The middle finger has to do with karmic responsibility and is aligned with Saturn and the lunar nodes. The ring finger is associated with the energies of the sun, Venus, and Mars. Mercury and the moon are aligned with the small finger. There are other systems supporting different practices, so to best align with your intention easily, work with a system with which you are already familiar.

WEARING GEMSTONES: JYOTISH ASTROLOGY		
FINGER	**PLANET**	**GEMSTONE**
First Finger or Forefinger	Jupiter	Yellow Sapphire
Middle Finger	Saturn	Blue Sapphire
	North Node	Hessonite Garnet
	South Node	Cat's Eye Chrysoberyl
Ring Finger	Sun	Ruby
	Venus	Diamond
	Mars	Coral
Little Finger	Moon	Pearl
	Mercury	Emerald
Thumb	Venus	Diamond
	Mars	Coral

The Jyotish system offers a model to aid in the alignment of body, gem-stone, and astrology. It is most important to wear gemstones with conscious, positive intention. When buying a ring for intentional purposes, use the practices outlined earlier for alignment, selection, purification, and programming. Mentally and spiritually dedicate the ring to a specific purpose and perhaps engrave the ring with a symbol, mantra, or power word. Jyotish astrologers have complex rituals aligned with ring dedication. Use rituals that are meaningful and memorable, support alignment to higher intentions, and connect the energy of the gem to the wearer. Wearing the ring connects mind, body, and energy. When you see the ring on your hand, you remember the purpose of the ring. The color, light, and energy of the gemstone magnifies the intention that is sent into the light of the eye and activates parts of your right brain that are programmed to manifest the intention. The ring is more than a magic talisman. It is an alchemical marriage bond to remember and act on a vow to yourself—your intention.

12

Chintamani Matrix Yoga

*Ten Transformational Practices with
Chintamani as Path and Goal*

> *The vast space of Vajrasattva**
> *the all-good expanse of the field of reality,*
> *this is the all-releasing and pure modality*
> *uncreated, unceasing, and unthinking.*
>
> VAIROTSANA, *EYE OF THE STORM*

WE HAVE ARRANGED THE PRACTICES in this chapter as a continuum from the previous chapter, from fundamental to more advanced, but we do not want you to jump to the last few pages first. We have practiced what we are presenting, and they do build upon one another. We recognize readers will have a wide range of self-cultivation skills and experiences, with some just beginning and some advanced. The dance is between not spending too much time immersing yourself in practices at which you are already skilled versus exploring unfamiliar practices that may lead to new insights and capabilities. Creating the energetic and conscious dynamic for meaningful self-transformation is the basis of each practice. You will have to find the tension of personal balance, tuning yourself like the strings of a harp ready to play.

---

*Vajrasattva is Sanskrit for "Diamond Being."

This collection of practices is known as chintamani matrix yoga. It is the moment to step beyond logic and information in order to find out what the chintamani means in your marrow.

At the heart of activating the chintamani are the divergent paths of me-first or you-first. It is not an exclusive choice of me versus them, because benefiting all sentient beings also brings greater benefit to oneself. Before we have even begun the first practice, however, we will already have committed to one side or the other of this paradox. Leaning right or left is an automatic, subconscious orientation unless we have exercised a conscious choice instead. The chintamani yoga discussed here will succeed as selfless practice. The mindset to benefit others operates below intention yet can also operate fused with the light of conscious intention. Examining this is the yoga before yoga.

Primary Vows

The first step is making a few deep vows to and for yourself:

to realize your own highest development, supreme enlightenment;
to find accomplished and trustworthy teachers to guide you;
to seek community with other serious yogis on this practice path; and
to benefit others unconditionally.

With any of these vows you are not imposing a time limit or set of specific performance expectations on yourself. The certainty and intensity of your commitment to these vows will change and ease your karma in that moment. As you take this vow again as you begin each day, your renewed focus will add to the force of your great purpose. Each day, you take smaller steps to realize these vows. There is an important Chinese adage that your first step takes you halfway to your goal.

Ishtadevata, Indwelling Divine

We discovered that the jewel net of Indra projects a net of illusion that engulfs all sentient beings in a dream cloud of misperception. The jewel net is an endless matrix of karmic causes and effects in the stream of time, spinning a very compelling delusion. The practice of ishtadevata (chosen, personal deity) is the yoga that can dispel the illusion that abides at the heart of self-perception, the ego. The illusion is about identifying yourself with something you are not. So before understanding your own primordial nature, you have to break the misidentification and the solid-seeming belief structure that constantly arises as deep dissatisfaction. Ishtadevata, or yidam practice, is a way to shift identification from ego to divine archetype. In this yoga, you begin by choosing a divine archetype that resonates at a gut level. In Vajrayana Buddhism, the choice is a yidam, a Buddha or Bodhisattva, who as a great, enlightened being, radiates infinite compassion, wisdom, and skill. You can also choose some other divine being that has meaning and inspires you. Later, you can choose a different ishtadevata that is more powerful for you. Familiarize yourself with a specific image of your chosen ishtadevata, because every symbol held by or displayed around your divine archetype shows how your yidam manifests in the world. We presented some ishtadevatas in chapter 3 that may prove helpful.

The yoga is to immerse yourself in the realm of your ishtadevata, visualizing and experiencing that world as clearly as possible. There are differing depths at which this yoga operates. You can visualize your ishtadevata three feet above your head either facing you or facing the same direction as you. Closer still, you can visualize your yidam as your same size facing you in mirror posture. Closer yet, if you have received a tantric empowerment with specific practice instructions, you can visualize yourself as the ishtadevata. In whichever yoga mode you practice, the yidam arises from emptiness and remains like rainbow light, present but not solid. Perceiving yourself as solid ego or solid ishtadevata only entangles you deeper in dense illusion. You will know that this yoga is transforming your life when any of a number of signs occur. The first is that the yidam appears spontaneously in your dreams or that symbols associated with the yidam appear in your daily life as topics, images, or implements. The second sign is that you experience the archetype not just as a static picture, but dynamically moving in your dreams or practice visualizations. The third sign is that you begin to interact with your yidam, perhaps asking questions and receiving answers. The fourth sign is that after testing guidance given by the yidam, you find it to be increasingly true, accurate, and reliable. As this yoga proceeds, you discover the fifth sign that you no longer identify with your body or ego and realize that the seat of your consciousness has shifted dramatically.

Since this is chintamani yoga, a chintamani is part of the symbols your ishtadevata manifests. If you choose a Vajrayana Buddhist yidam, almost all specific images include a gem or group of gems on fire, symbolizing the chintamani. Some Bodhisattvas will even hold a chintamani as discussed in chapter 3. If you have chosen an ishtadevata that is not usually pictured with a chintamani, try to find an image in which that deity does have a chintamani. For instance, although the important Hindu deity Ganesh usually does not display a chintamani, there are images in which he holds the chintamani in one of his central left hands. If there are no chintamani deity images you can find, visualize and experience the chintamani as a prominent symbol in the world of your chosen ishtadevata. Near the end of your practice session, you need to offer the chintamani of universal benefit as well as all the merit and positive energy generated in your practice session for the benefit of all sentient beings. This step will establish supreme generosity as integral in your life. The following section describes the specific steps of chintamani ishtadevata practice.

◎ Chintamani Ishtadevata Yoga

1. Sit in a comfortable posture that you can hold for the whole practice in a serene room.
2. Relax and take at least three deep breaths.
3. State your vows to become enlightened, to follow your outer and inner guru, to practice with the community of yoginis and yogis, and to seek to benefit all sentient beings without limit in all you do.
4. Chant this mantra once as your ishtadevata dynamically arises out of space: *Aum Swabhava Shuddha, Sarva Dharma Swabhava Shuddho Hung!**
5. Settle yourself in the realm of the ishtadevata, exploring and sensing

---

*This mantra means: "(Ishtadevata) self-arising purely, all phenomena self-arising purely!"

what is all around. Attune to any visions, sounds, aromas, tastes, or sensations of that realm.

6. Throughout all space there are Buddhas, Bodhisattvas, saints, sages, and realized masters. You send the light of your intentions to them. They all radiate light back to your heart, throat, and third eye chakras. They also radiate infinite light to the chintamani.

7. Focus on the chintamani and imagine it radiating limitless blessings to all beings. Imagine it blessing specific people, animals, plants, and the Earth.

8. Chant the mantra of your ishtadevata to focus your attention. For example, if Tara is your yidam, the mantra would be *Aum Tare Tuttare Ture So Ha!**

9. Dissolve the form vision of your ishtadevata in rainbow light while remaining aware of the empty presence of your yidam.

10. Meditate in this state comfortably for as long as you can remain self-aware.

11. Offer the wealth and blessings of the chintamani and the positive energy you have just generated to benefit all sentient beings.

12. As you move to get up, imagine the palpable presence of your yidam accompanying you in all your activities.

13. Periodically throughout the day, remember and reexperience the presence of your yidam.

Specific and Limitless Intention

In the introduction we asked the question: If you had the chintamani, what would you do with its potentials? This practice shifts that from an intellectual inquiry to a heart inquiry. You will continue to use your main ishtadevata practice but will add a few variations. You will need a quartz crystal as physical support for the chintamani. You will also use the practice instructions from chapter 11 on setting intentions and meditating with a crystal in this next sequence. Make sure that you have cleared the crystal you will use in this yoga as discussed in chapter 11. Below you will find the instructions for the full yoga with the new practice variations.

---

*A partial set of mantras for various ishtadevata/yidams is included in appendix 2.

◎ Intention and Visualizing the Chintamani

1. Sit in a comfortable posture that you can hold for the whole practice in a serene room.

2. Hold a clear quartz crystal at your navel chakra area. Relax and take at least three deep breaths.

3. Raise the crystal to your heart and hold it prayerfully. State your vows to become enlightened, to follow the truth of your outer and inner guru, to practice with the community of yoginis and yogis, and to seek to benefit all sentient beings without limit in all you do.

4. As you chant *Aum Swabhava Shuddha Sarva Dharma Swabhava Shuddho Hung!* once, the full presence of your ishtadevata dynamically arises out of the crystal.

5. Settle yourself in the realm of the ishtadevata, exploring and sensing what is all around. Attune to any visions, sounds, aromas, tastes, or sensations of that realm. Recognize the crystal you are holding as both yours and the yidam's chintamani.

6. Throughout all space there are Buddhas, Bodhisattvas, saints, sages, and realized masters. Send the light of your intentions to them. They all radiate infinite light back to your heart, throat, and third eye chakras. They also radiate infinite light to the chintamani.

7. Focus on the chintamani and imagine it radiating limitless blessings to all beings. Imagine it blessing specific people, animals, plants, and the Earth.

8. Chant the mantra of your ishtadevata to focus your attention. For example, if Avalokiteshvara is your yidam, the mantra would be *Aum Mani Padme Hum!*

9. If you have specific intentions to benefit others or to benefit your projects that bless others, state these intentions and release them completely.

10. Dissolve the form vision of your ishtadevata in rainbow light while remaining aware of the empty presence of your yidam now within your crystal chintamani.

11. Meditate in this state comfortably for as long as you can remain self-aware.

12. Offer the wealth and blessings of the chintamani and the positive energy you have just generated to benefit all sentient beings.

13. As you move to get up, imagine the palpable presence of your yidam accompanying you in all your activities.

14. Periodically throughout the day, remember and reexperience the presence of your yidam.

Chintamani Energy Body

In chapter 9 we discussed the complexities of transforming the energy body so that it works in synergy with other yoga practices. Energy body yoga opens a second and parallel branch of practice. If you have experience with regular practice of pranayama, qigong, or *tsa lung,* then continue. If you are new to the yoga of internal fire, then you need to seek out teachings in these disciplines. Also, if you are new to these practices, be open to discovering that one system may be more compatible for you than another as you test them. The authors practice the treasure teaching of Senton Dorje* and Master Quan called Xian Lung Fa Men, or Spiral Dragon Dharma System. Spiral Dragon leads to relaxing and opening the energy system so that it transforms itself naturally without artifice. It takes considerable, long-term discipline to transform the energy body, so in whichever system you practice, don't push for quick accomplishment. Working with the energy body causes each practitioner to create a cascade of changes in diet, exercise, vitality, lifestyle, and personal resilience as they attune to and transform the flow of subtler energies.

A practice that supports energy body work that will eventually lead to realizing the *vajrakaya,* or diamond body, is Vajrasattva meditation. Vajrasattva is a white or clear Buddha whose name means pure diamond being. The meditation is an outer and inner exploration of the world of diamond purity. In this tantric system, purity involves behavior, but even more it involves the basis of perception. The root impurity is that each of us looks in a mirror and perceives individual characteristics: height, weight, age, sex, and race. There are thousands more qualities that each of us perceive and are reflected back in the perception of others. These

---

*Senton Dorje was Master Quan's Guru. She discovered the treasure teaching of Xian Lung Fa Men, or Spiral Dragon Dharma System, while making an extensive thirteen-year retreat in a cave not far distant from Kumbum Monastery, a University Monastery for the study and practice of Kalachakra.

characteristics are not those of our original nature, but of our current karmic profile. The root ignorance, which is the root impurity, is identifying the collection of temporary characteristics as real instead of seeing the uncreated self. If, however, we were to perceive our original nature directly, it would appear more like Vajrasattva or his consort, Vajrasattvi, or you would appear more like your ishtadevata. This Vajrasattva practice works with our perception of what is real. In part, it challenges us to reexamine our perception both of the outside world and of our bodies as being solid, impenetrable, and permanent. Empirical science recognizes that our bodies and the outside world are mostly energy configurations with minimal matter. Yet our ordinary senses interpret the energy patterns as solid presence. Below, you will find the steps of Vajrasattva practice.

Figure 12.1. Supports for practice. The flaming gems symbolize
the visual presence of the chintamani. A Tibetan singing bowl represents the
realm of sound and physically creates resonant vibration along with mantra.
In the foreground is a Siberian blue quartz crystal vajra carved by Nicholas
Xu. The vajra symbolizes the indestructible and diamond-like nature of
absolute reality and is used in most Tibetan tantric rituals.
Photo by Kaleigh Brown

◎ *Vajrasattva Energy Body*

1. Relax your body, emotions, and mind while in a comfortable standing or sitting posture.

2. State your vows. If you are doing ishtadevata and Vajrasattva practice back to back, you can omit this step, as you have already set your great intention.

3. Visualize yourself as yidam, with Vajrasattva just above your crown. He radiates light to you. You in turn radiate light to Vajrasattva and to the presence of limitless Buddhas, Bodhisattvas, and realized spiritual masters surrounding you. In turn, all these great beings radiate light back to you to help transform your energy body.

4. Sincerely ask for light to dissolve all your physical, emotional, mental, and spiritual obscurations that have accumulated since before the beginning of time. Vow not to create further negativity for others or for yourself.

5. Chant Vajrasattva's mantra: *Aum Vajrasattva Hung!** Experience light radiating from Vajrasattva to clear all your illness, poisons, dark energies, and misdeeds. Feel the full release of disease and dissatisfaction.

6. Rest your mind and relax. Explore your body complex so that you begin to experience the empty, expansive, and open nature of your own presence. You may continue to chant the mantra if it does not interfere with your investigation. After enough practice sessions you may find chanting the mantra will help rather than hinder your focus.

7. Resume chanting the mantra. At this moment Vajrasattva pours *amrita* nectar into the top of your head. It is like a golden honey in consistency but is a form of light. It enters your spinal column and flows downward into your body to fill you with ease, energy, happiness, and peace. The nectar removes traces of negativity and suffering.

8. Send the great peace you are receiving to all beings to ease their cares. You can add specific people you know who will benefit from this light of peace.

---

*There is a hundred-syllable Vajrasattva mantra that you may want to learn later and chant instead of the six-syllable mantra.

9. Dissolve the vision of Vajrasattva and rest your mind in pure awareness. Experience your body and self as clear diamond and as being the same as the chintamani.

10. Offer the blessings of peace, happiness, and wealth of chintamani qualities you have just generated to benefit all sentient beings.

11. Before you move to resume your day's tasks, reexperience yourself as your yidam.

12. Whenever you can, recall your yidam as present at the center of all your actions unfolding over the course of the day.

Finding Your Chintamani

So far, your practices have included holding a clear quartz crystal as a physical support for the chintamani. You have also begun the yoga of increasingly experiencing yourself as a clear, diamond chintamani. As discussed, the chintamani has been associated with a great number of different gems of varying colors. In this yoga, you will identify particular characteristics of the chintamani, especially color, that resonate for you from within and scintillate in light. One method is external as you choose four different crystal minerals and blend their qualities. This was presented in chapter 11 in the practice called "Create a Mind Gem" on page 294. If you have complete confidence in the mind gem you fused, you can use that gem in all self and yidam visualizations for the remaining practices. If you still are in doubt, try the following inner method of manifesting the mind gem.

◎ Manifesting the Inner Mind Gem

If your yidam is connected to a particular chintamani gem, then as a phase of your yidam practice, focus on that chintamani. Experience its qualities as clearly as you can. If that chintamani continues to resonate strongly with you, then you have found a better support for your chintamani yoga than a clear quartz crystal or the created mind gem. If you have no confidence that the yidam's chintamani is also yours, or if your ishta-devata doesn't hold a chintamani, then use this next method for greater confidence.

In front of the image of each Buddhist yidam, there is one gem or a pile of gems with the top gem engulfed in flames. Those gems aflame are the symbol of the chintamani (figure 12.1, page 316). If your yidam is not Buddhist, then visualize that there is a pile of flaming gems in front of your ishtadevata. In this pile are gems of white/clear, red, green, yellow, and blue colors. During your practice session, focus on experiencing that pile of gems as you chant the yidam's mantra. It may take a number of practice sessions, but eventually the gems will glow and pulse with different intensities of brightness. Eventually as you view the imagined pile, one colored gem will become the brightest of the group consistently. That is a better support for your chintamani yoga. You can combine several methods in your search, but your inquiry process is not over until you have no doubt that you have experienced your chintamani. You may combine several practices to fuse a range of qualities into your mind gem as you seek clarity and greater certainty. By being present with the chintamani energy that resonates with you, you will be led to know your inner chintamani.

Chintamani Matrix Yoga

By this phase of practice, you will know your inner chintamani. You may be prompted to find a better support crystal for your outer practice that matches the inner discovery of your chintamani. This search may take a while because you are looking for a crystal that is approximately like the one you've identified. It need not be a large crystal, nor does it need to be expensive. As you move forward with the next practices, you can use the clear crystal as a physical support for your inner chintamani until you obtain a more apt crystal. Don't rule out that you may be led forward in a series of discoveries with each crystal being closer to the one you have identified. By this phase of practice, you will also have the experience of your own energy field as it overlaps that of the chintamani. This yoga continues to emphasize the inner chintamani connection to induce greater awareness of the jewel net of Indra. As you sought out a specific inner chintamani during the last practice, it may have rearranged your connection to the yidam. You can make another choice of ishtadevata for your practice. All yidams share the same enlightened and realized nature, so at their core, they are the same. The outer appearances of ishtadevatas differ as they appeal to the mindset of our karma. It is important to have enthusiasm for your practice as your practice shifts your energy and awareness. As you notice you have made a big shift, it is important to adjust accordingly. This adds a new phase to your chintamani ishtadevata yoga but continues the core process.

◎ Experiencing the Chintamani Matrix

1. In this yoga, as you focus on the chintamani support crystal, you will notice that the yidam's chintamani has blended with you.

2. Furthermore, you can see that the field of all the Buddhas, Bodhisattvas, and realized masters in your visualization has changed. As you send your intentions, then receive and send light, you will notice a detail that was always present: each Buddha has a chintamani in front of them. From the iconography we discussed, you will remember that all the enlightened masters have chintamanis embedded in their light auras. You may have seen this before, but this yoga draws you to focus your mind more intensely on this connection.

3. Endlessly, beyond as far as you can see, are Buddhas with chintamanis in front of them and surrounding their auras. They are connected by light rays to each other and to you. When you get to the step of radiating light to bless all beings, become aware that all the realized masters with their chintamanis are radiating blessings to all beings in general and to beings and situations you especially wish to benefit.

4. At the conclusion of that step of practice, begin to dissolve your visualization. First, your yidam and all the Buddhas dissolve into the chintamanis in front of them in a blaze of rainbow light. Next, all the connected network of chintamanis dissolve in rainbow light.

5. As usual, remain in a meditative state, aware and awake as you steadily release thoughts and intrusive emotions as you continue to rest your being completely in the moment.

6. Afterward, dedicate the positivity of your practice for the benefit of all sentient beings.

7. As you rise to continue your day, reassert the presence of your ishtadevata during all your activities.

Shambhala and Kalachakra

Kalachakra and Shambhala practice are different aspects of the same yoga. Within the Tibetan Vajrayana tradition, Kalachakra is the last official tantra of the practice (*kama*) lineage. That means Kalachakra yoga has been handed down directly from guru to disciple in an unbroken chain since 1027 CE. It is a complicated and complete system in and of itself. Here we will present ways to increase affinities with both Kalachakra and Shambhala using daylight and nighttime practices, while continuing to build on our earlier chintamani yoga. As discussed in chapter 4, Vajrayana guidebooks to Shambhala present an outer journey paired with a particular inner practice necessary to surmount the next obstacle. Recall that Shambhala is a realm encircled by mountains with a capital city and a central palace. The outer ruler is a Kalki King and the inner ruler is Kalachakra and consort, Kalachakri. At the palace center is Kalachakra and Kalachakri, who preside over countless Bodhisattvas and enlightened masters. In this next practice, we approach the Shambhala realm, the capital city of Kalapa, and the central palace. There, your ishtadevata is one of the infinite Bodhisattvas and is perfect as your inner guide to Shambhala. Your yidam's chintamani has perfect affinity with Shambhala and Kalachakra practice.

◎ *Entering Shambhala by Day*

1. You begin your yidam practice as always from a relaxed yet attentive posture. Breathing deeply and relaxing more, you release all that afflicts you physically, emotionally, and mentally.

2. You state your four vows, holding your new support chintamani or clear crystal prayerfully in your hands at your heart chakra.

3. Place your chintamani support crystal in your left hand and hold it at your navel chakra. As you chant *Aum Swabhava Shuddha Sarva Dharma Swabhava Shuddho Hung!* experience the presence of your yidam arising from the chintamani crystal.

4. Settle yourself into experiencing the realm of your ishtadevata. You may continue to hold the support chintamani or place it on the earth in front of you. Make sure that you recognize the support chintamani as the actual chintamani of your yidam.

5. Direct your attention to the Buddhas, Bodhisattvas, and enlightened masters throughout all space who have a chintamani with them and others woven in their auras. Radiate light to all these great beings with rays coming from your heart and chintamani to their hearts and chintamanis. Recognize that you and they all remain connected in a seamless, endless web of light.

6. Ask your ishtadevata and the great assembly of sky beings around you to guide you to Shambhala. In answer, your ishtadevata and assembly of Buddhas beam brilliant light rays to all your chakras and to your chintamani. During this shower of light, chant the mantra of your yidam many times. You in turn radiate brilliant light to benefit all sentient beings in general and to those you specifically wish to benefit.

7. In order to establish a closer connection to Kalachakra, chant his approach mantra as much as you can: *Aum Guru Kalachakra Ye So Ha!*

8. At the end of your practice session, visualize that all the Buddhas and your yidam dissolve into their chintamani gems. Then dissolve all the chintamanis into empty space alive with energy and all possibilities.

9. Meditate silently in this state for as long as you can, remaining self-aware.

10. Offer the wealth and blessings of the chintamanis throughout all space and the positive energy you have generated by your practice to benefit all sentient beings.

11. Before you move to attend to the activities of your day, reestablish the presence of your yidam in all you will do, feel, and think.

◎ Entering Shambhala by Night

1. The next step is to take this daylight practice into your dreams. Sit up in bed for a few minutes to prepare yourself for sleep. Breathe deeply, relax, and center yourself.

2. State your four vows, three of spiritual reliance and one to benefit all beings.

3. Chant the mantra once that invokes your ishtadevata: *Aum Swabhava Shuddha Sarva Dharma Swabhava Shuddho Hung!*

4. Next, chant this mantra a number of times to approach Kalachakra: *Aum Guru Kalachakra Ye So Ha!*

5. As you lie down, make the intention to encounter your yidam and to receive dream guidance to connect with Shambhala.

6. As the day and dream practices begin to saturate your mind and energy field over weeks or months, dreams will arise to answer your sincere intentions. Write them down and contemplate their meaning as to how you are being directed to your next step of connection with Shambhala and the Kalachakra. The difficulty for most of us is that we don't often want to take the advice we receive. But once you are confident you understand the direction emerging from your encounters with people and symbols in both your waking activities and in your dreams, you must follow that direction for the journey to Shambhala to unfold forward.

Light Energy and Rainbow Body

An end result of Kalachakra yoga, highest yoga, or atiyoga is the accelerated exhaustion of karma that might otherwise take millions of incarnations to accomplish. Karma provides the gravity that enmeshes us in time and illusion. Supreme enlightenment exhausts all positive and negative karma, collapsing the causal structure of linear time. To accomplish this in a lifetime is possible and is a return to the natural condition of mind. Here we introduce a meditation that leads to resting the mind in its natural state. Abiding in that deep state of samadhi automatically liberates the mind from attachment and karma. With persistent practice, your karma will be exhausted as you recognize that enlightenment is always present, saturating your ordinary awareness completely. This practice is an independent and parallel practice set that integrates with the ishtadevata and energy yogas we have worked with so far.

◎ Recognizing Essential Presence

1. Light three incense sticks as offerings to the entire universe to benefit all sentient beings.

2. State your vows to abide in the enlightened mind, to encounter all phenomena as it really is, to follow the light to the truth of your inner guru, to engage with others to create endless benefit, and to seek the good

of all sentient beings. You may also chant mantras to help settle your energy and mind.

3. Your posture is important. Sit in an upright posture with spine straight. You may sit in a cross-legged lotus or half-lotus posture on a zafu (pillow) on the floor or in a chair. Cross the right leg in front of the left. Place your right palm over your left and hold this mudra at your navel. Make sure your arms don't collapse at your sides but hold them open in a circle of energy moving through your shoulders, arms, and hands easily. Almost touch the two thumbs together, making an oval at your navel. As you become aware of body discomfort, check to see that your posture is correct. If not, make adjustments to correct it.

4. Take a few deep breaths. Then allow your breath to settle into a deep and natural rhythm. Let the breath help release any difficulty of body, emotion, or thought. Whenever you become unsettled, you can count breaths from one to ten for as many cycles as it takes to settle.

5. Focus your attention on your navel. If your mind drifts into images or thoughts, bring your attention back to your breath and the present moment. Let go of everything with simple, easy attention on the present moment.

6. You may focus your gaze in one internal or two external ways. You may close your eyes or keep them open while looking down at a 45-degree angle with your head upright. Let your visual focus be general, ready to respond to anything in the room but not scrutinizing anything in particular. If you practice outdoors, you may sky gaze in the day or night, looking into the open area of the sky but not staring directly at the sun or moon. Release control of your visual field and rest your mind in the sky. Depending on where you practice and what your internal condition is, choose a meditation that harmonizes with how agitated or settled your awareness is.

7. Dedicate the positivity of your practice to benefit all sentient beings and especially to help others in your life who are struggling with difficulties.

8. At the conclusion of your session, as you begin to move, you can either choose to remain in an open, aware state moment to moment or reexperience yourself as your ever-aware ishtadevata. You can experience your awareness as the chintamani. Renew the continuity of your

awareness whenever you notice that you have become distracted. Be patient and don't judge yourself. Move on with awareness moment by moment.

◎ *Integrating the Symbols of Shambhala*

In "Entering Shambhala by Day" and "Entering Shambhala by Night," you approached the Kalachakra yidams (figure 4.1, page 79) at the center of the Kalachakra mandala (figure 4.2, page 80) and created greater affinity with them. You have also begun the process of entering Shambhala by day and night. Next, establish presence in Shambhala and set about anchoring your presence there by contemplating symbols and activating yidams.

Every yidam has a presence in the Kalachakra mandala and in Shambhala, although some are more directly connected. In chapter 3, we introduced most of these yidams. Those Buddhas and Bodhisattvas explicitly holding a chintamani are the first natural connection. King Gesar is a future King of Shambhala and will be guided by Padmasambhava. White Mahakala is also connected to the wish-fulfilling gem, but not through the main storyline. Finally, White Tara arises in many personal quests to guide yogis directly to Shambhala and then back into ordinary life forever transformed. If your yidam is one of these, then your practice may be easier, but it does not directly depend on the close connection. Whatever ishtadevata practice you have done so far has established the necessary connections for you.

As preparation, contemplate the Kalachakra and Kalachakri image, the Kalachakra mandala, and two additional symbols. The first is the Ten of Power Kalachakra seed syllable (figure 10.1, page 239), which contains the concentrated visual presentation of the Kalachakra mantra. The second symbol (figure 12.2 on the following page) is the chintamani ascending. Look at both of these symbols when you are relaxed and let your gaze rest on one at a time. Do not strain your vision, rather become comfortably familiar with them. They awaken connections that will spontaneously arise at the right moment. Experience the world of the symbols as you have done with the world of your yidam. Be present and experience what arises without grasping or chasing. You can contemplate these symbols informally or more formally after establishing your intention to benefit all beings and performing

Figure 12.2. Symbol of Chintamani Yoga.
Design and art by J. Govert

a full session of chintamani matrix yoga. At the conclusion of your contemplation, offer the benefit of your practice for the welfare of all.

◎ Chintamani Presence in Shambhala

1. Light three incense sticks as an offering to the entire universe to benefit all sentient beings.
2. State your vows to abide in the enlightened mind, to encounter all phenomena as they really are, to follow the light to the truth of your inner guru, to engage with others to create endless benefit, and to seek the good of all sentient beings.

3. Arrange the four images and symbols so you can see them and sense their presence.

4. Breathe deeply and relax, then adopt a comfortable seated posture while holding your support crystal as your chintamani.

5. Invoke your yidam by chanting once: *Aum Swabhava Shuddha Sarva Dharma Swabhava Shuddho Hung!*

6. Experience the world of the yidam, especially sensing and connecting with the deity's chintamani.

7. Notice the infinity of Buddhas, Bodhisattvas, and realized spiritual masters who each have a chintamani. Send light to them and to your ishta-devata and receive light back into all your chakras and chintamani.

8. Chant one round of the mantra of your yidam while receiving light from the matrix of enlightened beings and sending it to benefit all sentient beings and especially those you wish to help.

9. Chant the mantra that connects your yidam, the chintamani, Kalachakra and Kalachakri, and Shambhala as a single presence: *Aum Chintamani Ma La Wa Ra Ya Swa Ha!*

10. At the end of chanting, dissolve the vision by first dissolving all the enlightened masters into their respective chintamanis, then dissolving all chintamanis into space.

11. Meditate in this state for as long as you comfortably can.

12. Dedicate the blessings of your practice to all sentient beings.

13. As you arise as your yidam, remember that you are in Shambhala. Everything you will experience in your daily life is an expression of Shambhala.

The sum of the practices in this chapter will allow your diamond body to arise as the seat of awareness. From this, the rainbow body can manifest at the end of your life as you integrate your practice into the death process. Over the course of your life, the more you have been able to let go of attachments and illusions, the more ably you can direct how you cross from embodied limitation into limitless vast expanse. As you have become lighter in every sense over the course of your life, you will be better able to dissolve your physical body and transform any remaining karma into golden light.

Epilogue

IN TIMES OF WIDESPREAD CALAMITY on Earth, refuge realms open. The Roerichs set out to find Shambhala in the era of grave suffering between the last two world wars. At the end of his *Altai-Himalaya* (1929) travel diary, Nicholas left the impression that they had found refuge in a cave entrance to Shambhala on the slopes of Mt. Kanchenjunga. At an elevation of 28,169 feet in the northern Himalayas, Kanchenjunga is one of the tallest, most dangerous mountains in the world. Tulshuk Lingpa, a Tibetan Lama, led an expedition there of three hundred inspired followers seeking entrance to a beyul (hidden land) in 1962, a time fraught with plausible global nuclear devastation by the United States or the Soviet Union.[1] Prior to Tulshuk Lingpa's death in a Mt. Kanchenjunga avalanche, survivors reported supernatural phenomena that were signs they were close to the beyul entrance. They believed the expedition's failure was rooted in the lack of faith of the followers, not due to Tulshuk Lingpa's lead.

Tashiding Monastery, located in Sikkim near the foothills of Kanchenjunga, is where Nicholas Roerich may have interviewed an enigmatic Lama about Shambhala. He recorded this conversation in his travel journal: "Lama Rinpoche knows that on the north side of Kinchenjunga, there lies a cave. Very narrow is the entrance to it, but it broadens and brings one to a whole city. The high priest knows many things, and asks not to speak of them until the appointed time. The consciousness of Geshe* is profound . . . Geshe knows about Shambhala and its complete significance. He takes care to revive the teachings."[2]

---

*Geshe is a title of a scholar Lama who is highly revered.

328

A mysterious stone door, invisible to observers, is embedded into the rock face at Drakkar Tashiding Monastery, believed to be a gateway to the secret valley of Beyul Demashong. Legend reports that at Drakkar Tashiding, meaning "White Rock of the Auspicious Centre,"[3] a Lama walked through the stone wall and entered the hidden realm. The area around the monastery was blessed and consecrated as holy ground by Padmasambhava. A beyul in its own right, the Tashiding area has a cave of longevity dedicated to Guru Rinpoche, sacred pools and wish-fulfilling lakes, caves with precious gemstones and crystals, healing plants, and magical occurrences. Songs from billions of dakinis mysteriously echo within its sacred caves. The monastery's site was selected when a light rainbow emanating from Kanchenjunga pointed to the spot. A contemporary and follower of the Roerichs, Andrew Tomas, reported that the tower of Shambhala is illuminated with a chintamani stone that emanates diamond ray beams like a beacon, which may be mistaken for lightning or the aurora borealis in the Himalayas. Tomas further speculated that the chintamani has an "inner heat" or radiation "mightier than radium," while being "highly sensitive to mental vibrations."[4] Light beams radiating from the chintamani tower in the sacred realm may have led Lamas to select Tashiding's location. Padmasambhava sealed the protective boundaries of the sacred beyul containing multiple entries to the hidden land. He hid several *termas* (secret teachings) around Tashiding to be discovered by treasure revealers and spiritual seekers in times of need and crisis. He also hid other treasures including a chintamani at Tashiding.[5]

Surrounding Tashiding, there are four sacred caves dedicated to and laid out in the four directions with Tashiding Monastery, and its cave, located at its spiritual heart and center:

1. The Hidden Cave in the East (*Sharchog Beyphug*)
2. The Secret Cave of the Dakini in the South (*Lho Kando Sangphug*)
3. The Cave of Great Bliss in the West (*Nub Dechenphug*)
4. The Cave of the Heart of the Deity in the North (*Jhang Lhari Nyingphug*)

Circumambulating these caves clockwise around Tashiding Monastery is part of a sacred pilgrimage practice. The caves offer unique spiritual challenges for self-cultivation. Laid out like the Kalachakra mandala, Tashiding has at least four likely gateways to the sacred realm. Like the Kalachakra mandala gates, each cave is connected to different paths to enlightenment. The monastery is located on a heart-shaped hill above the confluence of two rivers generating electromagnetic fields and portals. The stone door at Drakkar is as much an energetic as it is a physical barrier, preventing the unawakened from entry. To escape the matrix of physical illusion requires interior spiritual transformation.

The Dalai Lama has an especially strong connection to Padmasambhava and Shambhala. The Dalai Lamas are considered reincarnations of Pundarika, the second Kalki King of Shambhala. Curiously, another title for the Dalai Lama is Yishin Norbu, Tibetan for wish-fulfilling gem. The current Dalai Lama has given the Kalachakra empowerment over thirty-three times throughout the world, including once at Tashiding in 1993. Although Kalachakra is one of the highest and most secret tantric initiations, the Dalai Lama has given this empowerment globally to connect as many people as possible with Shambhala. He also has a strong connection to Tashiding, visiting it on several occasions, and has held a retreat there. His affinity to Tashiding seems directly related to the Kalachakra and the presence of Shambhala.

There could be multiple entrances to Shambhala or hidden lands, not just on Kanchenjunga. According to prophecies by Padmasambhava, there are beyuls throughout the Earth. Edwin Bernbaum, who wrote an extensive study about hidden realms and their connection to Kalachakra, suggests that these entrances could be tangible and/or spiritual.[6] Shambhala exists in a dimension outside our conventional worldview. Thomas Shor recounts a story by Tulshuk Lingpa who explained that the Kanchenjunga beyul cannot be found on a map because it "exists, but off the map . . . a map of Sikkim couldn't contain it, for the Great Hidden Valley in Sikkim is three times as large as the outer Kingdom of Sikkim."[7] Tulshuk Lingpa could be speaking literally that the sacred valley is connected by a vast network of caves beneath all of Sikkim and parts of Bhutan, Nepal, India, and China. The second possibility is that the beyul is interior and interdimensional, connecting to physical outer Earth near Kanchenjunga on a time cycle, alternately opening and closing interdimensional doors. Sacred locations, such as Shambhala and beyuls, are unlike ordinary places. Shambhala seems to pulse in synchronicity of time and place with Kanchenjunga, where each are periodically in and out of phase with one another. Kalachakra and the chintamani frequently appear in conjunction with Shambhala. The Kalachakra serves as an interdimensional map of time and space, while the chintamani is a key to unlock mysteries that allow us to transform stone barriers, both internal and external. The Roerichs were not explicit about the location of Shambhala because it is weakly tied to global position, but it is strongly invoked during global spiritual crisis, such as we are experiencing now. This is when the chintamani and its message appear as guiding lights to traverse the path to glorious Shambhala.

APPENDIX I

Five Dhyani Buddhas Correspondences

The table below presents detailed information about the five Buddha families adapted from Reginald Ray's *Secret of the Vajra World*.[1] You may find this table useful for finding a yidam with whom you wish to work in your practice.

QUALITY/ FAMILY	BUDDHA	VAJRA	RATNA	PADMA	KARMA
Dhyani Buddha	Vairochana	Akshobhya	Ratnasambhava	Amitabha	Amoghasiddhi
Consort	Dharma-datvishvari	Mamaki	Lochana	Pandaravasini	Tara
Family (English)	Awakened	Lightning	Jewel	Lotus	Action
Mudra	Teaching Dharma	Earth Touching	Generosity	Meditation	Fearlessness
Symbol	Wheel	Vajra	Jewel	Lotus	Sword
Direction	Center	East	South	West	North
Color	White	Blue	Yellow	Red	Green

QUALITY/ FAMILY	BUDDHA	VAJRA	RATNA	PADMA	KARMA
Wisdom	All-Encompassing Space	Mirror-Like	Equanimity	Discriminating Awareness	All-Accomplishing
Body association	None	Eyes	Stomach	Throat	Genitals, limbs
Skanda	Form	Consciousness	Feeling	Perception	Karmic formations
Element	Space	Water	Earth	Fire	Wind
Affliction	Ignorance	Anger	Pride	Passion	Envy
Realm	God, animal	Hell	Hungry ghost	Human	Jealous god
Season	None	Winter	Fall	Spring	High Summer
Time of Day	No time	Early morning	Mid-morning	Sunset	Dusk, dark, early night
Temperature	Neutral	Cool	Warm	Hot	Cold
Primary function	Being	Thinking	Consuming	Relating	Doing

APPENDIX 2

Practice Mantras

In the table below, you will find a set of mantras that can be used to work with certain yidams and/or ishtadevatas. Remember that there is no empowerment necessary to experience yourself as a yidam when working with Bodhisattvas Avalokiteshvara, Green Tara, or Medicine Buddha. There is also no empowerment necessary to chant the mantras of Manjushri or Amitabha, but an empowerment is required to practice oneself directly as either.

YIDAM	MANTRA	INTENTIONS*
Medicine Buddha	*Aum Bhekadze, Bhekadze, Maha Bhekadze Raja Samudgate Soha!*	Healing Acute, Chronic, and Root Disease Causes
Vajrasattva Vajrasattvi	*Aum Vajrasattva Hung!*	Purifying, Clearing, Renewing
Vairochana	*Aum Vairochana Aum!*	Awakening, Teaching Dharma, Radiance
Akshobhya	*Aum Akshobhya Hung!*	Accelerated Purification, Removing Negativity
Ratnasambhava	*Aum Ratnasambhava Tram!*	Generosity, Prosperity
Amitabha	*Aum Amitabha Hrih!*	Balanced Magnetism, Benefit for the Dying

*Each of the Buddhas and Bodhisattvas contains all possible enlightened qualities of compassion, wisdom, and skill. Some have taken vows to provide a particular benefit, which are also stimulated by reciting the yidam's mantra.

YIDAM	MANTRA	INTENTIONS*
Amoghasiddhi	*Aum Amoghasiddhi Ah!*	Accomplishment, Cutting Through Obstacles
Manjushri	*Aum Ah Ra Pa Tsa Na Dhi!*[1]	Wisdom, Knowledge, Learning
Avalokiteshvara	*Aum Mani Padme Hung!* After 108 repetitions add *"Hrih!"*[†2]	Compassion, Love, Chintamani
Green Tara	*Aum Tare Tuttare Ture Soha!* After 108 repetitions add *"Tam!"*[‡3]	Protection, Compassion, Swift Action
Akashagarbha	*Aum Vajra Ratna, Aum Trah Svaha!*	Prosperity, Generosity, Chintamani
To arise as any yidam[§]	*Aum Swabhava Shuddha Sarva Dharma Swabhava Shuddho Hung!*	Perceiving beyond the appearances of karma
Kalachakra approach	*Aum Guru Shri Kalachakra Ye!*	Connecting to Kalachakra and Shambhala
Kalachakra Chintamani	*Aum Chintamani Ma La Wa Ra Ya Svaha!*	Connecting to the Kalachakra, Chintamani, and Shambhala

*Each of the Buddhas and Bodhisattvas contains all possible enlightened qualities of compassion, wisdom, and skill. Some have taken vows to provide a particular benefit, which are also stimulated by reciting the yidam's mantra.

[†]*Bija* or seed syllables add essential and concentrated sound energy to mantras. In the Manjushri mantra, the last syllable, *"Dhi,"* is a *bija* syllable. In some mantras a *bija* syllable is not a main sound of every mantra recitation but is added at the end of a round of 108 repetitions. For Avalokiteshvara, add *"Hrih"* at the end.

[‡]For Green Tara, add *"Tam"* at the end (see note above re *bija* syllables).

[§]Recite this mantra once when you are about to visualize your yidam and experience that enlightened realm.

Materials Analysis
of Chintamani Orbs

Below you will find the results of the chemical analysis we ordered for two chintamani orbs from Thailand. Instrument used for analysis: Innov-X Hand Held XRF Device in "Mining Mode." The fact that the crust portion of the orbs have only trace amounts of the organic elements of sulfur and phosphorous implies that the crust is not funerary ash. The main constituents of the orb composition include the organic elements of carbon, oxygen, and nitrogen, but their individual amounts were not able to be determined with this test. As expected for glass or crystal, there is from 23 to 29 percent silicon composition, which is true of the crust as well as the orb. The next most significant elements are calcium, potassium, aluminum, and magnesium, all found in combination with silicon. These four elements are absent from the crust. Lead is notably absent from the results, which means the orbs are not leaded glass.

ELEMENT	ELEMENT	BLUE ORB*		GREEN ORB		BLUE ORB
		DARK BLUE	LIGHT BLUE	GREEN	CRUST	CRUST
Ag	Silver	0.0000%	0.0000%	0.0000%	0.0000%	0.0000%
Al	Aluminum	1.9440%	5.7860%	4.3960%	6.8930%	4.0010%
As	Arsenic	0.0000%	0.0000%	0.0000%	0.0000%	0.0000%
Bi	Bismuth	0.0000%	0.0000%	0.0000%	0.0000%	0.0000%
Ca	Calcium	7.1790%	3.6120%	6.0130%	2.1450%	3.6960%
Cd	Cadmium	0.0310%	0.0270%	0.0290%	0.0280%	0.0260%
Cl	Chlorine	0.0000%	0.0000%	0.0000%	0.0000%	0.0000%
Co	Cobalt	0.0000%	0.0000%	0.0000%	0.0000%	0.0000%
Cr	Chromium	0.0220%	0.0380%	0.0480%	0.0580%	0.0320%
Cu	Copper	0.3310%	0.4900%	0.0000%	0.0000%	0.5240%
Fe	Iron	0.4460%	0.4460%	0.5050%	0.5050%	0.3690%
Hf	Hafnium	0.0150%	0.0170%	0.0000%	0.0000%	0.0200%
K	Potassium	4.2310%	3.3940%	4.9490%	0.0000%	0.0000%
LE[†]	Light Element	59.8500%	54.8910%	54.3760%	62.9860%	62.8840%
Mg	Magnesium	1.4540%	0.0000%	1.3970%	0.0000%	0.0000%
Mn	Manganese	0.0140%	0.0220%	0.0290%	0.0190%	0.0170%
Mo	Molybdenum	0.0000%	0.0000%	0.0000%	0.0000%	0.0000%
Ni	Nickel	0.0000%	0.0075%	0.0026%	0.0034%	0.0077%
P	Phosphorous	0.4460%	0.2770%	0.4800%	0.0000%	0.0840%
Pb	Lead	0.0011%	0.0035%	0.0010%	0.0014%	0.0031%

*The blue glass orb had two zones in the same orb, one blue and another a lighter blue. Both areas were tested and the results recorded. Both orbs had a crust on the bottom, which were both tested and recorded in this table.

[†]LE refers to Light Elements, O, C, and N, less than Mg atomic weight.

ELEMENT	ELEMENT	BLUE ORB*		GREEN ORB		BLUE ORB
		DARK BLUE	LIGHT BLUE	GREEN	CRUST	CRUST
S	Sulfur	0.0950%	0.1420%	0.0930%	0.0000%	0.1330%
Sb	Antimony	0.0141%	0.1490%	0.0137%	0.0132%	0.0137%
Si	Silicon	23.6020%	29.5540%	27.4210%	26.6670%	27.8740%
Sn	Tin	0.1260%	0.0130%	0.0112%	0.0361%	0.0133%
Ta	Tantalum	0.0000%	0.0000%	0.0000%	0.0000%	0.0000%
Ti	Titanium	0.1550%	0.2740%	0.1820%	0.5930%	0.2620%
W	Tungsten	0.0000%	0.0000%	0.0000%	0.0000%	0.0000%
Zn	Zinc	0.0087%	0.0166%	0.0127%	0.0051%	0.0000%
Zr	Zirconium	0.0044%	0.0063%	0.0084%	0.0143%	0.0087%
Total		99.9893%	99.1949%	99.9996%	99.9955%	99.9985%

*The blue glass orb had two zones in the same orb, one blue and another a lighter blue. Both areas were tested and the results recorded. Both orbs had a crust on the bottom, which were both tested and recorded in this table.

Glossary

Agni Yoga: The "Yoga of Fire"; also refers to a book channeled by Helena Roerich.

amrita: Nectar of immortality that arose from the churning of the milk ocean by Vishnu.

anu-yoga: See Dzogchen.

Aswatthama: The last general of the Kauravas, who unleashes weapons of mass destruction in the Mahabharata.

asuras: Anti-gods, demons, or titans who continually war against the devas in Hindu cosmology.

Avalokiteshvara: Also known as Chenrezig, Kuan Yin, Kanzeon. Literally, the one who hears the suffering of all beings. Bodhisattva of compassion who wields the chintamani.

Avatamsaka Sutra: Also *Hua Yen, Kegon,* or *Flower Garland Sutra.* Buddhist Sutra that discusses the jewel net of Indra.

avatar: A periodic incarnation of the sustainer god, Vishnu, to rebalance when the world abandons divine order.

bardos: The six intermediate states of life and death and the transitions from one to another.

beyul: "Hidden Land" created by Guru Padmasambhava to serve as a refuge during later troubled times.

Book of Rites: Also *Li Ji,* one of the five ancient Confucian classic writings.

caduceus: Staff of the god Mercury, representing the central channel of the spine and the two side channels surmounted by the awakened mind.

chakravartin: A universal monarch who is completely focused on the happiness and benefit of all.

Chenrezig: See Avalokiteshvara.

chinta: Sanskrit root word for mind intention.

chintamani: Also *yishin norbu, ruyibaoshu,* or *nyoi-hoju.* The wish-fulfilling gem that brings great blessings or repression depending on who wields it to activate the intention.

Copper Colored Mountain of Padmasambhava: Also *Zandokpalri.* The pure land established by the vows of Guru Padmasambhava.

daigo: "Great Awakening," a higher type of enlightenment.

dakini: "Sky dancer," the most sacred aspect of the feminine in human, divine, and enlightened form.

devaloka: The realm of the Devas or gods.

devas: "Shining Ones" or gods in Hinduism.

dharani: A long mantra that invokes the qualities, presence, or blessings of a Buddha or Bodhisattva.

dhatu: A realm on Mount Meru, the world mountain, composed of three sections on the mountain: low, mid, and high. These form three corresponding realms: desire (*kama*), form (*rupa*), and formless (*arupa*).

Dwaraka: The capital city of Shri Krishna in the Mahabharata.

Dzogchen: The highest yoga practice system within the Nyingma order of Tibetan Buddhism. Also called the Great Perfection and is synonymous with atiyoga or yoga beyond yoga. The system builds on anu-yoga, the cultivation of the energy body leading to stages of direct cutting and crossing over that result in manifesting the rainbow body.

Eastern Land of Medicine Buddha: A pure dimensional land created by the vow of the Medicine Buddha to heal the root of all diseases and suffering of all sentient beings.

fei cui: A variety of very bright green jade from Burma.

Five Dhyani Buddhas: Also Five Jinas (Victors), archetypal Buddhas associated with the five types of consciousness, five colors, and five elements.

Gesar of Ling: Both the name of the longest epic in the world from the Tibetan and Mongolian tradition, and the king who is the central focus of it. King Gesar, reputed to have lived in 1027 CE, is the general who leads a successful war to defeat a demonic, world-threatening alliance. In the future, he will direct the armies of Shambhala to defeat the negative ones and usher in a golden age of peace.

Hastinapura: The capital city of the Pandavas in the Mahabharata.

IIED: Intention Imprinted Electrical Device designed by William Tiller.

indrajala: The jewel net of Indra.

ishtadevata: Also yidam, the indwelling divine self-nature externally experienced as a Buddha, Bodhisattva, or divine being. A chosen deity for visualization and mantra recitation.

Jambhala: A wealth-granting Bodhisattva, yellow in color, shown adorned with many gems holding the chintamani in his left hand.

kai guang: Chinese Buddhist ritual to consecrate a statue.

kaigen: Japanese Buddhist ritual to consecrate a statue.

Kalachakra: "Wheel of Time" tantra of Tibetan yoga associated with Shambhala. Kalachakra also refers to the central Buddha of the highest yoga tantra.

Kalachakri: Yidam consort of Kalachakra, expressing the bliss of enlightenment.

Kalki: In Hindu cosmology, the avatar of Vishnu next in line for reincarnation, who will subdue the masses of malevolent beings to usher in a golden age of peace.

Kalki King: The Shambhala kings, sixth through twenty-fifth in succession.

Kangxi: Manchu Emperor who commissioned the earliest extant copy of the *Gesar of Ling* epic in 1716.

Kauravas: The non-dharmic antagonists of the Mahabharata epic.

kaustubham: "Pervading the Universe." The chintamani arising from the churning of the milk ocean presented to Vishnu to benefit all of creation.

Krishna: The avatar of Vishnu featured in the Mahabharata and the Bhagavad Gita section of that epic.

Kshitigarbha: Also known as Dizang and Jizo. Bodhisattva with the chintamani who alleviates suffering of even those in the hell realms.

Laghutantra: The simplified Kalachakra teachings written by Manjushri Yashas, the first Kalki Shambhala King.

Lapis philosophorum: The Philosopher's Stone.

Mahabharata: The great hundred-thousand-verse Indian epic poem.

Mani Raja: An epithet for Gesar of Ling meaning "Jewel King."

Master Morya: Also El Morya. The Master, now ascended, who gave a chintamani to the Roerichs and from whom Helena received telepathic messages and channeled information.

Medicine Buddha: Also Sangye Menla, Bhaisajya Guru. Buddha who vowed to heal all roots of disease and alleviate suffering.

myrobalan: The main herb contained in the medicine bowl held by the Medicine Buddha.

Pandavas: The dharmic protagonists of the Mahabharata epic.

Pema Kod: A beyul located in southern Tibet east of Bhutan and north of the Indian province of Arunachal Pradesh.

Philosopher's Stone: The archetypic symbol at the heart of Western alchemical traditions and mystery schools.

Prasena: Brother of Satrajit who took the syamantaka chintamani and was subsequently murdered by thieves, as told in the Mahabharata.

ratna: A Sanskrit term for a jewel or precious object.

Ratnasambhava: With consort Vajradhatvishvari, the Dhyani Buddhas heading the ratna or jewel family of humble generosity.

Red Path to Shambhala: A secret guidebook to Shambhala rumored to be held at Hemis Monastery in Leh, Ladakh.

rigpa: Ever-present awareness.

Roerich Pact: An international treaty signed in 1932 agreeing to respect the cultural treasure places of all countries especially during war.

Rudra Chakrin: The twenty-fifth and last Kalki King of Shambhala, who will defeat the negative powers to usher in a golden age of peace.

samadhi: The state of deep and effortless flow of continuous meditation. The seventh practice limb of yoga according to Patanjali.

Samantabhadra: One of the eight great Bodhisattvas bearing a chintamani.

samudra manthana: Hindu myth of churning the milk ocean that produced the first chintamanis.

sangha: "Assembly" in Sanskrit. In Buddhism, it is one of the three jewels and refers to the gathering of spiritual friends who practice the way of enlightenment with focused commitment.

Satrajit: The clan elder to whom Surya, the sun god, gave the ruby-like syamantaka gem in the Mahabharata.

Shambhalai Lamyig: A guidebook written by the sixth Panchen Lama in 1775.

Shambhala: A subtle dimension populated by those who practice the Kalachakra tantra and who guide the evolution of life, culture, and consciousness on Earth.

Sowa Rigpa: Tibetan medical tradition.

spagyrics: A branch of alchemy concerned with elixirs and medicines.

Spiral Dragon Dharma System: An integrated practice *terma* revealed by Senton Dorje and taught by her disciple, Master Guan-liang Quan.

stupa: Buddhist architectural monuments that resonate with the human chakra system to bring enlightenment to Earth and to bless the land.

Surya: The sun deva or god.

syamantaka mani: The ruby-like chintamani that Shri Krishna secures for the greater benefit of humanity in the Mahabharata.

tachyolithic: The inherent technology involved in the instantaneous transfer and activation of information and intention to and from crystals.

Tara: A female deva in Hinduism or Bodhisattva of active compassion in Buddhism.

Tashiding Monastery: A Tibetan monastery in Sikkim, near Mount Kanchenjunga, connected to Shambhala teachings.

Tengyur: The collected and complete set of all Buddhist teaching commentaries in Tibetan Vajrayana.

terma: A tantric practice hidden by Guru Padmasambhava to be discovered by Treasure Revealers (Tertons) when humanity can most benefit from that teaching.

Tulshuk Lingpa: Tibetan Lama and Treasure Revealer (1932–1960) who set out to find the beyul near Kanchenjunga.

Ugrasena: Head of the Yadava clan into which Shri Krishna was incarnated, as related in the Mahabharata.

vaidurya: The chintamani-level gem of the Medicine Buddha that is either beryl, emerald, lapis lazuli, or blue sapphire.

vajrakaya: Diamond energy body.

Vajrasattva and Vajrasattvi: The Buddha and Buddha-consort known as "Diamond Beings."

Vajrayana: "Diamond Vehicle," another name for tantric Buddhism of Tibet, China, and Japan.

Vedas: The oldest sacred books of Hinduism that contain teachings on the worlds, spiritual development, and rituals for dissolving karma and harmonizing consciousness.

Vedic: Referring to the philosophy, learning, rituals, prayers, mantras, and tradition of the Vedas and subsequent sacred literature based on the Vedas.

Vimalaprabha: A Kalachakra teaching commentary known also as the *Ornament of Stainless Light* written by the second Shambhala Kalki King, Pundarika.

Western Paradise: Also Sukhavati and Dewachen. A pure land and blissful dimension to which humans can go after death to accelerate self-perfection.

White Mahakala: A wealth Bodhisattva referred to as "the Wish-Fulfilling Gem."

Xian Lung Fa Men: See Spiral Dragon Dharma System.

yakshas: Fierce nature spirits, lords of earth wealth.

yantras: Sacred diagrams often inscribed with mantras.

Yudhisthira: Eldest of the Pandavas and ultimately king of the Kuru nation in the Mahabharata.

yugas: Planetary cycles of 24,000 or 26,000 years described in the Indian religious traditions that are important in measuring the progress of Earth evolution.

Zhang Zhung: An ancient kingdom in northeastern Tibet around Mount Kailash that was a precursor of modern Tibetan culture and spiritual practice.

Notes

Introducing the Chintamani

1. Yeats, "The Second Coming," 117.
2. *Vishnu Purana,* 25.
3. Monier-Williams, *A Sanskrit English Dictionary,* 398.

Chapter 1. The Chintamani Quest

1. Tomas, *Shambhala,* 179–80.
2. Roerich, *Altai-Himalaya.*
3. Drayer, *Nicholas & Helena Roerich,* 303.
4. Roerich, *Shambhala,* 116.
5. Roerich, *Shambhala,* 1–33.
6. Roerich, *Shambhala,* 1.
7. Sopa et al., *Wheel of Time,* 54–55.
8. Roerich, *Altai-Himalaya,* 59–60.

Chapter 2. Chintamani and Intention

1. *Hymns of the Atharva Veda,* 343.
2. Monier-Williams, "indrajala," 166.
3. Lao-tsu, *Lao-tsu's Taoteching,* 14.
4. Monier-Williams, "dharma," 510.
5. Satyeswarananda, *Mahabharata,* 305.
6. Cook, *Hua-yen Buddhism,* 3.

Chapter 3. Jewels Everywhere East

1. Tsogyal, *Lotus-Born,* 31–36.
2. Tsogyal, *Lotus-Born,* 34.
3. Tsogyal, *Lotus-Born,* 34–35.
4. Tsogyal, *Lotus-Born,* 35.

5. Tsogyal, *Lotus-Born*, 35.

6. Birnbaum, *The Healing Buddha*, 65; Thrangu, *Medicine Buddha Teachings*, 95.

7. Spokensanskrit.org, "Vaiḍūrya."

8. Banerjee, *Ashtamahabodhisattva*, 16.

9. Banerjee, *Ashtamahabodhisattva*, 18.

10. Banerjee, *Ashtamahabodhisattva*, 10.

11. *Sutra of the Past Vows of Earth Store Bodhisattva*, 44–48.

12. Jayarava, *Visible Mantra*, 125.

13. Banerjee, *Ashtamahabodhisattva*, 63.

14. Banerjee, *Ashtamahabodhisattva*, 64.

15. Beer, *Handbook of Tibetan Buddhist Symbols*, 193.

16. Banerjee, *Ashtamahabodhisattva*, 43.

17. Dagyab, *Buddhist Symbols in Tibetan Culture*, 65.

18. Dagyab, *Buddhist Symbols in Tibetan Culture*, 70–71.

19. Beer, *Handbook of Tibetan Buddhist Symbols*, 192.

20. Beer, *Handbook of Tibetan Buddhist Symbols*, 193.

21. Norbu, *Crystal and the Way of Light*, 100.

22. Inagaki, *A Dictionary of Buddhist Terms*, 235.

23. O'Neill, *Essential Kanji*, 219.

24. O'Neill, *Essential Kanji*, 55.

25. Nelson, *Modern Readers' Japanese-English Character Dictionary*, 314.

26. O'Neill, *Essential Kanji*, 225.

Chapter 4. Shambhala, Kalachakra, and the Chintamani

1. Lodro, *Unveiling Your Sacred Truth*, 110.

2. Roerich, *Shambhala*, 5.

3. Bernbaum, *Way to Shambhala*, 185.

4. Thompson, *Vedic Cosmography and Astronomy*, 19.

5. Bernbaum, *Way to Shambhala*, 186.

6. Bernbaum, *Way to Shambhala*, 187–94.

7. Thomas Shor, *A Step Away From Paradise*, 210–14.

8. Maroney, *Book of Dzyan*, 12.

9. Godwin, "Saint-Yves d'Alveydre and the Agarttian Connection," 2.

10. Saint-Yves d'Alveydre, *Kingdom of Agarttha*, 48.

11. Ravenscroft, *Spear of Destiny*, 255–56.

12. Ravenscroft, *Spear of Destiny*, 256.

13. Ravenscroft, *Spear of Destiny*, 257.

14. Ravenscroft, *Spear of Destiny*, 256.

15. *Sri Kalki Purana,* 15.

16. *Mahabharata,* 391.

17. Rao, *The Lost City of Dwaraka.*

18. Patel, "The Bhagavad-Gita, Oppenheimer and Nuclear Weapons."

19. David-Neel and Yongden, *The Superhuman Life of Gesar of Ling,* 16.

Chapter 5. Power Crystals across Cultures

1. Lees, "Green Man of Cercles," 1–251.

2. Lees, "Green Man of Cercles," 228.

3. *Li Chi Book of Rites,* 463–64.

4. Levy and Scott-Clark, *Stone of Heaven,* 11–28.

5. *Kojiki,* 195–97; *Nihongi,* 57–65.

6. Ono, *Shinto,* 5, 64.

7. Nelson, *Modern Reader's Japanese-English Character Dictionary,* 103.

8. Sansom, *A History of Japan,* 19.

9. Shaer, "A Secret Tunnel"; Laity, "Lakes of Mercury."

10. Van der Sluijs, "The Wish-Granting Jewel," 1–7.

11. Folda, "An Icon of the Crucifixion at the Nativity in Sinai," 170–71.

12. Folda, *Crusader Art,* 140.

13. Von Eschenbach, *Parzival,* 251.

14. Von Eschenbach, *Parzival,* 251.

15. Rahn, *Crusade Against the Grail.*

16. Vronsky, "Montsegur."

17. Temple, *Crystal Sun,* 341.

18. Folda, *Crusader Art,* 124–27, 155.

19. Hancock, *Underworld.*

20. Donnelly, *Atlantis,* 338–440.

Chapter 6. Gems and Stones of Renown

1. Roerich, *Shambhala,* 245, 272.

2. Joseph and Beaudoin, *Opening the Ark of the Covenant,* 118.

3. Dalrymple and Anand, *Koh-i-Noor,* 36.

4. Tarling, "The Wars of British Succession"; Koh-i-Noor Diamond, "History."

5. Kurin, *Hope Diamond,* 97–123.

6. Gaillou et al., "The Hope Diamond."

7. Cobb, "The Pearl of Allah."

8. Genesis 28:16–17 (AV).

9. Genesis 28:22 (AV).

10. Green, *Interlinear Bible,* 24.

11. An Anglican Liturgical Library, "Form and Order of Service."

12. Gerber, *Stone of Destiny,* 128.

13. Green, *Interlinear Bible,* 24.

14. Saint-Hilare, *On Eastern Crossroads,* 131.

15. Temple, *Sirius Mystery.*

16. Simmons and Warner, *Moldavite,* 26.

17. Hanus et al., *Moldavite,* 26–29.

18. Simmons and Ahsian, *Book of Stones,* 394.

19. Wikipedia, "Cristobalite."

20. Russell Shor, "GIA Tests Extraterrestrial Gemstones."

21. Bauval and Gilbert, *Orion Mystery,* 203.

22. Temple, *Crystal Sun,* 287.

23. Heide and Wlotzka, *Meteorites,* 83.

24. Kotsugi et al., "Novel Magnetic Domain Structure in Iron Meteorite," 1.

25. Bibhuranjan and Meyer, "Tetrataenite in Terrestrial Rock," 209.

Chapter 7. Crystal Spiritual Technology

1. Baconnier et al., "Microcrystals in the Pineal Gland of the Human Brain," 204.

2. Smereka, "Spiral Crystal Growth," 282–301.

3. *I Ching or Book of Changes,* 721–23.

4. Temple, *Sirius Mystery,* 285–86.

5. On-line Encyclopedia of Integer Sequences, "Magic Numbers of Nucleons."

6. Hudson Institute of Mineralogy, "Crystallography."

7. Holtkamp, "Crystal Shapes."

8. Gienger, *Crystal Power, Crystal Healing,* 42–82.

9. Gienger, *Crystal Power, Crystal Healing,* 94–103.

10. Kazansky et al., "Eternal 5D Data Storage."

11. University of South Australia, "Using Light for Next-Generation Data Storage."

12. Tiller, *Psychoenergetic Science,* xiv–xv.

13. Tiller, *Psychoenergetic Science,* 48.

14. Tiller, "White Paper IV: It Is Time for a Consciousness-Inclusive Science," 10.

15. Tiller, "White Paper IV: It Is Time for a Consciousness-Inclusive Science," 12.

16. Lifestream Associates, "The Power of Love."

17. Schrodinger, *What Is Life,* 5.

18. *Oxford English Dictionary,* "Crystal."

19. Chemicool Dictionary, "What Is a Crystal?"

20. Schrodinger, *What Is Life,* 5.

21. Wilczek, "Crystals in Time," 28–36.
22. International Union of Crystallography, "Aperiodic Crystal."
23. Schrodinger, *What Is Life,* 61.
24. Lipton, *Biology of Belief,* 43–45.
25. Lipton, *Biology of Belief,* 109.
26. Lipton, *Biology of Belief,* 122–23, 229–32.

Chapter 8. The Crystal Matrix

1. Metropolitan Museum of Art, "Menat Necklace from Malqata."
2. Wikipedia, "Brisingamen."
3. Wikipedia, "Necklace of Harmonia."
4. Johari, *Numerology*; Johari, *Healing Power of Gemstones.*
5. Cerulli and Guenzi, "Mineral Healing," 75.
6. Johari, *Healing Power of Gemstones,* 16.
7. Josephus, *Works of Flavius Josephus,* 83.
8. Harrell et al., "Hebrew Gemstones in the Old Testament," 45.
9. Green, *Interlinear Bible,* 72.
10. Muss-Arnolt, "The Urim and Thummim," 192–224.
11. Hancock, *Sign and the Seal,* 68–69.
12. Joseph and Beaudoin, *Opening the Ark of the Covenant,* 118.
13. Losack, *Saint Patrick and the Bloodline of the Grail,* 17, 119, 128, 146.
14. 2 Maccabees 2:1–8.
15. Piso, "Flavius Josephus aka Arrius Calpurnius Piso."
16. Revelation 23:16–21 (AV).
17. Revelation 4:3,7 (AV).
18. Burckhardt, "The Heavenly Jerusalem and the Paradise of Vaikuntha."
19. Collins, *Cygnus Mystery,* 125.

Chapter 9. Chintamani Alchemy

1. Hauck, *Emerald Tablet,* 18.
2. Merriam-Webster Online Dictionary, "Smaragd."
3. Wiktionary, "Smáragdos (σμάραγδος)."
4. Wisdom Library, "Marakata."
5. Wisdom Library, "Marakata."
6. Merriam-Webster Online Dictionary, "Alchemy."
7. Beretta, *Alchemy of Glass,* ix.
8. Hauck, *Emerald Tablet.*
9. Endredy, *Shamanic Alchemy.*
10. Beretta, *Alchemy of Glass,* 2, 4.

11. Hauck, *Emerald Tablet*, 168

12. Jung, *The Red Book*.

13. Jung, *Psychology and Alchemy*, 257.

14. Jung, *Psychology and Alchemy*, 260.

15. Jung, *Alchemical Studies*, 242.

16. Jung, *Alchemical Studies*, 96.

17. Hauck, *Emerald Tablet*, 328.

18. Kaptchuk, *The Web That Has No Weaver*, 78.

19. Wong, *Shambhala Guide to Taoism*, 180–82.

20. Wong, *Shambhala Guide to Taoism*, 183.

21. Houston, *Yoga Sutra Workbook*, I.3.

Chapter 10. Creating the Chintamani

1. Bryant, *Wheel of Time Sand Mandala*, 17.

2. Baigent and Leigh, *Elixir and the Stone*, 174.

3. *Chemical Wedding of Christian Rosenkreutz*, 16.

4. Egan, *Meaning of the Monas Hieroglyphica*.

5. Egan, *Meaning of the Monas Hieroglyphica*, 7.

6. Newman, *Newton the Alchemist*, 3.

7. Drob, "The Sefirot."

8. Kaplan, *Sefer Yetzirah*, 261.

9. Kaplan, *Sefer Yetzirah*, 261.

10. Beretta, *Alchemy of Glass*.

11. Beretta, *Alchemy of Glass*, 9.

12. Beretta, *Alchemy of Glass*, 4.

13. Beretta, *Alchemy of Glass*, 41.

14. Beretta, *Alchemy of Glass*, 59.

15. Temple, *Crystal Sun*, 314.

16. Mitchell-Hedges, *Danger My Ally*, 225, 241–47.

17. Morton and Thomas, *Mystery of the Crystal Skulls*, 41–49, 224, 326.

18. Mt. Shasta, *My Search in Tibet*, 33.

19. Mt. Shasta, *My Search in Tibet*, 127.

20. *Tibetan Medicine*, 68.

21. Tibetan Spirit, "Drikung Chintamani Medicinal Incense."

Chapter 11. Crystal Alignment and Intention

1. Interstellar Light Applications, "Research."

2. Jensen, *Introduction to Vogel Healing Tools*, 13–15.

3. 1 Kings 3 (AV).

4. Merriam-Webster, "Elixir."

5. Josephus, *Works of Flavius Josephus,* 202.

6. Roerich, *Shambhala,* 245.

7. Johari, *Healing Power of Gemstones,* 29.

Epilogue

1. Thomas Shor, *A Step Away from Paradise.*

2. Roerich, *Altai-Himalaya,* 391–92.

3. Thomas Shor, *A Step Away from Paradise,* 115.

4. Tomas, *Shambhala,* 60–61.

5. Tenzing, "Legacy of Guru Padmasambhava."

6. Bernbaum, *Way to Shambhala,* 68–69, 133.

7. Thomas Shor, *A Step Away from Paradise,* 182.

Appendix 1. Five Dhyani Buddhas Correspondences

1. Ray, *Secret of the Vajra World,* 144.

Appendix 2. Practice Mantras

1. Jayarava, *Visible Mantra,* 186.

2. Jayarava, *Visible Mantra,* 188.

3. Jayarava, *Visible Mantra,* 196.

Bibliography

An Anglican Liturgical Library. "The Form and Order of Service that is to be performed and the Ceremonies that are to be observed in The Coronation of Her Majesty Queen Elizabeth II in the Abbey Church of St. Peter, Westminster, on Tuesday, the second day of June, 1953." Oremus (website). Accessed May 28, 2021.

Baconnier, Simon, Sidney Lang, Maria Polomska, Garry Berkovic, and Guilia Mesh. "Calcite Microcrystals in the Pineal Gland of the Human Brain: First Physical and Chemical Studies." *Bioelectromagnetics* 23 (2002): 488–95.

Baigent, Michael, and Richard Leigh. *The Elixir and the Stone.* London: Arrow, 2005.

Banerjee, Radha. *Ashtamahabodhisattva: The Eight Great Bodhisattvas in Art and Literature.* New Delhi: Abha Prakashan, 1994.

Bauval, Robert, and Adrian Gilbert. *The Orion Mystery.* New York: Crown, 1994.

Beer, Robert. *The Handbook of Tibetan Buddhist Symbols.* Boston: Shambhala, 2003.

Beretta, Marco. *The Alchemy of Glass: Counterfeit, Imitation, Transmutation in Ancient Glassmaking.* Sagamore Beach, Mass.: Science History Publications, 2009.

Bernbaum, Edwin. *The Way to Shambhala: A Search for the Mythical Kingdom Beyond the Himalayas.* Los Angeles: Jeremy P. Tarcher, 1980.

Bibhuranjan, Nayak, and Franz Michael Meyer. "Tetrataenite in Terrestrial Rock." *American Mineralogist* 100, no. 1 (January 2015): 209–14.

Birnbaum, Raoul. *The Healing Buddha.* Boulder, Colo.: Shambhala, 1979.

Bryant, Barry. *The Wheel of Time Sand Mandala.* Ithaca, N.Y.: Snow Lion, 1992.

Burckhardt, Titus. "The Heavenly Jerusalem and the Paradise of Vaikuntha." *Studies in Comparative Religion* 4, no. 1 (Winter 1970).

Cerulli, Anthony, and Caterina Guenzi. "Mineral Healing: Gemstone Remedies in Astrological and Medical Traditions." In *Soulless Matter, Seats of Energy: Metals, Gems and Minerals in South Asian Traditions*, edited by Fabrizio M. Ferrari and Thomas W. P. Dähnhardt, 73–93. Sheffield, UK: Equinox, 2016.

Chemical Wedding of Christian Rosenkreutz. Translated by Joscelyn Godwin. Boston: Phanes Press, 1991.

Chemicool Dictionary (website). "What Is a Crystal?" Accessed September 17, 2019.

Cobb, Wilburn Dowell. "The Pearl of Allah." *Natural History Magazine,* November 1939.

Collins, Andrew. *The Cygnus Mystery*. London: Watkins, 2010.

Cook, Francis, H. *Hua-yen Buddhism: The Jewel Net of Indra*. University Park, Pa.: Penn State University, 1977.

David-Neel, Alexandra, and Lama Yongden. *The Superhuman Life of Gesar of Ling*. Boston and London: Shambhala, 1987.

Dagyab, Rinpoche. *Buddhist Symbols in Tibetan Culture*. Boston: Wisdom Publications, 1995.

Dalrymple, William, and Anita Anand. *Koh-i-Noor: The History of the World's Most Infamous Diamond*. New York: Bloomsbury, 2017.

Donnelly, Ignatius. *Atlantis: The Antediluvian World*. 1882. Reprint, New York: Dover, 1976.

Drayer, Ruth A. *Nicholas & Helena Roerich: The Spiritual Journey of Two Great Artists and Peacemakers*. Wheaton, Ill.: Quest Books, 2005.

Drob, Sanford L. "The Sefirot." The New Kabbalah (website). 2001.

Egan, Jim. *The Meaning of the Monas Hieroglyphica with Regards to Geometry*. Newport, R.I.: Cosmopolite Press, 2010.

Endredy, James. *Shamanic Alchemy: The Great Work of Inner Transformation*. Rochester, Vt.: Inner Traditions, 2019.

Folda, Jaroslav. "An Icon of the Crucifixion at the Nativity in Sinai: Investigating the Pictorial Language of its Ornamental Vocabulary: Chrysography, Pearl-dot Haloes and Çintemani." In *In Laudem Hierosolymitani*, edited by Ronnie Ellenblum, Iris Shagrir, and Jonathan Riley-Smith. London: Routledge, 2007.

———. *Crusader Art: The Art of the Crusaders in the Holy Land 1099–1291*. London: Lund Humphries, 2008.

Freeland, Elena. *Under an Ionized Sky: From Chemtrails to Space Fence Lockdown*. Port Townsend, Wash.: Feral House, 2018.

Gaillou, E., J. E. Post, and J. E. Butler. "The Hope Diamond: Blue by Day, Red by Night." *MinBlog*. May 22, 2012.

Garje, Khamtrul. *The Jewel Ladder: A Preliminary Nyingma Lamrim*. Dharamsala, India: Library of Tibetan Works and Archives, 1990.

Gerber, Pat. *Stone of Destiny*. Edinburgh: Canongate, 1997.

Gienger, Michael. *Crystal Power, Crystal Healing: The Complete Handbook*. Translated by Astrid Mick. London: Cassel Illustrated, 2004.

Godwin, Joscelyn. "Saint-Yves d'Alveydre and the Agarttian Connection." In

The Kingdom of Agarttha: A Journey into the Hollow Earth. Translated by Jon E. Graham. Rochester, Vt.: Inner Traditions, 2008.

Green, Jay P., Jr., ed. *The Interlinear Bible: Hebrew-Greek-English*. 2nd ed. London: Hendrickson, 1985.

Gyaltsen, Lobzang Chokyi. "Aspiration to Fulfill the Stages of the Glorious Kalachakra Path." In *The Practice of Kalachakra,* by Glenn H. Mullin. Ithaca, N.Y.: Snow Lion, 1991.

Gyaltsen, Losang Chokyi. *Medicine Buddha: Wish-Fulfilling Jewel*. Translated by David Molk. Portland, Ore.: Foundation for the Preservation of the Mahayana Tradition, 2009.

Hancock, Graham. *The Sign and the Seal*. New York: Crown, 1992.

———. *Underworld: The Mysterious Origins of Civilizations*. New York: Crown, 2002.

Hanus, Radek, et al. *Moldavite: Mysterious Tears from Heaven*. Czech Republic: Granit, 2016.

Harrell, James E., James K. Hoffmeier, and Kenton F. Williams. "Hebrew Gemstones in the Old Testament: A Lexical, Geological, and Archaeological Analysis." *Bulletin for Biblical Research* 27, no. 1 (2017): 1–52.

Hauck, Dennis William. *The Emerald Tablet: Alchemy of Personal Transformation*. New York: Penguin, 1999.

Heide, Fritz, and Frank Wlotzka. *Meteorites: Messengers from Space*. Translated by R. S. Clarke Jr. and Frank Wlotzka. Berlin: Springer-Verlag, 1995.

Holtkamp, Mark. "Crystal Shapes." Smorf (website). Accessed May 27, 2021.

Houston, Vyaas. *The Yoga Sutra Workbook*. Warwick, N.Y.: American Sanskrit Institute, 1995.

Hudson Institute of Mineralogy. "Crystallography." Mindat.org. Accessed May 27, 2021.

Hymns of the Atharva Veda. Translated by Ralph T. H. Griffith. Benares, India: E. J. Lazarus & Co., 1895.

I Ching or Book of Changes. 24th ed. Translated by Richard Wilhelm and Carl Baynes. Princeton, N.J.: Princeton University Press, 1990.

Inagaki, Hisao. *A Dictionary of Japanese Buddhist Terms*. Union City, Calif.: Heian, 1989.

International Union of Crystallography. "Aperiodic Crystal." *Online Dictionary of Crystallography*. Last edited November 8, 2017.

Interstellar Light Applications, LLC. "Research." Amazingmoonlight.com. Accessed July 21, 2020.

Jayarava. *Visible Mantra*. Cambridge, UK: Visible Mantra Books, 2011.

Jensen, Paul. *Introduction to Vogel Healing Tools*. A Foundation for the Advancement of Vogel Healing Techniques, 1999.

Johari, Harish. *The Healing Power of Gemstones*. Rochester, Vt.: Destiny, 1988, 1996.

———. *Numerology*. Rochester, Vt.: Destiny, 1990.

Joseph, Frank, and Laura Beaudoin. *Opening the Ark of the Covenant*. Franklin Lakes, N.J.: New Page, 2007.

Josephus, Flavius. *The Works of Flavius Josephus*. Translated by William Whiston. London: Ward, Lock & Co., 1879.

Joyce, James. *A Portrait of the Artist as a Young Man*. New York: Viking, 1961.

Jung, Carl. *Alchemical Studies*. Vol. 13, *Collected Works*. Translated by R. F. C. Hull. Princeton, N.J.: Bollingen, 1967.

———. *Memories, Dreams, Reflections*. Rev. ed. New York: Vintage, 1989.

———. *Psychology and Alchemy*. Vol. 12, *Collected Works*. Translated by R. F. C. Hull. Princeton, N.J.: Bollingen, 1968.

———. *The Red Book: Liber Novus*. Edited by Sonu Shamdasani. Translated by Mark Kyburz and John Peck. New York: W. W. Norton & Co., 2009.

Kaplan, Aryeh. *Sefer Yetzirah: The Book of Creation*. Boston: Weiser, 1997.

Kaptchuk, Ted J. *The Web That Has No Weaver: Understanding Chinese Medicine*. New York: Congdon and Reed, 1983.

Kazansky, Peter, Ausra Cerkauskaite, Martynas Beresna, Rokas Drevinskas, Aabid Patel, Jingyu Zhang, and Mindaugas Gecevicius. "Eternal 5D Data Storage Via Ultrafast-laser Writing in Glass." *SPIE Optoelectronics & Communications* (March 2016): 1–3.

Koh-i-Noor Diamond (website). "History of Kohinoor Diamond." Accessed September 12, 2020.

Kojiki: Records of Ancient Matters. 5th ed. Translated by Basil Hall Chamberlain. Tokyo: Tuttle, 1993.

Kotsugi, Masoto, Chiharu Mitsumata, Hiroshi Maruyama, Takanori Wakita, Toshiyuki Taniuchi, Kanta Ono, Motohiro Suzuki, et al. "Novel Magnetic Domain Structure in Iron Meteorite Induced by the Presence of $L1_0$-FeNi." *Applied Physics Express* 3, no. 1 (2010): 1–3.

Kurin, Richard. *Hope Diamond: The Legendary History of a Cursed Gem*. New York: Harper, 2006.

Laity, Paul. "Lakes of Mercury and Human Sacrifices—After 1,800 Years, Teotihuacan Reveals its Treasures." *The Guardian* (online), September 24, 2017.

Lao-tsu. *Lao-tsu's Taoteching*. Translated by Red Pine. San Francisco: Mercury House, 1996.

Lees, Julianna. "The Green Man of Cercles." Yumpu (website). Accessed June 25, 2021.

Levy, Adrian, and Cathy Scott-Clark. *Stone of Heaven: The Secret History of Imperial Green Jade*. London: Weidenfeld and Nicolson, 2001.

Li Chi Book of Rites: An Encyclopedia of Ancient Ceremonial Usages, Religious Creeds, and Social Institutions. Vol. II. Translated by James Legge. 1885. Reprint, Whitefish, Mont.: Kessinger, 2003.

Lifestream Associates. "The Power of Love." VogelCrystals.net. Last updated June 15, 2018.

Lipton, Bruce, H. *The Biology of Belief.* 2nd ed. Carlsbad, Calif.: Hay House, 2016.

Lodro, Shar Khentrul Jamphel. *Unveiling Your Sacred Truth Through the Kalachakra Path. The Enlightened Reality.* Vol. 3. Belgrave, Australia: Tibetan Buddhist Rime Institute, 2016.

Losack, Marcus. *Saint Patrick and the Bloodline of the Grail: The Untold Story of St. Patrick's Royal Family.* Belfast, Ireland: Nicholson & Bass, 2011.

Mahabharata of Krishna-Dwaipayana Vyasa Translated into English Prose. Vol. 3. Translated by Mohan Kisari. Calcutta: Ganguli Bharata Press, 1883–1896.

Maroney, Tim, ed. *The Book of Dzyan.* Hayward, Calif.: Chaosium, 2000.

Merriam-Webster Online Dictionary. "Alchemy." Accessed August 6, 2020.

———. "Elixir." Accessed September 7, 2020.

———. "Smaragd." Accessed August 2, 2020.

Metropolitan Museum of Art (website). "Menat Necklace from Malqata." Accessed May 28, 2021.

Mitchell-Hedges, F. A. *Danger My Ally: True Life Adventures of F. A. Mitchell-Hedges.* 1954. Reprint, Ontario: St. Catherines, 1995.

Monier-Williams, M. *A Sanskrit-English Dictionary.* 1899. Reprint, Delhi: Motilal Banarsidass, 1997.

Morton, Chris, and Ceri Louise Thomas. *The Mystery of the Crystal Skulls: Unlocking the Secrets of the Past, Present and Future.* Rochester, Vt.: Bear and Company, 2002.

Mt. Shasta, Peter. *My Search in Tibet for the Secret Wish-Fulfilling Jewel.* Mt. Shasta, Calif.: Church of the Seven Rays, 2016.

Muss-Arnolt, W. "The Urim and Thummim. A Suggestion as to Their Original Nature and Significance." *The American Journal of Semitic Languages and Literatures* 16, no. 4 (July 1900): 192–224.

Nelson, Andrew N. *The Modern Readers' Japanese-English Character Dictionary.* 35th ed. Tokyo: Tuttle, 1993.

Newman, William R. *Newton the Alchemist: Science, Enigma, and the Quest for Nature's "Secret Fire."* Princeton, N.J.: Princeton University Press, 2018.

Nihongi: Chronicles of Japan from the earliest Times to A.D. 637. 10th ed. Translated by A. G. Aston. Tokyo: Tuttle, 1993.

Norbu, Namkhai. *The Crystal and the Way of Light: Sutra, Tantra and Dzogchen.* Edited by John Shane. Boulder, Colo.: Snow Lion, 2000.

O'Neill, P. G. *Essential Kanji*. New York: Weatherhill, 1973.

On-line Encyclopedia of Integer Sequences. "Magic Numbers of Nucleons." Last modified September 18, 2020.

Ono, Sokyo. *Shinto: The Kami Way*. Tokyo: Tuttle, 1962.

Oxford English Dictionary. "Crystal." Accessed online September 17, 2019.

Patel, Rajesh. "The Bhagavad-Gita, Oppenheimer and Nuclear Weapons." Hindu Human Rights (website), August 12, 2012.

Piso, Roman. "Flavius Josephus aka Arrius Calpurnius Piso." June 2, 2017. Available on Academia.edu website.

Rahn, Otto. *Crusade Against the Grail*. Translated by Christopher Jones. Rochester, Vt.: Inner Traditions, 2006.

Rao, S. R. *The Lost City of Dwaraka*. New Delhi: Aditya Prakashan, 1999.

Ravenscroft, Trevor. *The Spear of Destiny*. New York: Samuel Weiser, 1973.

Ray, Reginald. *Secret of the Vajra World: The Tantric Buddhism of Tibet*. Vol. 2. Boston: Shambhala, 2002.

Roerich, Nicholas. *Altai-Himalaya: A Travel Diary*. Brookfield, Conn.: Arun Press, 1929, 1983.

———. *Flame in Chalice*. "Sacred Signs." New York: Nicholas Roerich Museum, 2017.

———. *Shambhala: In Search of a New Era*. 1930. Reprint, Rochester, Vt.: Inner Traditions, 1990.

Saint-Hilare, Josephine. *On Eastern Crossroads: Legends and Prophecies of Asia*. New York: Frederick A. Stokes, 1930.

Saint-Yves d'Alveydre, Alexandre. *The Kingdom of Agarttha: A Journey into the Hollow Earth*. Translated by Jon E. Graham. Rochester, Vt.: Inner Traditions, 2008.

Sansom, George. *A History of Japan to 1334*. Redwood City, Calif.: Stanford University Press, 1958.

Satyeswarananda, Giri Maharaj. *The Mahabharata with Lahiri Mahasay's Commentaries on the Bhagavad Gita*. San Diego, Calif.: Sanskrit Classics, 1986.

Schrodinger, Erwin. *What Is Life: The Physical Aspect of the Living Cell*. 1922. Reprint, Cambridge, UK: Cambridge University Press, 1967.

Shaer, Matthew. "A Secret Tunnel Found in Mexico May Finally Solve the Mysteries of Teotihuacán." *Smithsonian Magazine* (online), June 2016.

Shelley, Percy Bysshe. "Ozymandias." In *English Romantic Writers*, edited by David Perkins. New York: Harcourt, Brace and World, 1967.

Shor, Russell. "GIA Tests Extraterrestrial Gemstones for Down-to-Earth Elements." GIA (website). Accessed May 28, 2021.

Shor, Thomas K. *A Step Away from Paradise: The True Story of a Tibetan Lama's Journey to a Land of Immortality*. Haryana, India: Penguin Ananda, 2011.

Simmons, Robert, and Kathy Warner. *Moldavite: Mysterious Tears from Heaven.* Gloucester, Mass.: Heaven and Earth, 1988.

Simmons, Robert, and Naisha Ahsian. *The Book of Stones.* Berkeley, Calif.: North Atlantic, 2007.

Smereka, Peter. "Spiral Crystal Growth." *Physica D: Nonlinear Phenomena* 138, no. 3 (April 15, 2000): 282–301.

Sopa, Lhundub, Roger Jackson, and John Newman. *The Wheel of Time: The Kalachakra in Context.* Ithaca, N.Y.: Snow Lion, 1985.

Spokensanskrit.org. *"Vaiḍūrya."* Accessed May 2020.

Sri Kalki Purana. Translated by Das Bhumipati. Mathura, India: Tai Nitai Press, 2006.

Sutra of the Past Vows of Earth Store Bodhisattva. Dharma Realm Buddhist Association, Nederland (website). Accessed June 30, 2021.

Tabula Smaragdina (Emerald Tablet). Translated by Isaac Newton. Keynes MS. 28, King's College Library, Cambridge University. The Chymistry of Isaac Newton (website). Accessed May 2021.

Tarling, Nicholas. "The Wars of British Succession." *New Zealand Journal of History* 15, no. 1 (April 1981): 24–34.

Temple, Robert. *The Crystal Sun.* London: Century, 2000.

———. *The Sirius Mystery.* Rochester, Vt.: Destiny, 1998.

Tenzing, Thupten. "The Legacy of Guru Padmasambhava in the Dissemination of Buddhism in Sikkim." Sahapedia (website). September 2, 2019.

Thompson, Richard L. *Vedic Cosmography and Astronomy.* Los Angeles: Bhaktivedanta Book Trust, 1989.

Thrangu, Khenchen. *Medicine Buddha Teachings.* Ithaca, N.Y.: Snow Lion Publications, 2004.

Thurman, Robert. *The Jewel Tree of Tibet: The Enlightenment Engine of Tibetan Buddhism.* New York: Free Press, 2005.

Tibetan Medicine. Translated by Jampal Kunzang Rechung. Berkeley: University of California Press, 1973.

Tibetan Spirit (website). "Drikung Chintamani Medicinal Incense." Accessed July 3, 2020.

Tiller, William A. *Psychoenergetic Science: A Second Copernican Scale Revolution.* Walnut Creek, Calif.: Pavior, 2007.

———. "White Paper IV: It Is Time for a Consciousness-Inclusive Science." The Tiller Foundation (website). 2009.

Tiso, Francis V. *Rainbow Body and Resurrection: Spiritual Attainment of the Material Body and the Case of Khenpo A Cho.* Berkeley, Calif.: North Atlantic, 2016.

Tomas, Andrew. *Shambhala: Oasis of Light*. 1977. Reprint, San Bernardino, Calif.: New Saucerian, 2019.

Tsogyal, Yeshe. *The Lotus-Born: The Life Story of Padmasambhava*. Edited by Marcia Binder Schmidt. Translated by Erik Pema. Boston: Shambhala, 1993.

University of South Australia. "Using Light for Next-Generation Data Storage." ScienceDaily (website). July 11, 2018.

Vairotsana. *Eye of the Storm: Vairotsana's Five Original Transmissions*. Translated by Keith Dowman. Kathmandu: Vajra Publications, 2006.

Van der Sluijs, Marinus. "The Wish-Granting Jewel: Exploring the Buddhist Origins of the Holy Grail." *Viator* 42, no. 2 (2011): 1–48.

Vishnu Purana. Translated by B. K. Chaturvedi. New Delhi: Diamond Books, 2016.

Von Eschenbach, Wolfram. *Parzival*. Book IX. Translated by Helen M. Mustard and Charles E. Passage. New York: Vintage, 1961.

Vronsky, Peter. "Montsegur: Identities of Cathars Executed on March 16, 1244." Russianbooks.org. Accessed April 15, 2019.

Walker, J. Samuel. "The New Deal and the Guru." *American Heritage* 40, no. 2 (March 1989).

Wikipedia (website). "Brisingamen." Accessed September 5, 2020.

———. "Cristobalite." Accessed September 1, 2020.

———. "Necklace of Harmonia." Accessed September 5, 2020.

Wiktionary (website). "Smáragdos" (σμάραγδος). Accessed August 2, 2020.

Wilczek, Frank. "Crystals in Time." *Scientific American* 321, no. 5 (November 2019): 28–35.

Wisdom Library (website). "Marakata: 9 definitions." Accessed August 2, 2020.

Wong, Eva. *The Shambhala Guide to Taoism*. Boston: Shambhala, 1997.

Yeats, William Butler. "The Second Coming." In *Modern British Poetry,* edited by Louis Untermeyer, 117. New York: Harcourt, Brace & World, 1969.

Index